The State
of
Public Bureaucracy

Bureaucracies, Public Administration, and Public Policy

Kenneth J. Meier
Series Editor

Bureaucracies, Public Administration,
and Public Policy

The State
of
Public Bureaucracy

Larry B. Hill	Hal G. Rainey
Gary L. Wamsley	Bert A. Rockman
Charles T. Goodsell	Grace Hall Saltzstein
John A. Rohr	Theodore J. Lowi
Orion White	James Q. Wilson
James Wolf	Martin Landau
B. Guy Peters	Francis E. Rourke

LARRY B. HILL, EDITOR

M. E. Sharpe, Inc.
Armonk, New York
London, England

Library of Congress Cataloging-in-Publication Data

The State of public bureaucracy / edited by Larry B. Hill:
contributors, Larry B. Hill . . .[et al.].
p. cm.

Includes index.
ISBN 1-56324-007-6 (Cloth)
ISBN 1-56324-008-4 (Paper)
1. Bureaucracy—United States.
2. Public administration—United States.
I. Hill, Larry B.
JK421.S72 1992
353′.01—dc20
91-3983090-19138
CIP

Printed in the United States of America

The paper used in this publication meets the minimum requirements of the
American National Standard for Information Sciences—
Permanence of Paper for Printed Library Materials,
ANSI Z39.48–1984.

MV (c) 10 9 8 7 6 5 4 3 2 1
MV (p) 10 9 8 7 6 5 4 3 2

For Brian Wellington Hill

Contents

Part Two: The Future State of Public Bureaucracy

The Contributors

CHARLES T. GOODSELL is Professor of Public Administration at the Virginia Polytechnic Institute and State University and Director of its Center for Public Administration and Policy. Among his books are *The Social Meaning of Civic Space: Studying Political Authority through Architecture; The Case for Bureaucracy: A Public Administration Polemic*; and *The Public Encounter: Where State and Citizen Meet* (editor).

LARRY B. HILL is Professor of Political Science at the University of Oklahoma. He is a past chair of the Section on Public Administration of the American Political Science Association. His writings include *The Model Ombudsman* and *Essentials of Public Administration* (with F. Ted Hebert).

MARTIN LANDAU is Professor of Political Science at the University of California, Berkeley. *The Public Administration Review* has twice given him the William E. Mosher Award for distinguished scholarship. In addition to his many articles and monographs, he is the author of *Political Theory and Political Science: Studies in the Methodology of Political Inquiry*.

THEODORE J. LOWI is John L. Senior Professor of American Institutions at Cornell University. He was president of the American Political Science Association for 1990–91. His books include *At the Pleasure of the Mayor: Patronage and Power in New York City, 1898–1958; The Pursuit of Justice* (with Robert F. Kennedy); *The End of Liberalism: The Second Republic of the United States; The Politics of Disorder*; and *The Personal President: Power Invested, Promise Unfulfilled*.

B. GUY PETERS is Maurice Falk Professor of American Government and Chair of the Department of Political Science at the University of Pittsburgh. His publications include *The Politics of Bureaucracy; Comparative Public Administration: Problems of Theory and Method*; and *Public Administration: Challenges, Choices, Consequences* (with Charles H. Levine and Frank Thompson).

HAL G. RAINEY is Professor of Political Science at the University of Georgia. He has served as Chair of the Public Sector Division of the Academy of Management and as a member of the editorial boards of several academic journals. He is the author of *Understanding and Managing Public Organizations*.

BERT A. ROCKMAN is Senior Fellow in Governmental Studies at The Brookings Institution and University Professor of Political Science and Research Professor in the University Center for International Studies at the University of Pittsburgh. He is a past president of the Section on Presidency Research of the American Political Science Association, and his book *The Leadership Question* received the section's Richard E. Neustadt award in 1985. He also is coauthor of *Bureaucrats and Politicians in Western Democracies,* and coeditor of *Elite Studies and Communist Politics; Do Institutions Matter?* and *The Bush Presidency: First Appraisals.*

JOHN A. ROHR is Professor of Public Administration at the Virginia Polytechnic Institute and State University. He is the Managing Editor of *Administration and Society.* His books include *To Run a Constitution: The Legitimacy of the Administrative State; Ethics for Bureaucrats: An Essay on Law and Values;* and *Prophets without Honor: Public Policy and the Selective Conscientious Objector.*

FRANCIS E. ROURKE is the Benjamin H. Griswold III Professor of Public Policy at The Johns Hopkins University. He is the author of a number of books and articles on American government and politics, including *Bureaucracy, Politics, and Public Policy; Bureaucracy and Foreign Policy;* and *Secrecy and Publicity: Dilemmas of Democracy.*

GRACE HALL SALTZSTEIN is Associate Professor and Chair of the Department of Political Science at the University of California, Riverside. She has written extensively on the concept of bureaucratic responsiveness.

GARY L. WAMSLEY is Professor of Public Administration at the Virginia Polytechnic Institute and State University. He is the editor of *Administration and Society* and the author of a number of articles and books, including *Selective Service and a Changing America* and *The Political Economy of Public Organizations* (with Mayer Zald).

ORION WHITE is Professor of Public Administration at the Virginia Polytechnic Institute and State University. He has written extensively on organizational development and behavior, and mediation.

JAMES Q. WILSON is James Collins Professor of Management and Public Policy at the University of California, Los Angeles. He was for twenty-six years Shattuck Professor of Government at Harvard University. He is president of the

American Political Science Association for 1991–92. He is author or coauthor of twelve books, including *Bureaucracy; Thinking about Crime; Varieties of Police Behavior; Political Organizations; The Investigators; Crime and Human Nature* (with Richard J. Herrnstein); and *City Politics* (with Edward C. Banfield).

JAMES WOLF is Associate Professor of Public Administration at the Virginia Polytechnic Institute and State University. His writings include *The Human Resource Crisis in the Public Sector: Rebuilding the Capacity to Govern* (with Larry M. Lane) and *Building City Council Leadership Skills: A Casebook of Models and Methods* (coeditor with Stephen W. Burks).

Foreword

The M.E. Sharpe, Inc., series on bureaucracies, public policy, and public administration is designed as a forum for the best work on bureaucracy and its role in public policy and governance. Although the series is open with regard to approach, methods, and perspectives, especially sought are three types of research. First, the series hopes to attract theoretically informed, empirical studies of bureaucracy. Public administration has long been viewed as a theoretical and methodological backwater of political science. This view persists despite a recent accumulation of first-rate research. The series seeks to place public administration at the forefront of empirical analysis within political science. Second, the series is interested in conceptual work that attempts to clarify theoretical issues, set an agenda for research, or provide a focus for professional debates. Third, the series seeks work that challenges the conventional wisdom about how bureaucracies influence public policy or the role of public administration in governance.

The State of Public Bureaucracy is an effort to redefine the field of public administration to focus on the political rather than the management side of bureaucracy. Larry Hill proposes that we view bureaucracy as a political institution similar to the presidency, the Congress, or the courts. By doing so, Professor Hill accomplishes two ends. Public administration is immediately distinguished from business administration. Students of public management constantly face the question: "How is public administration (management) different from business administration (management)?" Despite a myriad of differences—documented in this book by Hal Rainey—many still contend that public administration and business administration are essentially the same. This book focuses on the unique public sector aspects of governmental organizations. Second, the focus on public bureaucracy serves to integrate public administration with the vast tradition of studying political institutions and how they affect public policy in the United States. The study of public bureaucracy deserves an equal billing with the study of the Congress, the presidency, or the courts.

For the past several years, Larry Hill has encouraged, urged, and provoked scholars in the field to think about what defines the field of public administration. The essays collected in this volume are one result of his exhortations. Part one of the book attempts to focus on what is known about public bureaucracy in the existing literature. In many cases these essays are written by individuals who have been at the leading edge of research on public bureaucracy. The focus is empirical. In at least one case, the essay by Gary Wamsley and his colleagues, the view is distinctly normative. The Blacksburg Manifesto, as this chapter has become known, is an aggressive defense of public administration and the role it should play in the governance of the United States. Part two of the book looks to the future. The essays attempt to set an agenda for public bureaucracy research, to instruct the field as to where it should go. Since future directions are a topic about which scholars often disagree, these essays take a variety of different viewpoints.

Professor Hill has provided the discipline with a provocative book. *The State of Public Bureaucracy*, however, is only the first step in the process of defining a field of study. It invites discussion and challenges. Professor Hill would like nothing more than to hear from others who disagree with him. I urge you to write him.

Kenneth J. Meier
University of Wisconsin,
Milwaukee

Introduction:

Public Bureaucracy and the American State

Larry B. Hill

Few topics are more distasteful to most Americans than *bureaucracy*. Mere mention of the term is likely to bring to mind a series of negative images: dizzying mazes of impersonal, irresponsible, hierarchically arranged offices; those populated by rigid, unimaginative, risk-averse, time-serving, lazy functionaries "going by the book," "feathering their nest," and otherwise behaving like—well—behaving like "bureaucrats"! Considering its dismal place in the public imagination, why should we choose to study bureaucracy and, indeed, feature the term in a book title? The brief answer is that in the United States, as elsewhere around the world, bureaucracy has become an important focus of political power—however, and ironically, a focus whose study has been relatively neglected.

The *Oxford English Dictionary* specifies that "bureaucracy" has two meanings: "a. . . . Government by bureaux; usually officialism. b. Government officials collectively." John Stuart Mill, who is quoted on the "inexpediency of concentrating in a dominant bureaucracy . . . all the power of organized action . . . in the community," was the *OED's* authority for the definition of bureaucracy as constituting *rule* by bureaus and bureaucrats. Sometimes we use the term mainly in the *OED's* second sense—merely as a collective noun referring to governmental officials—but speaking of bureaucracy always invokes the sense that we speak also of the exercise of political power.

In addition to Mill, a number of other nineteenth- and early twentieth-century authors analyzed bureaucracy by focusing on its political power. Included among them are Hegel, Marx, Mosca, Michels, Weber, and Laski.[1] For example, al-

1

though Harold Laski was a proponent of welfare-state programs for Britain, he began his famous entry on "Bureaucracy" in the *Encyclopaedia of the Social Sciences* with this negative image of bureaucratic power: "Bureaucracy is the term usually applied to a system of government the control of which is so completely in the hands of officials that their power jeopardizes the liberties of ordinary citizens."

The following passages from *Economy and Society* indicate that Max Weber, bureaucracy's most important academic expositor, was well attuned to the political power of the growing social phenomenon:

> —As an instrument of rationally organizing authority relations, bureaucracy was and is a power instrument of the first order for one who controls the bureaucratic apparatus. . . . Where administration has been completely bureaucratized, the resulting system of domination is practically indestructible.
> —The power position of a fully developed bureaucracy is always great, under normal conditions overtowering. The political "master" always finds himself, vis-à-vis the trained official, in the position of a dilettante facing the expert.
> —In a modern state the actual ruler is necessarily and unavoidably the bureaucracy, since power is exercised neither through parliamentary speeches nor monarchical enunciations but through the routines of administration.
> —In view of the growing indispensability of the state bureaucracy and its corresponding increase in power, how can there be any guarantee that any powers will remain which can check and effectively control the tremendous influence of this stratum?[2]

Although Weber sometimes has been viewed as an advocate of bureaucracy, the following gloomy passage indicates that in actuality he was pessimistic about the future of humanity in the coming bureaucratic age: "What have we to set against this machinery, in order to preserve a remnant of humanity from this parceling-out of the soul, from this exclusive rule of bureaucratic life ideals?"[3] One need not share all of Weber's pessimism to endorse his conclusion that bureaucracy has become an important force in modern life.

Defining Public Bureaucracy

> *"When I use a word," Humpty Dumpty said in a rather scornful tone, "it means just what I choose it to mean—neither more nor less." "The question is," said Alice, "whether you can make words mean so many different things." "The question is," said Humpty Dumpty, "which is to be master— that's all."*
>
> —Lewis Carroll, *Through the Looking-Glass*

However much we may share Alice's concern regarding the violation of conventional understandings about words, Humpty Dumpty was, of course, correct in maintaining that we have discretion in naming things. But the best names usually do not stray too far from accepted meanings, and they are highly evocative of the things being described. Furthermore, the words we choose may have important consequences for what we see and how we think about it.

The tradition of writers who focus on bureaucracy's political power has continued, but the American public's distaste both for government and for bureaucracy has inhibited interest in a subject so labeled. In addition, many scholars who are interested in the general subject have—for a variety of professional and ideological reasons—chosen not to use the rubric of bureaucracy to describe their research. For example, they may speak of the process of administration, or they may describe the entities in question as organizations, institutions, or agencies.

First, why do I choose to speak of bureaucracy rather than of *administration?* Schools and departments of administration—with or without the prefixes *business* or *public*—have proliferated in American universities, and the American Society for Public Administration has attracted thousands of members. Focusing on a process is a sound approach to the study of political phenomena, and as a practical matter the focus allows courses of study in "how-to-do-it." Nonetheless, administration is a relatively value-neutral process, and its study may be mainly descriptive and far removed from political analysis. Bureaucracy, on the other hand, is likely to conjure up images of politics.

Second, why do I choose to describe the objects of study as bureaucracies rather than as organizations, institutions, or agencies? Bureaucracies certainly are *organizations*, and the stream of literature that often is described as organizational theory has been useful in analyzing bureaucracies, as well as such other sorts of organizations as matrix organizations or open-systems organizations. Although it is important to understand how bureaucracies are like and unlike other kinds of organizations, using the term bureaucracy emphasizes the focus on a distinctively political form of organization. Furthermore, bureaucracies also are likely to be *institutions*, but the latter term lacks sufficient specificity—as well as a direct political connotation—so that it does not serve as an adequate substitute for bureaucracy. Finally, although bureaucracies may be called *agencies*, the idea of bureaucracies as agents is unsatisfactory. Does it not seem inconsistent to talk of rule by bureaus that are merely acting on behalf of others, as agents do?

To be sure, a case can be made for talking of administration and of organization, institution, agency, instead of bureaucracy. And we shall frequently use each of these terms below—with the implied understanding that we focus on their political aspects. But reasons also exist for preferring to talk of bureaucracies in order to emphasize the political dimensions of these entities. And, at the same time that we continue to use the other terms mentioned above to describe the phenomena under analysis, we join the writers who have continued to use the term "bureaucracy" in their analyses.[4]

Invoking Humpty Dumpty's warrant, when I use the word *bureaucracy* I mean to refer to rule by bureaus or bureaucrats, but only in a limited sense. I do not assume that they have achieved control of the political process. Instead, I always think of bureaucracy as an unproven hypothesis; bureaucratic power may be formidable or weak. I find the word useful because *bureaucracy* brings to mind the political dimensions of the objects under study.

Bureaucratization is a phenomenon that has affected nearly all aspects of modern life,[5] but we shall concentrate on *public*, or governmental, bureaucracies. I use the term "public" to emphasize a primary interest in those organizations whose purpose is stated in legislative terms and whose powers ultimately are supported by legitimate political coercion. I appreciate the streams of literature that emphasize the "public" character of many seemingly "private" organizations and that identify "publicness" as a continuous variable.[6] Nonetheless, for present purposes I would be most interested in such matters as the private organizations' roles as captors, contractors, or regulatees of organizations that are clearly public. This focus is not intended to exclude more or less private organizations from analysis—third-sector agencies clearly play an increasingly important policy role in this country, for example—but rather is designed to indicate a primary orientation toward overtly public organizations.

The Foundations of Bureaucratic Power

What makes public bureaucracy a politically powerful force in modern society? The following discussion of bureaucracy's bases of power is synthesized from Weber and many other sources. The first division of the discussion focuses on those power bases that are inherent in the nature of bureaucracy; the second features those that are peculiar to the position of bureaucracies in American society.

Power Bases Inherent in the Nature of Bureaucracy

All bureaucracies share certain legal, material, and strategic-organizational resources. These resources translate into power when bureaucratic action agencies use them to develop political capacities.

Legal Resources

The law is a principal power resource for bureaucracy. According to Weber, the bureaucratization of modern states, which was nascent as he wrote, is but a consequence of the adoption of a rational-legal basis—as opposed to a traditional or a charismatic basis—for structuring official authority relations. In fact, he identified bureaucracy as a subcategory of rational legalism, calling it the "purest type of exercise of legal authority."[7]

The law provides a basis for bureaucracy's existence, specifies its powers and jurisdiction, and enables its decisions to be enforced. Because bureaucrats are official, legally endowed representatives of the state, their actions are usually considered to be legitimate by other actors, who are predisposed to comply with bureaucrats' instructions. Citizens and other political actors know that bureaucratic actors have the legal authority to reward and punish—to encourage or forbid many activities, to subsidize or to prosecute. Thus, they are likely to defer to bureaucrats' wishes and treat them as authority figures.

Material Resources

Bureaucracies' monetary and other capital resources, which are likely to be greater than those of competitors, are important power resources. Simply having access to multimillion-dollar budgets, computers and other equipment, data analysts, caseworkers, secretaries—all are likely to be significant sources of political power. In addition, material resources may provide a basis for the building of further bureaucratic power. For example, as bureaucracies spend money in the normal course of events, they often "buy" the allegiance of constituent groups, which may multiply the agencies' political power.

Strategic-Organizational Resources

Bureaucracies frequently are monopoly providers of services for the public and for other key actors in governance. Thus, these actors may have nowhere else to turn to have their needs met and may feel highly dependent on the agency. That dependence is increased by the widespread appreciation of the importance of bureaucracy's ability to process large numbers of routine cases quickly. In addition, whereas many of the other actors in the governance process are temporary and their involvement may be episodic and limited to certain issues, bureaucracies—largely staffed by career employees—are permanent actors and enjoy the power resource of continuity.

Expertise, knowledge, and specialization are further strategic-organizational ingredients of bureaucracy's power. As professionalization—and sub-professionalization—becomes ever more important in modern society, bureaucracies employ more and more professionals, who gain additional authority by virtue of their professional credentials. Bureaucratic expertise is frequently founded upon nothing more exotic, however, than repetitive experience in making mundane decisions.

Another important strategic-organizational source of bureaucracy's power is the ability to affect the context of decision making, particularly through controlling the flow of information and the timing of decisions. Bureaucracies frequently control information crucial to governance. In fact, they often maintain a near monopoly over important information, whose existence may be unknown to other actors, and bureaucracies may aggressively protect their secrets.[8] A special aspect of bureaucracy's informational control is the organizational memory, which is frequently stored in computerized data banks under the bureaucracy's control. Bureaucracies also may have an impact on the context of decision making through affecting the timing of decisions. Thus they may act quickly or delay in order to maximize their input. The fact that many occasions for making decisions are presented to bureaucracies on an emergency basis—ranging from natural disasters or oil spills to wars or recessions—certainly increases their power.

Political-Action Resources

Bureaucratic agencies are behaving entities, or organizations in action. They have the ability to harness all of their legal, material, and organizational resources and develop a capacity to accomplish their missions. The members of a bureaucracy become committed to those missions, they socialize new members of the organization, and their leaders strive to achieve the bureaucracy's objectives.

Finally, in the long run, political issues become bureaucratic issues, and the inherent power of implementation is a key to bureaucracy's political power. Bureaucrats have the action. They are expected by other actors to exercise discretion, meet their responsibilities, and get on with the job—even if the bureaucrats' choices may differ from those of other actors.

Power Bases Related to the Peculiar Nature of American Politics

Although bureaucracies everywhere share the preceding power resources, American bureaucracies—disliked and disparaged as they are—actually enjoy some unusual power resources. Owing to the sharing/separation of powers between the executive and the legislature, American bureaucracies face fragmented, multiple controls; since no single institution is in charge of American bureaucracies, they may play their nominal controllers off against each other. At the same time, American bureaucracies do not have an official political protector. The obvious contrast is with the parliamentary regimes of Western Europe whose executive— fused with the legislature—is able to offer such political protection. Hence, in order to defend itself and accomplish its mission, an American bureaucracy must be politically proactive.

Furthermore, the unusual strength of American political groups of various sorts—along with the fragmentation of the state's controls over bureaucracy— encourages agencies to convert the interests they share with their constituencies into an independent power base. Since it is an iron law of politics that groups flow to power, they seek out agencies that have jurisdiction over the groups' interests, and the groups and the agencies pursue their common cause.

Also, in the postwar period, most American laws have been vaguely drafted— whether because of a decision to defer to bureaucratic expertise, a lack of political consensus, or cowardice on the part of politicians. The vagueness of statutes allows bureaucrats to create policies—especially when writing rules to implement the law. Largely owing to rivalry with the executive, however, in recent years Congress often has attempted to write somewhat more detailed legislation.

In addition, in the highly partisan American political environment, where consensus on specifics seldom exists among official and nonofficial actors, bureaucrats often are viewed as nonpartisan, honest brokers between factions. Notwithstanding the heat of the never-ending political battle, all parties eventually realize that somehow the work of government must be accomplished. Especially at the state and the local levels, bureaucrats may be trusted more than any other political force and allowed to exercise much discretion.

Finally, because distrust of "politics" is a key component of the American political culture, decisions that would clearly be considered political and appropriate for handling by politicians in most other countries may be translated into technical, managerial, and other supposedly nonpolitical issues—issues subject to the jurisdiction of American bureaucrats. For example, regulating the money supply is entrusted to the "nonpolitical" Federal Reserve, and urban areas hire "nonpartisan" city managers. As suspicious as Americans are of bureaucrats, they are sometimes even more suspicious of politicians.

Conclusion: The Problem of American Bureaucratic Power

The inventory of power bases discussed above is, of course, only a list of resources that may be available to a bureaucracy. Whether bureaucracies are successful in using those resources to establish "a system of domination"—in Weber's terms—over the political process remains an open question. As the book proceeds we shall examine such matters as the ability of bureaucracies to assert their wills over other unofficial and official political actors and the power of both sets of actors over bureaucracies.

Although American bureaucracies have access to the important power resources discussed above, they are not monolithic; they also are burdened with significant vulnerabilities. For example, the executive and the legislature share control over a bureaucracy's existence and structure, its legal authority, and its material resources. And the judiciary may issue rulings that profoundly affect its activities. Furthermore, the distinctive American practice of naming large numbers of political appointees to significant positions in agencies allows politicians to penetrate bureaucracies. Private groups may penetrate bureaucracies as well—even "capture" them. All in all, despite their significant powers, agencies may be highly vulnerable to other political forces. Bureaucracies are at constant risk of losing authority, missions, and their very existence. Bureaucratic power seems highly variable, depending on such matters as the particular power position of a given agency, the stage of the policy process under consideration, the policy arena in question, the type of policy scrutinized, and the level of policy involved.

Thus, to talk of American bureaucracy as a state unto itself—as implied by one meaning of the double entendre in the book's title—seems extravagant. Although I am not persuaded that American government is best described as *bureaucracy* in the sense of *rule by* bureaucrats, the issue of just how much political power bureaucracies actually wield raises interesting questions for students of politics. The essays in part one continue to explore bureaucratic power—mainly, but not exclusively in the United States. And (in the second meaning of the title) part one's essays also explore a number of other important dimensions of the current state of public bureaucracy. The essays in part two look to the future state of public bureaucracy.

Notes

1. The *OED* quotation of Mill is from *Principles of Political Economy, With Some of Their Applications to Social Philosophy* (London: J.W. Parker, 1848), p. 529. See Hegel, *Philosophy of Right* [1821], trans. T.M. Knox (London: Oxford University Press, 1952); Marx, *Critique of Hegel's 'Philosophy of Right'* [1843], ed. Joseph O'Malley, trans. Annette Jolin and Joseph O'Malley (Cambridge: Cambridge University Press, 1970); Mosca, *The Ruling Class* [1896], ed. Arthur Livingston, trans. Hannah D. Kahn (New York: McGraw-Hill, 1939); Michels, *Political Parties: A Sociological Study of the Oligarchical Tendencies of Modern Democracy* [1911], trans. Eden and Cedar Paul (London: Jarrold and Sons, 1915); Weber, *Economy and Society: An Outline of Interpretive Sociology* [1914-29], ed. Guenther Roth and Claus Wittich (Berkeley: University of California Press, 1978); Laski, "Bureaucracy," in *Encyclopaedia of the Social Sciences*, vol. 3, ed. R.A. Seligman (New York: Macmillan, 1930), pp. 70-74.

2. *Economy and Society*, vol. 2, pp. 987, 991, 1393, 1403.

3. Quoted in Arthur Mitzman, *The Iron Cage: An Historical Interpretation of Max Weber* (New York: Alfred A. Knopf, 1970), p. 232.

4. A chronological listing over the past half-century of prominent examples of writers who have featured the rubric of *bureaucracy* in their studies follows:

The Decade of the 1940s. Robert K. Merton, "Bureaucratic Structure and Personality," *Social Forces* 18 (1940): 560-68; Peter Selznick, "An Approach to a Theory of Bureaucracy," *American Sociological Review* 8 (1943): 47-54; John Donald Kingsley, *Representative Bureaucracy: An Interpretation of the British Civil Service* (Yellow Springs, OH: Antioch Press, 1944); Ludwig von Mises, *Bureaucracy* (New Haven, CT: Yale University Press, 1944); Reinhard Bendix, "Bureaucracy: The Problem and Its Setting," *American Sociological Review* 12 (1947): 493-507.

The Decade of the 1950s. Charles S. Hyneman, *Bureaucracy in a Democracy* (New York: Harper, 1950); Norton E. Long, "Bureaucracy and Constitutionalism," *American Political Science Review* 46 (September 1952): 808-18; Robert K. Merton, Alisa Gray, Barbara Hockey, and Hanan C. Selvin, eds., *Reader in Bureaucracy* (Glencoe, IL: Free Press, 1952); Arnold Brecht, "How Bureaucracies Develop and Function," *Annals of the American Academy of Political and Social Science* 292 (1954):1-10; Dwaine Marvick, *Career Perspectives in a Bureaucratic Setting* (Ann Arbor: University of Michigan Press, 1954); Peter M. Blau, *The Dynamics of Bureaucracy: A Study of Interpersonal Relationships in Two Government Agencies* (Chicago: University of Chicago Press, 1955); Alvin Gouldner, "Metaphysical Pathos and the Theory of Bureaucracy," *American Political Science Review* 49 (1955): 496-507; Monroe Berger, *Bureaucracy and Society in Modern Egypt* (Princeton, NJ: Princeton University Press, 1957); Fritz Morstein Marx, *The Ad-*

ministrative State: An Introduction to Bureaucracy (Chicago: University of Chicago Press, 1957).
   The Decade of the 1960s. Victor A. Thompson, *Modern Organization* (New York: Random House, 1961); S.N. Eisenstadt, *The Political System of Empires* (Glencoe, IL: Free Press, 1963); Joseph La Palombara, ed., *Bureaucracy and Political Development* (Princeton, NJ: Princeton University Press, 1963); Peter Woll, *American Bureaucracy* (New York: Norton, 1963); Michel Crozier, *The Bureaucratic Phenomenon* (Chicago: University of Chicago Press, 1964); Fred W. Riggs, *Administration in Developing Countries: The Theory of Prismatic Society* (Boston: Houghton Mifflin, 1964); Francis E. Rourke, ed., *Bureaucratic Power in National Politics* (Boston: Little, Brown, 1965); Gordon Tullock, *The Politics of Bureaucracy* (Washington, DC: Public Affairs Press, 1965); Matthew Holden, Jr., " 'Imperialism' in Bureaucracy," *American Political Science Review* 60 (December 1966): 943-51); G. Sjöberg, R.A. Brymer, and B. Farris, "Bureaucracy and the Lower Class," *Sociology and Social Research* 50 (1966): 325-37: Anthony Downs, *Inside Bureaucracy* (Boston: Little, Brown, 1967); Nicos P. Mouzelis, *Organisation and Bureaucracy: An Analysis of Modern Theories* (London: Routledge and Kegan Paul, 1967); James Q. Wilson, "The Bureaucracy Problem," *The Public Interest* 6 (1967): 3–9; Reinhard Bendix, "Bureaucracy," in *International Encyclopedia of the Social Sciences*, vol. 2 (New York: Macmillan and Free Press, 1968), 206-19; Robert Alford, *Bureaucracy and Participation* (Chicago: Rand-McNally, 1969); Lewis C. Gawthrop, *Bureaucratic Behavior in the Executive Branch: An Analysis of Organizational Change* (New York: Free Press, 1969); Theodore J. Lowi, *The End of Liberalism: Ideology, Policy, and the Crisis of Public Authority* (New York: Norton, 1969); Francis E. Rourke, *Bureaucracy, Politics, and Public Policy* (Boston: Little, Brown, 1969); Victor A. Thompson, *Bureaucracy and Innovation* (University: University of Alabama Press, 1969).
   The Decade of the 1970s. Martin Albrow, *Bureaucracy* (New York: Praeger, 1970); Warren G. Bennis, ed., *American Bureaucracy* (Chicago: Aldine, 1970); Graham T. Allison, *Essence of Decision: Explaining the Cuban Missile Crisis* (Boston: Little, Brown, 1971); William Niskanen, *Bureaucracy and Representative Government* (Chicago: Aldine-Atherton, 1971); Francis E. Rourke, *Bureaucracy and Foreign Policy* (Baltimore: Johns Hopkins University Press, 1972); Eugene P. Dvorin and Robert H. Simmons, *From Amoral to Humane Bureaucracy* (San Francisco: Canfield Press, 1972); Elihu Katz and Brenda Danet, eds., *Bureaucracy and the Public: A Reader in Official–Client Relations* (New York: Basic Books, 1973); Lewis C. Mainzer, *The American Public Service: Political Bureaucracy* (Glenview, IL: Scott, Foresman, 1973); Donald P. Warwick, *A Theory of Public Bureaucracy: Politics, Personality, and Organization in the State Department* (Cambridge, MA: Harvard University Press, 1973); Morton H. Halperin, *Bureaucratic Politics and Foreign Policy* (Washington, DC: Brookings Institution, 1974); Samuel Krislov, *Representative Bureaucracy* (Englewood Cliffs, NJ: Prentice-Hall, 1974); Ezra N. Suleiman, *Politics, Power, and Bureaucracy in France: The Administrative Elite* (Princeton, NJ: Princeton University Press, 1974); Matthew Crenson, *The Federal Machine: Beginnings of Bureaucracy in Jacksonian America* (Baltimore: Johns Hopkins University Press, 1975); Lee Fritchler, *Smoking and Politics: Policy Making and the Federal Bureaucracy* (Englewood Cliffs, NJ: Prentice-Hall, 1975); Daniel Katz, Barbara A. Gutek, Robert L. Kahn, and Eugenia Barton, *Bureaucratic Encounters: A Pilot Study in the Evaluation of Government Services* (Ann Arbor: Institute for Social Research, University of Michigan, 1975); Kenneth J. Meier, "Representative Bureaucracy: An Empirical Analysis," *American Political Science Review* 69 (June 1975): 526–42; Lester B. Salamon and Gary L. Wamsley, "The Federal Bureaucracy: Responsive to Whom?" in *People vs. Government: The Responsiveness of American Institutions*, ed. Leroy N. Rieselbach (Bloomington, IN: Indiana University Press, 1975), pp. 151–88; Arnold J.

Meltzner, *Policy Analysts in the Bureaucracy* (Berkeley: University of California Press, 1976); Morris S. Ogul, *Congress Oversees the Bureaucracy: Studies in Legislative Supervision* (Pittsburgh: University of Pittsburgh Press, 1976); Randall B. Ripley and Grace A. Franklin, *Congress, the Bureaucracy, and Public Policy* (Homewood, IL: Dorsey Press, 1976); Bengt Abrahamsson, *Bureaucracy or Participation: The Logic of Organization* (Beverly Hills, CA: Sage, 1977); Guy Benveniste, *Bureaucracy* (San Francisco: Boyd and Fraser, 1977); Hugh Heclo, *A Government of Strangers: Executive Politics in Washington* (Washington, DC: Brookings Institution, 1977); Ralph P. Hummel, *The Bureaucratic Experience* (New York: St. Martin's, 1977); Eugene Lewis, *American Politics in a Bureaucratic Age: Citizens, Constituents, Clients, and Victims* (Cambridge, MA: Winthrop, 1977); B. Guy Peters, *The Politics of Bureaucracy: A Comparative Perspective* (New York: Longman, 1978); John Rohr, *Ethics for Bureaucrats: An Essay on Law and Values* (New York: Marcel Dekker, 1978); R. Douglas Arnold, *Congress and the Bureaucracy: A Theory of Influence* (New Haven, CT: Yale University Press, 1979); Colin Campbell and George Zablowski, *The Superbureaucrats: Structure and Behaviour in Central Agencies* (Toronto: Macmillan, 1979); Kenneth J. Meier, *Politics and the Bureaucracy: Policymaking in the Fourth Branch of Government* (North Scituate, MA: Duxbury Press, 1979); Marshall W. Meyer, *Change in Public Bureaucracies* (Cambridge: Cambridge University Press, 1979); Jeffrey M. Prottas, *People-Processing: The Street-Level Bureaucrat in Public Service Bureaucracies* (Lexington, MA: Lexington Books, 1979); Robert K. Yin, *Changing Urban Bureaucracies: How New Practices Become Routinized* (Santa Monica, CA: Rand Corp., 1979).

The Decade of the 1980s. Frederic A. Bergerson, *The Army Gets an Air Force: Tactics of Insurgent Bureaucratic Politics* (Baltimore: Johns Hopkins University Press, 1980); William P. Browne, *Politics, Programs, and Bureaucrats* (Port Washington, NY: Kennikat, 1980); Bryan D. Jones, *Service Delivery in the City: Citizen Demand and Bureaucratic Rules* (New York: Longman, 1980); Eugene Lewis, *Public Entrepreneurship: Toward a Theory of Bureaucratic Power: The Organizational Lives of Hyman Rickover, J. Edgar Hoover, and Robert Moses* (Bloomington: Indiana University Press, 1980); Michael Lipsky, *Street-Level Bureaucracy* (New York: Russell Sage, 1980); David Nachmias and David H. Rosenbloom, *Bureaucratic Government USA* (New York: St. Martin's, 1980); Carol H. Weiss and Allen H. Barton, *Making Bureaucracies Work* (Beverly Hills, CA: Sage, 1980); Joel D. Aberbach, Robert D. Putnam, and Bert A. Rockman, *Bureaucrats and Politicians in Western Democracies* (Cambridge, MA: Harvard University Press, 1981); Charles T. Goodsell, ed., *The Public Encounter: Where State and Citizen Meet* (Bloomington: Indiana University Press, 1981); Christopher Hood and Andrew Dunsire, *Bureaumetrics: The Quantitative Comparison of British Central Government Agencies* (University: University of Alabama Press, 1981); Herbert Kaufman, "Fear of Bureaucracy: A Raging Pandemic," *Public Administration Review* 41 (January/February 1981): 1–9; Samuel Krislov and David H. Rosenbloom, *Representative Bureaucracy and the American Political System* (New York: Praeger, 1981); B. Guy Peters, "The Problem of Bureaucratic Government," *Journal of Politics* 43 (February 1981): 56–82; Frank J. Thompson, *Health Care and the Bureaucracy: Politics and Implementation* (Cambridge, MA: MIT Press, 1981); Michael Nelson, "A Short, Ironic History of American National Bureaucracy," *Journal of Politics* 44 (August 1982): 747–78; Bernard Rosen, *Holding Government Bureaucracies Accountable* (New York: Praeger, 1982); Douglas Yates, *Bureaucratic Democracy: The Search for Democracy and Efficiency in American Government* (Cambridge, MA: Harvard University Press, 1982); Colin Campbell, *Governments under Stress: Political Executives and Key Bureaucrats in Washington, London, and Ottawa* (Toronto: University of Toronto Press, 1983); Eva Etzioni-Halevy, *Bureaucracy and Democracy: A Political Dilemma* (London: Routledge and Kegan Paul,

1983); Charles T. Goodsell, *The Case for Bureaucracy: A Public Administration Polemic* (Chatham, NJ: Chatham House, 1983); Jerry L. Mashaw, *Bureaucratic Justice: Managing Social Security Disability Claims* (New Haven: Yale University Press, 1983); H. Brinton Milward and Hal G. Rainey, "Don't Blame the Bureaucracy!" *Journal of Public Policy* 3 (October 1983): 149–68; Patricia W. Ingraham and Carolyn Ban, eds., *Legislating Bureaucratic Change: The Civil Service Reform Act of 1978* (Albany: State University of New York Press, 1984); Robert D. Miewald, *The Bureaucratic State: An Annotated Bibliography* (New York: Garland, 1984); John P. Burke, *Bureaucratic Responsibility* (Baltimore: Johns Hopkins University Press, 1986); Joel F. Handler, *The Conditions of Discretion: Autonomy, Community, Bureaucracy* (New York: Russell Sage, 1986); Gary C. Bryner, *Bureaucratic Discretion: Law and Policy in Federal Regulatory Agencies* (New York: Pergamon, 1987); Jack H. Knott and Gary J. Miller, *Reforming Bureaucracy: The Politics of Institutional Choice* (Englewood Cliffs, NJ: Prentice-Hall, 1987); Richard J. Stillman, II, *The American Bureaucracy*, (Chicago: Nelson-Hall, 1987); Judith E. Gruber, *Controlling Bureaucracies: Dilemmas in Democratic Governance* (Berkeley: University of California Press, 1987); B. Guy Peters, *Comparing Public Bureaucracies: Problems of Theory and Method* (Tuscaloosa: University of Alabama Press, 1988); Brenda Danet, *Pulling Strings: Biculturalism in Israeli Bureaucracy* (Albany: State University of New York Press, 1989); William T. Gormley, Jr., *Taming the Bureaucracy: Muscles, Prayers, and Other Strategies* (Princeton, NJ: Princeton University Press, 1989); James Q. Wilson, *Bureaucracy: What Government Agencies Do and Why They Do It* (New York: Basic Books, 1989).

5. See Peter M. Blau and Marshall W. Meyer, *Bureaucracy and Modern Society*, 2d ed. (New York: Random House, 1971).

6. Barry Bozeman, *All Organizations are Public: Bridging Public and Private Organization Theory* (San Francisco: Jossey-Bass, 1987).

7. *Economy and Society*, vol. 1, p. 220.

8. Weber emphasized that administrative secrecy was an important bureaucratic power base: "Bureaucratic administration always tends to exclude the public, to hide its knowledge and action from criticism as well as it can." Furthermore, he said: "The concept of the 'office secret' is the specific invention of bureaucracy, and few things it defends so fanatically as this attitude which, outside of the specific areas mentioned, cannot be justified with purely functional arguments" (ibid., vol. 2, p. 992).

Part One

The Current State
of Public Bureaucracy

1

Taking Bureaucracy Seriously

Larry B. Hill

—A major scandal arises in the procedures for governmental contracting.
—A bold new treaty to limit nuclear weapons is being negotiated.
—The president says he will implement a comprehensive war on drugs.
—Plans are underway for restructuring Medicaid.

When this book's authors hear about these kinds of developments, we are likely to ask: *What is the role of the relevant public agencies?* We take public bureaucracy seriously. That is, we believe public agencies play important roles in the processes by which policy is made and citizens are governed. Of course, we know that the three branches of government and such other political actors as pressure groups and the mass media may play even more important roles in these processes; but we choose to focus on the roles of public agencies—including the impact of the other political actors upon these agencies.

By any measure, the United States has developed an extensive public sector. To be sure, many of our public programs are structured and delivered in unusual ways; some might say in eccentric and chaotic ways. But when the instrumentalities of the state and the local governments are added to those at the federal level, the total size of the American welfare state is roughly similar to that of most Western European countries. Of course, large public bureaucracies have been created to administer these programs. What is the state, or condition, of American public bureaucracy, and how much do we really know about the subject? These questions are addressed in this part of the book.

Conducting a periodic inventory of the state of the presidency, the Congress, or any other institution of American government seems appropriate, but special reasons exist for considering the state of public bureaucracy. Foremost among them is that, considered as groups, the American public and its political leaders

15

and American social scientists have thus far failed to take bureaucracy seriously. That is, although public bureaucracy has emerged as a significant political phenomenon in recent decades, Americans have neglected to integrate this development into their general understandings of the political process. As a result of this failure to acknowledge the importance of public bureaucracy and to focus on it dispassionately, we know much less than we should know about the phenomenon, and the justification for undertaking an inventory of its state becomes compelling.

The Public's Failure to Take Bureaucracy Seriously

How can I argue that Americans fail to take public bureaucracy seriously when stories dealing with the subject appear in nearly every issue of our daily newspapers, and our politicians constantly comment on the performance of bureaucrats? The apparent contradiction is resolved when we recall that most of the public discussion is at the level of sloganeering rather than analysis. Americans have found that, as Gibbon said of Corsica, deploring bureaucracy is easier than describing its actual condition.

Although few pollsters have attempted to find out just how deeply Americans deplore the subject, a guess that "bureaucracy" would rank as our third-most salient negative political symbol—after "communism" and "socialism"—probably would not be far off the mark. The guess is buttressed by the following polling data. When *U.S. News and World Report* asked a sample of the American people to rank a list of twenty-six private and public institutions on their "ability to get things done," the "federal bureaucracy" was ranked last; it was next to last when the sample ranked the institutions on "honesty, dependability, and integrity."[1] Compounding the problem with these allegedly ineffective and untrustworthy institutions is the fact that bureaucracies also are widely seen as being politically powerful. Two-thirds of another sample agreed that: "The trouble with government is that elected officials have lost control over the bureaucrats, who really run things."[2] About a decade ago, Americans' aversive feelings toward bureaucracy became so strong that some commentators turned to medical terminology in attempting to characterize them: Thompson talked of "bureausis" as "a kind of social disease," and Kaufman called the fear of bureaucracy a "raging pandemic."[3]

But the possibility remains that the prevalent antibureaucratic sentiment is mainly a matter of rhetoric and of labels and does not necessarily represent Americans' true feelings toward the phenomena in question. If the pollsters mentioned above had asked about the "civil service" and "civil servants" rather than "bureaucracy" and "bureaucrats," would the responses have been different? Although the question is unanswerable, we shall attempt to shed light on it by examining polling data that have inquired about citizens' attitudes toward and experiences with bureaucracy—however it may be labeled. Because attitudes about bureaucracy are inextricably intertwined with those about governance in general, we shall first explore briefly how citizens feel about government and being governed by the institutions created for this purpose.

Attitudes toward Government in the Abstract

Many Americans become uncomfortable when they think explicitly about government in the abstract. In recent years, when the Gallup organization has asked, "Which of the following will be the greatest threat to the country in the future— big business, big labor, or big government?," majorities of the samples nominated government as the greatest threat; about one-fifth each chose labor and business, and the remainder had no opinion.[4]

Over several years, the University of Michigan's Survey Research Center (SRC) has documented citizens' high levels of cynicism and low levels of trust in government, as indicated by the responses to the following three questions.[5] First: "How much of the time do you think you can trust the government in Washington to do what is right . . .?" In 1986, hardly any of the respondents (3 percent) believed one "always" can trust the government, about one-third (35 percent) believed such trust was due "most of the time," about three-fifths (57 percent) felt able to give it only "some of the time," and the same small numbers (2 percent) didn't know or volunteered "none of the time." Second: "Would you say the government is pretty much run by a few big interests looking out for themselves or that it is run for the benefit of all the people?" In 1984, far more respondents believed the government was run by a few big interests (55 percent) than believed it was run for the benefit of all (39 percent); 6 percent "didn't know." Third: "Do you think that people in the government waste a lot of the money we pay in taxes, waste some of it, or don't waste very much of it?" In 1984, two-thirds believed a lot of tax money was wasted (65 percent), and nearly all of the remainder believed some was wasted (30 percent); only 4 percent thought not very much was wasted, and 2 percent didn't know.

These SRC results reveal high levels of cynicism; an examination of earlier *National Election Surveys* indicates that levels of trust have fallen considerably since these questions were first asked in 1958. Of course, not everyone is cynical, but substantial numbers of citizens perceive their government as untrustworthy, elite-dominated, and wasteful. That they also should feel alienated from the bureaucratic instrumentalities of that government seems only natural.

Attitudes toward the Scope of Government

Debates about the proper scope of government are a staple of American political discourse. The public's responses to polling questions vary from time to time and seem to be very sensitive to how questions are framed. The following responses to an SRC question in 1986 illustrate the public's range of opinion. Thirty-one percent of the sample agreed that "the government in Washington is trying to do too many things that should be left to individuals and private businesses," but nearly as large a group (27 percent) disagreed and felt that "the government should do even more to solve our country's problems," while the largest group (43 percent) reported having "opinions somewhere in between." Pollsters who have asked a broad range of questions about government's scope—including preferred levels of services and spending—and its ability to solve problems have discovered that public opinion is far from unified. Although substantial numbers of Americans view government as too powerful, too active, or too ineffective, other large groupings hold contrary opinions or have ambivalent or unformed views on the subject.[6]

Progovernmental views are especially apparent when citizens are asked how they feel about spending levels for particular programs; even those who are in favor of spending cuts in the abstract seldom show the courage of their convictions when asked about preferred expenditure levels for programs concerning crime, the environment, education, health, or other special interests. Despite widespread cynicism about government and disagreement about its scope and performance, Americans broadly endorse the continuation of their welfare state.

Attitudes toward Bureaucratic Encounters

Although we cannot be certain about the extent to which Americans' governmental attitudes are based upon cultural traditions or actual experiences with governments' instrumentalities, citizen–governmental contacts have expanded so that attitudes *may* be based upon bureaucratic contacts. In 1981, when the Census Bureau investigated who received which noncash assistance programs from the federal government, one of every three households was found to receive one or more of the following benefits: food stamps, school lunch aid, subsidized housing, Medicare, or Medicaid. Employing a different perspective, *U.S. News and World Report* compiled listings of the numbers of recipients of various "transfer payments" (e.g., Social Security, unemployment insurance, governmental pensions, welfare benefits, veterans' benefits). Their conclusion, which is in accord with the conventional estimate (but which I suspect is inflated by recipients of multiple benefits), is that "about half of the population receives transfer payments of some kind."[7]

Various national polls confirm that Americans' contact with bureaucracy is quite extensive and indicate that they are generally satisfied with their bureaucratic encounters. The best known of these studies, conducted by the SRC in 1973, found that 58 percent of a sample reported ever receiving "any help from government offices or agencies" with a list of such problems as unemployment compensation, finding a job, retirement benefits, public assistance, or job training. About one in three respondents reported contacts with more than one service agency. Despite what one would expect, based on our antibureaucratic traditions, 72 percent were satisfied—most were "very" satisfied—with the bureaucracy's handling of their problem. In addition, 15 percent reported "difficulties or problems" with constraint agencies over such matters as taxation or policing. As one might expect, citizens were less pleased about their encounters with these agencies: only 40 percent thought their problem was handled "well," 58 percent answered "poorly," and 2 percent "didn't know."[8]

A Harris poll, also taken in 1973, generally reinforced the SRC's findings, although, probably owing to differences in how the questions were worded, far fewer members of Harris's sample recalled having bureaucratic encounters. Eleven percent recalled encounters with the federal government; 46 percent of them proclaimed themselves as "highly satisfied," 29 percent were "only somewhat satisfied," and 25 percent were "not satisfied at all." Thirteen percent of the respondents remembered an involvement with a state government, and 24 percent did so with a local government. The same degrees of satisfaction were reported for both levels of government: 39 percent were highly satisfied, 26 percent were only somewhat satisfied, and 35 percent were not satisfied at all.[9]

Furthermore, a *Washington Post* poll, taken a decade later, found that about one-third of its sample reported doing "any business with the federal government in the past year. . . ." And 71 percent of them said they were "pleased" with their encounter. Virtually all other studies of citizens' evaluations of their bureaucratic encounters (at least, with service-related encounters) have found similarly high levels of satisfaction.[10]

How is the finding that Americans usually are satisfied with their bureaucratic encounters related to the negative attitudes toward government and bureaucracy that seem to be the predominant element of our political culture? Obviously, the finding conflicts with a uniformly antigovernmental, antibureaucratic cultural interpretation. Although the negative cultural interpretation of bureaucracy is strong enough that its detractors know they are unlikely to be criticized for expressing their views, the following evidence indicates that our ideas on the subject actually are complex, ambivalent, and contradictory.

In general terms, most Americans approve of the performance of their government and their bureaucracy. Even during the Watergate scandal in 1973, 61 percent of the SRC's sample reacted positively to the following question: "By and large, do most government offices do a good job?" Table 1.1 reports the results of a national poll conducted twelve years later by *USA Today*, which further confirm the public's high level of approval for government:

Table 1.1

"How Satisfied Are You with the Work and Service of the Federal Government?"

Very dissatisfied	Somewhat dissatisfied	Not sure	Somewhat satisfied	Very satisfied
7%	22%	1%	58%	12%

Source: USA Today, September 12, 1985.

A total of 70 percent of the public reported being satisfied with the federal government; slightly higher levels of satisfaction were reported for local government.[11] Recall that this level of satisfaction is similar to the level typically reported with respondents' own bureaucratic encounters. Clearly, these findings indicate that most Americans do not harbor the hatred for bureaucracy that is often assumed.

In fact, Americans have a complex, love–hate relationship with bureaucracy. For example, when the SRC asked those reporting an encounter with a service agency to evaluate it on such dimensions as fairness, 80 percent said they were treated fairly. But only 42 percent of the same group gave a positive general evaluation of governmental offices on "giving fair treatment." A similar pattern was found when other dimensions—including giving considerate treatment, correcting mistakes, and taking care of problems—were explored in the same way. On the average, about a 40 percent gap was found between the percentages of respondents giving positive evaluations of their encounters on each dimension and those giving positive evaluations of governmental offices in general on the same dimension.[12]

The authors of the SRC study ascribe the differences between people's evaluations of their particular experiences and their generalized assessments of bureaucracy to the well-known psychological finding that two distinct modes of response may exist, the pragmatic and the ideological.[13] According to this interpretation, asking about the details of respondents' interactions with specific governmental workers "sets a reality framework for response. It may be influenced by global attitudes, but such influence is minor compared to the facts of the experience itself." The nature of the bureaucratic experience seems to affect general evaluations of governmental bureaucracies only in certain circumstances: "Bad experiences reduce the appraisal of public agencies, but good experiences do not improve the appraisal." A strong and consistent pattern emerged in which many people reported having favorable bureaucratic encounters, but also gave an unfavorable evaluation of bureaucracies in general. The authors conclude: "This discrepancy is readily explained if one accepts the notion that the global attitudes reflect the general stereotypes of the culture about public bureaucracy."[14] Hence, many people shift between the pragmatic and the ideological modes in evaluating government and bureaucracy—apparently without experiencing significant cognitive stress.

General Evaluations of Bureaucratic Characteristics

The complexity of Americans' love–hate relationship with bureaucracy is further illuminated by Table 1.2, which contains data from the surveys by the University of Michigan's SRC and by the Harris organization probing citizens' perceptions of bureaucracy's negative and positive characteristics. The SRC sample was asked to respond to each statement "about the government and government

Table 1.2

Perceptions of Bureaucratic Characteristics

Negative Bureaucratic Characteristics

University of Michigan poll	Agreement with statement as description of bureaucracies (in percents)
1. Too many government offices do the same thing	78
2. Agency officials gain the most from government offices	58
3. No official takes responsibility for anything	56
4. No one person takes an interest in your problems	47
5. Government pries into the citizen's private life	43
6. Officials use their authority to push you around	37

Harris poll	Qualities best describing most bureaucracies (in percents)
1. Do things by the book	23
2. Play it safe	21
3. Just serving time	21
4. Out for themselves	18
5. Bureaucratic	14
6. Couldn't care less	12
7. Make red tape	12
8. Only want power	10
9. Make promises that are never kept	6
10. Dull	6
11. Corrupt	4

Positive Bureaucratic Characteristics

University of Michigan poll	Agreement with statement as description of bureaucracies (in percents)
1. Governmental workers work hard and try to do a good job	72
2. Governmental workers are usually very helpful	68

Harris poll	Qualities best describing most bureaucracies (in percents)
1. Dedicated to hard work	25
2. Want to help people	23
3. Intelligent, bright	21
4. Public spirited	18
5. Honest	16
6. Efficient.	14
7. Care about freedom	9
8. Idealistic	9
9. Courageous	8
10. Creative, imaginative	4
11. Tell it like it is	3

Sources: The University of Michigan data are compiled from Daniel Katz, Barbara Gutek, Robert L. Kahn, and Eugenia Barton, *Bureaucratic Encounters: A Pilot Study in the Evaluation of Government Services* (Ann Arbor: SRC, 1975), p. 136; The Harris Poll data are compiled from Louis Harris and Associates, *Confidence and Concern: Citizens View American Government, A Survey of Public Attitudes*, 93d Cong., 1st Sess., 1973, p. 310.

agencies" on a four-point, agree–disagree scale. The Harris respondents were asked to choose "the qualities which best describe most people who work in a career government job." Thus, the percentages reported for each poll were derived in different fashions.

Most of the SRC statements characterized bureaucracy negatively. Many more respondents agreed that "too many government offices do the same thing" than agreed with any other statement—perhaps because the charge was unrelated to bureaucratic performance and vague enough to serve as an outlet for the stereotypical antibureaucratic images prevalent in the culture. The statements ranked two through four, each of which attracted substantially lower levels of agreement, did concern performance and accused agency officials of being self-serving, ducking responsibility, and behaving impersonally—in short, of acting "bureaucratically." Only two statements made serious antibureaucratic allegations: "It is becoming difficult for an individual to have any private life because government pries and interferes in his personal affairs"; "The people in government offices like to use their authority to push you around." These antibureaucratic statements received the lowest levels of agreement, but about two-fifths of the sample did agree with them.

The Harris poll gave respondents a list of eleven negative and eleven positive qualities and asked them to choose which best described most bureaucrats. The negative qualities covered a wide range of supposed bureaucratic sins. Perhaps surprisingly, the results were quite scattered; no one quality was chosen as best describing most bureaucrats by as many as one quarter of the respondents. Only three negative qualities were selected by more than one-fifth of the sample: "Do things by the book," "Play it safe," and "Just serving time." The allegation that bureaucrats were self-serving attracted only one-third as many Harris respondents as SRC respondents (the statement was phrased differently by each organization; see SRC statement 2 and Harris statement 4). The remaining negative qualities, which covered a miscellany of the conventional bureaucratic diatribes, were endorsed by only a handful of respondents. In last place was the allegation that bureaucrats are corrupt.

The SRC included only two positive bureaucratic qualities in its list, but about seven-tenths of the respondents agreed that "Most of the people who work for governmental offices work hard and try to do a good job," and that "The people in governmental offices are usually very helpful." These statements were ranked second and third among the entire list of negative and positive statements. Surely it is not coincidental that the qualities of being hardworking and helpful also were the leading positive qualities cited by the Harris respondents. The Harris questioners offered a full panoply of other bureaucratic virtues: varying numbers of respondents chose each. Fewer people identified bureaucrats with creativity, imagination, and candor than with other virtues.

In addition, the Harris poll asked which "qualities best describe the people who *should* work in the government" (the results are not shown in the table). Two-thirds of the respondents said honesty was the most ideal quality. The qualities given the next three places on the "ideal" list were the same ones, in the same order, as the top three on the table's "actual" list. In general, the list of preferred bureaucratic virtues was quite similar to the respondents' list of perceived virtues.

According to the table, when they get down to specifics, the American people are not hostile to their bureaucratic agencies and the people who work in them. If citizens occasionally complain that government is "bureaucratic," they certainly are not alienated from its administrative agencies, and few bureaucratic sins are thought of as being particularly noteworthy. On the other hand, many Americans respect their bureaucrats as being hardworking, helpful, intelligent, public-spirited, honest, and efficient.

Conclusions

The principal findings from our review of a number of public opinion surveys may be stated simply. Many Americans harbor antigovernmental, anti-bureaucratic attitudes in the abstract, but most approve in general of current governmental policies and services—at least, when asked about individual programs. Furthermore, most citizens are quite pleased with their personal bureaucratic encounters, and favorable evaluations of governmental bureaucracies on a number of specific dimensions are widespread. These negative and positive bureaucratic perceptions are found against a background of disinterest. Most citizens are inclined not to think about government and bureaucracy unless needs arising from their daily lives—particularly those coming from their families and jobs—bring such issues to mind. Misinformation—sometimes of a spectacular variety—also is prevalent. For example, according to a Roper poll, the average citizen believes that more than half ($52.10) of every $100 coming into the Social Security system goes to pay for administration rather than benefits, when Social Security's actual expenditures for nonbenefit costs are only $1.30 per $100.[15] Attempting to interpret Americans' attitudes toward government and bureaucracy is highly frustrating. Opinions seem varied, contradictory, ambiguous. One may feel that the key to understanding how these opinions actually are internally consistent could be found in the next set of survey results. But the key always remains elusive.

I conclude that the quest for a comprehensive explanation is mistaken: the key to Americans' attitudes on these matters is understanding that no comprehensive explanation is possible. Our attitudes toward government and bureaucracy really are varied, contradictory, ambiguous, as well as ephemeral. Because I assume that a symbiotic relationship exists between the public and its politicians, I do not find it surprising that our politicians also do not take bureaucracy seriously.

The Politicians' Failure to Take Bureaucracy Seriously

We must abolish and consolidate hundreds of obsolete and unnecessary federal programs and agencies. . . . The vast bureaucracy of government often fails to deliver needed social services to our people.
—Jimmy Carter, 1975

The federal bureaucratic monster who would slay private enterprise is learning a new command. It's called—heel!
—Ronald Reagan, 1983

In the post–World War II period, bureaucracy and bureaucrats have become favorite targets of the venom of American politicians. Beginning in the late 1960s, George Wallace found he was guaranteed tumultuous applause whenever he delivered what became his classic line: "Send me to Washington and I will push those pointy-headed bureaucrats off their bicycles and throw their briefcases in the Potomac River!" Both Jimmy Carter and Ronald Reagan were listening to Wallace's applause; they elevated bureaucratic criticism to an art form and gave it an important place in their presidential campaigns and in their presidencies.

Innumerable examples of antibureaucratic comments could easily be found among the public utterances of most prominent politicians.[16] In fact, politicians' negative views of public bureaucracy are so well known that fully documenting them would be superfluous. Also, the views are usually expressed in such simplistic terms that attempting to analyze their content would be of questionable utility. Instead, I shall briefly consider some explanations for these views. The explanations are not intended to be mutually exclusive.

First, politicians could believe their antibureaucratic statements. After all, politicians are products of the American political culture. Finding that their views about public bureaucracy mirror those of the predominant strain of the culture should not be surprising. Because politicians always look for ways to emphasize their affinities with the public, antibureaucratic fulminations may be simply a natural expression of their beliefs.

Second, politicians who may not themselves have any particular animus against bureaucracy may sense that significant numbers of their constituents do and may decide to pander to those feelings in hopes of increasing their popularity and their electoral chances.

Third, however politicians may feel personally about bureaucracy, they are likely to understand that railing against it is a way of safely drawing positive attention to themselves without danger of offending an articulate, "probureaucracy" faction. At the same time, most politicians take care to make clear that their attack pertains only to bureaucracy, per se, and not to the programs it administers. Although even the most conservative politicians understand clearly that the public is staunchly committed to the benefits flowing from the programs,[17] politicians also understand that the commitment is essentially pragmatic and is unlikely to result in the creation of strong affective linkages between individual citizens and bureaucrats or their agencies.

Fourth, politicians are especially likely to attack bureaucracy because they understand that—owing to their own unpopularity—it is one of the few safe targets for them. At the beginning of this chapter, reference was made to a survey finding that Americans ranked the federal bureaucracy last among twenty-six private and public institutions on its "ability to get things done" and next to last on its "honesty, dependability, and integrity." Politicians were just ahead of the bureaucracy on the former ranking and behind it on the latter ranking. Sensing their own political marginality, politicians may view the prospect of reviling a group that is more unpopular than they are—even if only slightly—as an especially attractive political strategy.

Fifth, politicians may engage in bureaucrat bashing because they know that bureaucrats make excellent scapegoats. Whenever a policy is shown to be politically costly, appealing to the public's distaste for bureaucracy may deflect the criticism. For example, when the Reagan administration's attempt to save money from the school lunch program's budget by declaring ketchup and pickle relish to be vegetables was discredited, the president attempted to evade responsibility for his appointees' actions. At a news conference, he said: "Somebody got overambitious in the bureaucracy with their ketchup as a vegetable and we had to pull back some regulations that had been suggested."[18] Politicians may expect this particular variety of scapegoating to work because few members of the public are able to distinguish politicians from bureaucrats. Even though career bureaucrats were not implicated in the Watergate scandal, for example, it was popularly viewed as an indictment of bureaucracy.

In addition, politicians frequently make bureaucrats scapegoats by assigning them to make unpopular policy decisions. For example, laws dealing with highly controversial subjects on which a consensus cannot be forged often are deliberately written so vaguely that bureaucrats must create regulations saying what the law means. Then politicians, who have abdicated their law-making responsibility, may feel free to criticize public administrators for "usurping" the legislative prerogative.

Thus, for a variety of reasons, politicians find it useful to engage in anti-bureaucratic rhetoric—which may lead one to assume that they take bureaucracy seriously. Tracing the linkages between politicians and bureaucrats probably would reinforce such an assumption. As far as federal bureaucracies are concerned, elected politicians—in the aggregate—are the most important actors in their environments. Presidents appoint agency heads and some subordinate officials, for example, with the intention of providing policy direction. And presidents may, with congressional acquiescence, reorganize agencies. Agencies also are dependent upon the president and his executive bureaucracy for their budgetary life blood, for approval of their regulations, and for continuing policy guidance. For reasons such as the following, the Congress also looms large in the agencies' views. Only Congress can pass laws creating agencies, and congressional approval is required before proposed reorganizations become effective. Congress must act on the agencies' budgets, and it must authorize and appropriate funds for new programs. Furthermore, some members become enthusiasts of bureaucratic oversight. A few—perhaps William Proxmire was the most visible example—have made a career of playing the role of scourge of bureaucracy; the committee responsibilities of many others have caused them to become experts on the operations of particular agencies. And all members gain some familiarity with agencies through performing the casework function.

Despite the volume of the antibureaucratic rhetoric and the formal linkages between politicians and bureaucrats, as a group our politicians seldom take bureaucracy seriously. A comprehensive explication of the contention is beyond the scope of this chapter, but the tendency of politicians to vacillate between two approaches to bureaucracy is illustrative. On the one hand, many politicians focus at the macrolevel. They may be attracted to such "sledgehammer" tactics as attempting to eliminate agencies or programs, imposing across-the-board spending freezes or cuts, or giving appointees the general charge of sabotaging agency initiatives. On the other hand, many politicians focus on the microlevel. The president may place a telephone call giving instructions to a desk officer at the State Department, or a congressional committee may focus on supposed instances of minor bureaucratic malfeasance.

Whatever one may think of the policy goals being pursued, examples may be cited from recent administrations that may seem to indicate that bureaucracy was being taken seriously, for example, creating the Senior Executive Service and other aspects of the Civil Service Reform Act of 1978, vesting in the Office of Management and Budget the authority to vet regulations, contracting out ever-larger shares of the government's business in order to shrink bureaucracy, conducting the Iran-Contra hearings. When such examples are examined closely, however, questions arise as to whether bureaucracy really was taken seriously. As examples: the SES was never funded as envisioned; during the Reagan administration, the OMB was charged with abusing the regulatory process in order to reward political friends; contractors have been accused of providing shoddy and overpriced products; evidence of significant institutional reforms in the conduct of foreign policy has yet to emerge from the Iran-Contra hearings. It remains true that few politicians maintain a consistent interest in the ordinary range of agencies' activities and view agencies either as partners or trusted subordinates to be taken seriously in an ongoing process of public management.

The Political Implications of the Public's and the Politicians' Failure to Take Bureaucracy Seriously

It used to be said that the British Empire was acquired in a fit of absent-mindedness. The same could be said about the way in which the United States acquired its public bureaucracy. No political party or group of politicians ever said, "Elect us and we will erect a large welfare state with its attendant bureaucracies." Citizens did not say to themselves, "I want more benefits from government and understand that delivering the programs demanded by me and my fellow citizens will require the creation of large bureaucratic agencies, which will assume a legitimate place in our system of government." Rather than taking such a rationalist stance, most Americans have demanded particular programs, which politicians have been eager to supply, while either allowing those who espouse antigovernmental, antibureaucratic rhetoric to dominate political discourse or participating in the rhetoric themselves. Clearly, the prospects for a "Big Government Party" would be nil: bureaucracy is likely to continue to grow more powerful at the same time that antibureaucratic themes remain predominant in American politics.

Why these themes should be such important stereotypes in American political culture is not entirely clear, but our commitment to individualism surely is an essential component of the explanation.[19] If we continue to perceive of ourselves as rugged individuals (never mind that this conception has very little to do with the truth) admitting that we live in a bureaucratic society and are dependent on a bureaucratic government may seem a bitter pill to swallow. In addition, Americans have not developed a strong cultural tradition of viewing the state in instrumental terms; thus, bureaucracy may seem scary rather than an appropriate tool to accomplish agreed-upon objectives. Finally, as the American welfare state created large-scale bureaucracies, an image of those entities quickly developed that was congruent with the prevailing antigovernmental values in the culture; this image has been perpetuated and reinforced by the various agencies of political socialization.

Investigating the causes of our failure to take government and bureaucracy seriously may be less important, however, than investigating the consequences. Of course, we cannot be certain about all of the consequences. At the system level, our relatively low rates of voting and of participation in the policy process surely are related to the failure to take government seriously. Prominent among the consequences most closely related to bureaucracy are an unwillingness to consider the impact of incremental program increases upon the total size of the governmental sector and an unwillingness to consider how to deliver and pay for the programs. That is, we do not want to know that providing a group of additional services will in the aggregate increase governmental expenditures by a certain amount and require the hiring of additional personnel; we do not want to explore dispassionately the alternative ways of structuring programs so as to minimize costs, provide better services, or pursue whatever goals seem apposite; we do not want to acknowledge that the increased costs must be met by raising either the rate of taxation or the level of the deficit. Furthermore, our aversion to bureaucracy causes us to avoid thinking about how well any particular program actually operates, as well as how the various pieces of government fit together and how they might be re-formed more coherently and made to work more smoothly. For all the supposed rationalism of American life, we have taken the instrumental view of the state only so far—to the point of creating numerous programs to cure various ills. Although programs tend to develop protective constituencies, neither the general run of citizens nor that of elected officials ordinarily has much interest in most programs after their creation.

Another important set of consequences of our failure to take bureaucracy seriously concerns the issue of accountability. One might speculate that the ideologically marginal position of American bureaucracies would cause their every action to be scrutinized minutely. But—ironically—this seldom occurs. Instead, public and official concerns about the legitimacy of bureaucracy seem to encourage us to avoid any serious consideration of public agencies. If we believe that large bureaucracies are somehow "un-American" and do not wish to face up to the fact that we have demanded their creation, then neglecting them benignly may seem more appropriate than engaging in such prosaic chores as developing mechanisms to assure their accountability. Commentators frequently remark that our bureaucratic agencies are placed in a highly politicized, competitive, and frequently hostile environment so that they must develop political coping strategies in order to survive.[20] We need also to acknowledge that bureaucracies are given considerable degrees of autonomy in exercising these strategies because we do not want to grasp the nettle and engage in bureaucratic control—which would constitute an admission that public agencies have become significant political actors.

Finally, this failure to take government and bureaucracy seriously allows the public to be attracted by politicians promising quick fixes for the supposed maladies of big government. Considering the public's feelings of aversion toward bureaucracy—at least, at the ideological level—as well as its lack of an accurate informational base, is it surprising that candidates proffering a flashy new budgeting system, running against government itself, or pledging a continuation of high levels of services (in an era of inflation and large budgetary deficits) with no new taxes—to cite the Carter, Reagan, and Bush examples—could persuade many voters that these candidates were visionary statesmen? Expecting politicians to lead in taking a sophisticated approach to bureaucracy hardly seems reasonable when the failure of the average citizen to do so is highly apparent.

From the viewpoints both of citizens and of politicians, the state of public bureaucracy is always somewhat suspect. From the viewpoint of public bureaucracy, this refusal to take bureaucracy seriously contributes, paradoxically, both to its insecurity and to its political power.

The Political Scientists' Failure
to Take Bureaucracy Seriously

Like the public at large and the politicians, scholars also have failed to take public bureaucracy seriously. Because the scholars' job is to train their eyes unwaveringly on important developments within their purview, the failure of these men and women to devote adequate attention to the emerging phenomenon of public bureaucracy is puzzling. The excuse that scholars are simply products of the American political culture and have absorbed its animus against bureaucracy is only a partial explanation for the failure.

A more comprehensive explanation of why scholars have failed to take bureaucracy seriously may be found by tracing the histories of the relevant academic disciplines. A thorough analysis, which is beyond the scope of this chapter, would require delving into the histories of at least the following social sciences: political science, sociology, economics, psychology, and history. Also, a thorough analysis would require that investigations be made of the treatment of bureaucracy by such applied social sciences as public administration, business administration, social work, criminology, urban planning, human relations, industrial psychology, and public health.

Traditionally, the study of public bureaucracies has been thought to belong to political science more than to any other social science discipline, and the following historical sketch concentrates on developments in that discipline. Several of the topics treated here are sometimes discussed during investigations of the relationship between political science and public administration. Rather than recounting the full history of this disciplinary relationship, my hope is to treat the topics freshly by concentrating on the study of the phenomena in question—public bureaucracies—without becoming encumbered by the nonessential intellectual baggage that usually accompanies such discussions. As a device intended to further this objective, I shall arbitrarily create an academic field called "public bureaucracy," and shall conduct an admittedly anachronistic study of its history.[21]

The sketch of the history of public bureaucracy within political science will reveal that for nearly the first half of the twentieth century, public bureaucracy was important to the discipline, but soon after midcentury such studies had very nearly died out within organized political science. For the past decade or so, however, interest in public bureaucracy has been resurrected in political science. This book reflects that resurrection.

The Birth of Public Bureaucracy within Political Science

During the late nineteenth and the early twentieth centuries, political science emerged as a separate discipline in many American universities. Predominant among the early approaches to the new discipline was what we may call a legal-historical-normative approach. The topics for the first set of standing committees of the American Political Science Association (APSA) are indicative of the early focus: comparative legislation; comparative jurisprudence; international law and diplomacy; constitutional law; [public] administration; politics; and political theory.[22]

From the outset, the field of public bureaucracy was important to the discipline. At the APSA's first meeting in 1904, its president, Frank J. Goodnow (Professor of Administrative Law at Columbia University), said the subject of the new discipline of political science could be divided into three parts: (1) the "expression of the State will," involving the study of political theories and of extralegal customs and organizations (such as political parties) relevant to the formulation of the state will; (2) the "content of the State will," concerning the study of public law; and (3) the "execution of the State will, or the enforcement of law," pertaining to the "ascertainment and application of correct principles of administration." Because attention focused on the state, pursuing all three parts of the subject required that close consideration also be given to the state's instrumentalities—public bureaucracies—which he believed should be central objects of study for political scientists.[23]

The study of public bureaucracy predated the formation of the new discipline. In 1900, Goodnow had made a significant contribution to the field in his book *Politics and Administration,* where he proclaimed: "[P]ractical political necessity makes impossible the consideration of the function of politics apart from that of administration." In that book, he distinguished the functions of expressing and executing the state will—in terms similar to those quoted in the previous paragraph—but he refused to allocate the performance of the functions strictly to particular institutions: "[W]hile the two primary functions of government are susceptible of differentiation, the organs of government to which the discharge of these functions is intrusted cannot be clearly defined."[24]

A prominent early piece of literature in public bureaucracy was Woodrow Wilson's 1887 article, "The Study of Administration." Wilson saw clearly that bureaucracies are deeply imbedded in the political process. Furthermore, his conception of the differences between administrative and political functions was quite sophisticated; for example, he was well aware that civil servants—far from being mindless automata—normally make significant decisions about implementation: "the administrator should have and does have a will of his own in the choice of means for accomplishing his work."[25] But the civil servant's proper role went beyond implementation to involvement in the general policy process. Wilson considered this involvement important enough that serious questions arose concerning the exercise of administrative authority. Rather than curbing administrators, however, he suggested they be made clearly responsible for their actions: "large powers and unhampered discretion seem to me the indispensable conditions of [administrative] responsibility."[26] Wilson's understanding of the political character of governmental agencies is further illustrated by the emphasis he placed on examining the linkages between administration and public opinion. American political culture, he insisted, had a crucial effect on our administrative arrangements—so much so that he advocated borrowing foreign methods fearlessly because we would inevitably Americanize them.[27]

Both Wilson and Goodnow drew analytical distinctions between political and administrative functions, but I believe they did not intend to establish the strictly dichotomous relationship between the two (or between those who perform the functions) for which subsequent generations have often blamed them. Their intent, as I understand it, in contemporary language, was that politicians, who are principally charged with making top-level policy, ought not to bring partisan considerations into the administrative process; if they do so, this would be a legitimate object of study for scholars and reformers. At the same time, administrators, who are principally charged with making secondary-level policy designed to flesh out the top-level policy legitimated by politicians and with implementing both levels of policy, should be given broad authority to do so and should be held responsible for their performance.

If we were to adopt a modern-day vantage point for evaluating public bureaucracy as practiced by Goodnow, Wilson, and their coevals, we probably would criticize them for being overly normative and reformist and overly legalistic and descriptive. Nonetheless, they took public bureaucracy seriously and viewed its study as an integral part of the subject of political science. For the most part, this view was predominant during the discipline's first half-century of existence.

In 1926, Leonard D. White set an essentially political tone for public bureaucracy within political science in his pathbreaking *Introduction to the Study of Public Administration,* in which he defined public administration as "the management of men and materials in the accomplishment of the purposes of the state."[28] Certainly, White saw public administration as a managerial art or science involving "the execution of the public business"[29] and emphasizing the objectives of efficiency and economy; furthermore, his thorough treatment of forms of organization and reorganization and his exhaustive coverage of personnel issues (nine chapters were devoted to the latter subject) are likely to seem overly descriptive to the modern reader. But he believed his approach to administration "minimizes its legalistic and formal aspect."[30]

And White clearly viewed public administration as a political phenomenon: one chapter of his book was devoted to the external relationships of public administration with the legislature, the courts, political parties, and private groups; two chapters treated control of administration by the legislature, the electorate, and the courts. White even proclaimed in the preface that "administration has become, and will continue to be the heart of the modern problem of government."[31] The preface also contains evidence that White was operating in the mainstream of contemporary political science; he acknowledged the "invaluable systematic help in organizing the material of this volume" provided by his

Chicago colleagues Charles Merriam and Harold Lasswell—two of the discipline's most prominent figures, who became guiding lights for the behavioral revolution.

A comprehensive review of the public bureaucracy literature produced by political scientists during the quarter-century following the first publication of White's text, which went through four editions (the last appearing in 1955), is beyond this chapter's scope. An illustrative list of prominent works in the genre—most of which did not use the rubric of "bureaucracy" to define their subject—would include:

Carl Friedrich and Taylor Cole, *Responsible Bureaucracy*, 1932;
Gabriel Almond and Harold Lasswell, "Aggressive Behavior by Clients toward Public Relief Administrators," 1934;
E. Pendleton Herring, *Public Administration and the Public Interest*, 1936;
John Gaus, Leonard White, and Marshall Dimock, *The Frontiers of Public Administration*, 1936;
V. O. Key, *The Administration of Federal Grants to States*, 1937;
Carl Friedrich, "Public Policy and the Nature of Administrative Responsibility," 1940;
Herman Finer, "Administrative Responsibility in Democratic Government," 1941;
Robert Cushman, *The Independent Regulatory Commissions*, 1941;
James Fesler, *The Independence of State Regulatory Agencies*, 1942;
Avery Leiserson, *Administrative Regulation*, 1942;
J. Donald Kingsley, *Representative Bureaucracy*, 1944;
Lynton K. Caldwell, *The Administrative Theories of Hamilton and Jefferson*, 1944;
Paul Appleby, *Big Democracy*, 1945;
Herbert Simon, *Administrative Behavior*, 1947;
Robert Dahl, "The Science of Public Administration," 1947;
Dwight Waldo, *The Administrative State*, 1948;
Norton Long, "Power and Administration," 1949;
Oliver Garceau, *The Public Library in the Political Process*, 1949;
Charles Hyneman, *Bureaucracy in a Democracy*, 1950;
Herbert Simon, Donald Smithburg, and Victor Thompson, *Public Administration*, 1950.[32]

Over time, scholars in the field of public bureaucracy lost interest in the state, which came to be seen as a metaphysical concept, and focused on government, instead. That focus became blurred for many scholars, however, when they became interested in ideas about the political process. These ideas featured the roles of various private and public groups in a process that was viewed as being fluid and competitive. Such governmental institutions as bureaucracies frequently were counted simply as competitors for power along with pressure groups, parties, and so forth. Otherwise, the above-listed, disparate body of scholarship cannot easily be characterized.

So long as concrete political institutions—including, especially, political parties, pressure groups, and the various components of "government"—remained the discipline's principal focus, studies by political scientists who adopted the public bureaucracy perspective were commonplace. Such studies frequently were incorporated into more general works; two excellent examples are V. O. Key's chapter "Administration as Politics" in *Politics, Parties, and Pressure Groups*, and Charles Merriam's chapter "The Organs of Government" in *Systematic Politics*.[33] Furthermore, a given scholar might undertake a study in public bureaucracy, then move into quite a different field; for example, Carl Friedrich wrote "Responsible Government Service under the American Constitution" for the Commission of Inquiry on Public Service Personnel, before turning to further studies on law, history, and political theory.[34]

During this period, studies from the public bureaucracy perspective by political scientists were commonplace; also, such studies were considered to be mainstream social science. For example, in the 1930s the Social Science Research Council established a Committee on Public Administration, which sponsored a number of studies as well as a publication series; the study by Key listed above, which was a part of a larger committee project, was the first book published in the series. Other elements of the social science establishment also were sympathetic to the perspective; for example, Fesler's above-listed project was sponsored by the Rockefeller Foundation.

The Death of Public Bureaucracy within Political Science

Something happened to change the situation in which political scientists viewed studies in public bureaucracy as ordinary and legitimate projects. That something was political science's behavioral revolution. According to the concepts popularized by Thomas Kuhn, traditional political science clearly was "pre-paradigmatic"; thus, these developments did not constitute a "scientific revolution" in which allegiances shifted from one paradigm to another.[35] Nonetheless, some consequential changes certainly occurred in the discipline.

The behavioral revolution had no definite beginning, occurred over a considerable period, and lacked a definite ending; but most scholars probably would agree with dating it around midcentury or a few years before. Somit and Tanenhaus, who talk of the "post-1945 behavioral movement," abstracted from the extensive literature on the subject eight "key behavioralist articles of faith."[36] From the point of view of the fervent behavioralist, the preponderance of the literature in public bureaucracy clearly violated each article. I summarize the articles of faith below and follow each with my specification of the transgression public bureaucracy appeared to commit against it:

1. Political science should rigorously and systematically analyze political behavior and become an explanatory and predictive science (on the model of physics); public bureaucracy studies tended to be descriptive, unsystematic, noncumulative, and generally "unscientific."

2. Political science should study observable phenomena rather than supposed "institutional" phenomena, which are manifest only in the behavior of those who compose the institutions; public bureaucracy studies normally focused on such institutions as governmental agencies and pressure groups.

3. In order to increase scientific exactness, political scientists should try to quantify their data; but little quantification and no data bases comparable to those for voting behavior existed for public bureaucracy.

4. Political scientists should try to operationalize hypotheses and build empirical theories; but the public bureaucracy literature contained few such hypotheses or theories.

5. Political science should concentrate on basic research and avoid applied research; research in public bureaucracy frequently was applied or had obvious applied ramifications.

6. Because normative values (such as the public interest) were not scientifically provable, their discussion should be irrelevant to political science; much of the public bureaucracy literature was explicitly reformist.

7. Political science should be interdisciplinary (insights from psychology, sociology, and economics were especially valued); public bureaucracy was hardly influenced by these disciplines.

8. Political science should use such high-powered methodological tools as sample surveys, multivariate analysis, mathematical models, and simulation; public bureaucracy tended to use simple description in conducting old-fashioned case studies.

All in all, public bureaucracy's list of transgressions against behavioralism persuaded many of the new faith's true believers that, although public bureaucracy had from the discipline's founding been a constituent part, the old field was beyond redemption and (like other elements of traditionalism) should be cast beyond the pale of political science. Certainly, no formal action was taken to expel the field from the discipline, yet the message was delivered in unmistakable terms that studies in public bureaucracy were out of step with a behavioral political science.

On the authority of some public bureaucracy specialists who experienced the behavioralists' gradual victory, the message was delivered in a variety of ways. For example, sympathetic book and journal editors frequently were replaced with new ones hostile to public bureaucracy; the number of panels dealing with the perspective at meetings of the American Political Science Association was dramatically reduced; and some prominent departments of political science refused to hire, promote, and grant tenure to adherents of the perspective. Nonetheless, few behavioralists seemed to feel a particular animus against public bureaucracy, per se. The field's approach to research simply branded it as a particularly noteworthy bastion of traditionalism, the real enemy. Thus, warning others—especially impressionable graduate students—against such a perspective became the dedicated behavioralist's obvious duty.

Over time, the message about public bureaucracy's unacceptability as a prospective research field was delivered so successfully that overt statements of the message seldom were necessary. By the mid-1960s the messages that graduate students received on the subject were likely to be subtle ones, perhaps so subtle that few could articulate fully the reasons why public-bureaucracy research was out of bounds. But the reasons hardly mattered because the possibility of undertaking such research was unlikely to occur to most budding political scientists, who were pulled in other directions. The attractions of behavioralism stirred the imaginations of young scholars, who were unlikely to have occasion to think of the possibility of conducting a project that used the conventional public bureaucracy approach—nor were they likely to think of using the new developments to tackle a problem in public bureaucracy.

As far as public bureaucracy was concerned, branding institutional research as illegitimate was one of the most noteworthy consequences of the behavioral revolution. "Institutionalist" became one of the strongest epithets in the behavioralist's lexicon. Not all institutional research was forbidden, however. Prominent examples of allowable institutional research included studies of individuals within institutions (focusing on such matters as attitudes and role conceptions), explorations of group dynamics, and system theory approaches (focusing on such concepts as equilibrium). Very little of this research featured individuals as behaving actors within institutions, and almost none of it conceived of institutions as behaving entities.[37] Among the few institutional studies undertaken, most concerned legislatures and courts. Hardly any studies of public bureaucracies were conducted.

Traditionalists frequently charged that a principal effect of the behavioral approach was to take the politics out of political science. Many behavioralists regarded this as a virtue in the sense that their objective was to rid the discipline of the study of current events, of the "inside-dopster" perspective, of debates about "good" government, of ungeneralizable case studies featuring political institutions. In quite a different sense, however, the behavioralists hoped their approach would lead to a scientific understanding of politics, properly construed. However one may evaluate the success of that quest, much of the resulting political science may be characterized as abstract in form. To a considerable degree, the abstract quality of the writings in question comes from their dearth of political actors, largely a consequence of the behavioralists' injunctions against studying political institutions.[38]

I do not contend that no significant writing was done in public bureaucracy while political science was in the throes of the behavioral revolution.[39] Particularly, those who identified with the developing discipline of public administration (they have a separate story that is briefly mentioned below), simply continued with their work. Nor do I contend that political science conducted a thoroughgoing conspiracy against the field of public bureaucracy. For example, even after midcentury, while the behavioral movement was in full flower, the following exponents of public bureaucracy were elected presidents of the American Political Science Association: Luther Gulick, 1951-52; Pendleton Herring, 1952-53; Charles McKinley, 1954-55; V. O. Key, Jr., 1957-58; R. Taylor Cole, 1958-59; Emmette S. Redford, 1960-61; Charles S. Hyneman, 1961-62; and Carl J. Friedrich, 1962-63.[40] Perhaps the culture-lag hypothesis would be useful in explaining this finding.

In any event, another exponent of the field was not elected president of the association until Avery Leiserson in 1973-74.[41] Many students of public bureaucracy left the field during the behavioral revolution because they were attracted by the glamour of the new foci and techniques; others who did not wish to abandon the field became so estranged from political science that they left it for another discipline, usually public administration.

The Resurrection of Public Bureaucracy within Political Science

Of course, the public bureaucracy field did not completely die out in political science during the heyday of the behavioral revolution. But practitioners of the field felt distant from the new "mainstream," and many left the discipline.[42] Chief among the theoretical developments that contributed to public bureaucracy's eventual resurrection within political science were the public policy movement and the neo-institutional movement.

The Public Policy Movement

Interest in public policy began to mount during World War II. From the beginning the new emphasis was closely related to public bureaucracy. The first volume of *Public Policy: A Yearbook of the Graduate School of Public Administration, Harvard University* (edited by Carl J. Friedrich and Edward S. Mason), which collected eleven essays on a variety of policy topics, was published in 1940. At about the same time, Harold Lasswell started to write about and campaign in favor of the "policy sciences."[43] The orientations of early policy studies tended to be historical, descriptive, legalistic, normative, problem-centered, and applied; they focused on a variety of aspects—frequently administrative aspects—of programs in such substantive areas as foreign policy, transportation policy, education policy, health policy, and fiscal policy.[44] In short, the policy orientation was quintessentially "traditional" and, thus, subject to the behavioralist's derision.

During the behavioral revolution, through processes that remain somewhat mysterious, the policy orientation shed this image, however, and created for itself a new, far more robust, respectable, even romantic image. A principal explanation for the change was that policy studies became more "behavioral" in several senses. Of course, policy studies always had been empirically based; now, many researchers deemphasized individual case studies while bodies of quantitative data were collected and analyzed, using powerful techniques and the comparative method. In addition, theory became more important, hypotheses were tested, categorization schemes were developed (for example, Theodore Lowi's immensely popular scheme distinguished among regulatory, distributive, redistributive, and constituent policies).[45]

The policy studies movement also provided an opportunity to address the question of relevance. While political science was under the sway of behavioralism and logical positivism provided its underlying philosophical basis, scholars tended to avoid contentious political issues on the assumption that "science" could say nothing about them. Some behavioralists prided themselves on the irrelevance of their research, and it was often noted that one could read the principal political science journals during the 1960s without becoming aware that America's cities were seething, millions of people were held in poverty's steel grip, and a war was raging in Southeast Asia.

Motivated by a determination to move political science toward policy relevance and other normative concerns, in the late 1960s a number of those who had noted such obliviousness formed the Caucus for a New Political Science, which became a strong voice within the American Political Science Association. Many other political scientists not affiliated with the caucus agreed with its indictment of the discipline. Gradually, professional associations, academic institutions, and individual scholars began to respond. David Easton labeled the discipline's response the "postbehavioral revolution," which featured a "credo of relevance."[46]

To apply the term "revolution" to these developments may seem a bit grandiose, but studies increasingly focused on indisputably important policy issues. Once political scientists were confronted with the issues, who could contend that they should be forced to ignore such matters as racial discrimination, poverty, or war? After selecting these kinds of matters for study, policy analysts found that it was very difficult to operationalize the behavioralists' ironclad distinction between facts and values, especially in conducting applied research. And many analysts saw themselves as policy engineers offering prescriptions for society's ills. Few attempts were made to refute logical positivism's philosophical basis, however. For the most part, the doctrine was simply sidestepped in favor of policy relevance.[47]

A proclivity toward building policy-oriented institutions also became noticeable during this period. In an earlier day, institutes of government were popular; in order to take advantage of the new term's magic, many of these were rechristened with "policy" in the title. More important, new policy programs—frequently of an interdisciplinary character—were created at virtually all universities. These covered the entire gamut of policy concerns; in addition to the standard topics, new ones dealing with such matters as science, technology, and the future were especially popular. Some policy programs became degree-granting departments or even colleges; others concentrated on research, much of it applied. Such research was greatly stimulated by the availability of large sums of money from foundations and governmental agencies—especially applied programs within the National Science Foundation. New professional groups, such as the Policy Studies Organization, were formed; and such journals as the *Policy Studies Journal* and *Policy Sciences* were established. Public policy became an academic field, even a new, usually interdisciplinary, discipline.

Public policy certainly took public bureaucracy seriously. Indeed, distinguishing between the two was often impossible, for policy studies frequently featured the roles of public administrative agencies in all stages of the policy process. Studies of the "implementation" stage tended to focus on the bureaucratic actors; such studies were greatly stimulated in 1973 by the publication of *Implementation* by Jeffrey Pressman and Aaron Wildavsky.[48] Books, articles, and courses focusing on implementation proliferated during the next decade.[49] In fact, implementation became an identifiable subfield of public policy.

The policy movement within political science was auspicious for the field of public bureaucracy for two main reasons. First, scholarship in the field was advanced. Focusing either on the general policy process in a given policy arena or on such specific aspects as outcomes was likely to produce a study that featured the roles of public bureaucracies. Whether the project was called a policy implementation study or a public bureaucracy study was unimportant to the result. Second, using the policy label allowed studies in public bureaucracy to be viewed as respectable endeavors. Commentators on this phenomenon frequently referred to the policy "umbrella," under which many "traditional" subjects, including public bureaucracy, could be studied with impunity. Although public policy served as a bridge enabling studies in public bureaucracy to be reestablished as legitimate subjects for political scientists, this is not to say that public policy and public bureaucracy are equivalent. The focus of public policy normally is on outputs or outcomes; even implementation studies from the policy perspective usually underplay the roles of bureaucratic actors and neglect their internal dynamics.[50]

The Neo-Institutional Movement

Another development that facilitated the resurrection of public bureaucracy within political science was what we may call the "neo-institutional" movement. An obvious index of the strength of behavioralism's anti-institutional bias is that striking the word "government" from departmental titles became a significant symbolic struggle during the revolution's heyday. The "scientists" won out over the "institutionalists" at all but a few departments, and virtually all of the new departments created during this period (in which the discipline was a full participant in higher education's great expansion) were called political science. Nonetheless, by the late 1960s, a number of scholars—many of whom were quite prominent in the discipline—had begun to move toward institutional studies.

Most of the new institutionalists took a somewhat circuitous route to the subject: they examined the *concept* of institutionalization, which was normally viewed as a process, rather than the institutions themselves. Talking about such criteria of institutionalization as complexity, coherence, adaptability, and autonomy (offered by Samuel Huntington[51]) was permissible because these obviously were the sorts of categories used by sociologists, who were viewed as respectable. Since any meaningful conception of institutionalization must imply the existence of concrete institutions, focusing on this process proved a productive way of bringing institutions back into political analysis.

Nonetheless, advocating the study of political institutions was considered an avant garde perspective as much as two decades after the height of the behavioral revolution. In an essay published in 1970, for example, Fred Riggs cautiously suggested that institutions should not be excluded from comparative analyses:

> [I]t now seems to me that we do need institutional analysis. . . . The truth, I believe, is that institutions, social structures, patterns of action do indeed matter. . . . [I]t is suggested that some important advantages may accrue to us if we occasionally look on patterns of government as independent variables, treating other aspects of social and political systems as dependent variables.[52]

In recommending that governmental institutions be viewed as independent variables, Riggs was anticipating by a decade or more a body of comparative research that rediscovered the concept of the state.[53]

As late as the mid-1980s, authors who purported to offer a "theoretical" analysis of institutions usually presented their thesis as a somewhat radical departure from conventional wisdom and adopted a diffident posture in doing so.[54] An important instance of an article displaying both characteristics was published by James March and Johan Olsen in 1984: "The New Institutionalism: Organizational Factors in Political Life."[55] Although March and Olsen presented themselves as reporters rather than advocates, the mere publication of the article (which was a rare "think piece" and did not present any new data) in the discipline's most prestigious journal provided a significant boost for the neoinstitutional movement.

For the most part, according to March and Olsen, the five anti-institutional assumptions paraphrased as follows have been a part of "the basic vision that has characterized theories of politics since about 1950":

1. Political life is a dependent rather than an independent variable. Politics is simply a product of such contextual forces as class, demography, geography, ethnicity, culture, technology, or economics.

2. In general, politics is best understood as the aggregate consequences of individual behavior; institutions do not affect individual motives or act autonomously. According to this reductionist interpretation, "we make assumptions about individual consumers to understand markets, about voters to understand politics, and about bureaucrats to understand bureaucracies."

3. Political events are the result of deliberate, calculated decisions, or choices, rather than the product of an institutional structure affected by rules, norms, and traditions. Highly complex theories of choice have been elaborated.

4. "[Political] institutions and behavior are thought to evolve through some form of efficient historical process"; they do not just "happen" as a result of idiosyncratic historical events. Such a process depends on environmental conditions, as in a market, that are viewed as tending toward equilibrium: "For example, when it is predicted that political parties will come to identical positions in an environment of single-peaked voter preferences, it is assumed that party adjustment will be much more rapid than will be changes in voter preferences."

5. Governance is viewed in purely instrumental terms, and the focus is on outcomes. The process of political decision making is not seen as having intrinsic worth or as being useful for creating a sense of community purpose or for promoting civic education.

In the face of such hostility, the paucity of institutional studies—including studies of public bureaucracy—in the aftermath of the behavioral revolution seems quite understandable. March and Olsen point out, however, that in recent years each of the assumptions listed above has been challenged by a resurgent institutionalism, whose ideas:

> deemphasize the dependence of the polity on society in favor of an interdependence between relatively autonomous social and political institutions; they deemphasize the simple primacy of micro processes and efficient histories in favor of relatively complex processes and historical inefficiency; they deemphasize metaphors of choice and allocative outcomes in favor of other logics of action and the centrality of meaning and symbolic action.[56]

Nonetheless, March and Olsen emphasize that many of these ideas remain in the formative stages, they may be somewhat inconsistent with each other, and some institutionalists may accept one idea and reject another: "The institutionalism we have considered is neither a theory nor a coherent critique of one. It is simply an argument that the organization of political life makes a difference." Without campaigning in favor of the new orientation, they merely point out that institutionalists are beginning to mount a significant challenge to the anti-institutionalist mainstream, and conclude that the new institutionalism is only "an empirically based prejudice."[57]

Despite March and Olsen's diffidence, their assertion—presented under the prestigious auspices of the *American Political Science Review*—that a new institutional movement was underway in political science, their generally favorable analysis of its theoretical underpinnings, and especially their treatment of it as an intellectually respectable development—all helped give the movement legitimacy. Many recent participants in the neo-institutional movement have cited March and Olsen as authorities who have, in effect, given the discipline permission to recommence institutional studies.[58] Of course, that warrant extends to the field of public bureaucracy.

One cannot be certain that the current interest in policy and institutions—which has stimulated studies in public bureaucracy—will be sustained, yet I conclude that the interest is not merely a fad. During the behavioral revolution, political scientists desperately wanted to be respected as real scientists, and they believed that behavioralism would enable them to do the same kind of science that they thought physicists did. In chasing this chimera, members of the discipline were willing for a long time to ignore important *political* questions concerning public policy processes and outputs and the roles of large public institutions—none of which behavioralism could address satisfactorily. Unless another large-scale lapse of consciousness such as behavioralism occurs—perhaps it was false consciousness—a continuing place for public bureaucracy within political science seems assured.[59]

Organizational Developments

In addition to these theoretical developments contributing to public bureaucracy's resurrection within political science, some significant organizational developments also occurred. During the ascendancy of behavioralism, the linkages between the field and the discipline became tenuous. To be sure, the American Political Science Association continued annually to confer the Leonard D. White Dissertation Award, encompassing "the general field of public administration, broadly defined," but some adherents of public bureaucracy viewed the award as merely a vestigial marker of the field's former connection with the discipline. For many practitioners of public bureaucracy, the symbolic nadir of the field's relationship with political science came in 1982, when "the state of the discipline" was chosen as the theme for the APSA annual meeting and no paper was commissioned to review the traditional subfield of public administration.[60]

Ironically, this omission probably was indicative of the next phase of the culture-lag phenomenon, for public bureaucracy had begun to gain organizational strength within the APSA during the early 1980s. The most important manifestation of strength was the burgeoning of the Section on Public Administration, which was the association's first "organized section" and which has been mainly concerned with promoting research and teaching in public bureaucracy.[61]

Since 1983, when the section first met as an officially recognized entity, it has sponsored an average of fourteen panels at the association's annual meetings. The Public Administration Section has become one of the association's five large sections, whose membership levels fluctuate but are roughly comparable. The level of membership in the Public Administration Section was at about 700 in 1991. The Section on Public Administration has become the principal organization for scholars who take a political view of public administration, and—based on impressionistic evidence—the section appears already to have made significant contributions to the resurrection of public bureaucracy within political science.[62]

Several additional pieces of evidence indicate that the American Political Science Association has begun to take public bureaucracy seriously. Many panels at the annual meeting other than those of the section feature public bureaucracy research. On the average, probably twice as many panels dealing with public bureaucracy are offered at the convention under other titles—such as Public Administration and Organization Theory, Bureaucracy, and the Political Executive—as are offered by the Public Administration Section. And many more individual papers on public bureaucracy are offered at each meeting under such rubrics as public policy or comparative politics.

The creation of the John Gaus Lectureship by the APSA in 1985 was another indicator of public bureaucracy's resurrection within organized political science. Certainly, it was appropriate that the APSA Council decided to use an unrestricted bequest from the Gaus estate to "honor a scholar who best embodies the joint tradition of political science and public administration, and more generally, to recognize achievement and encourage scholarship in public administration."[63] The first six choices for the lectureship—Herbert Kaufman, Dwight Waldo, James Fesler, Aaron Wildavsky, Frederick Mosher, and Norton Long—were immediately recognizable as leading exponents of the public bureaucracy approach.

As public bureaucracy gained momentum within political science during the 1980s, the movement received assistance from sympathetic officers and staff of the APSA; particular mention should be made of presidents Aaron Wildavsky and Samuel Huntington (both important representatives of the movement) and of staff members Tom Mann and Catherine Rudder. It would be an exaggeration to claim that public bureaucracy has reached nirvana within political science—the APSA has yet to define precisely the role of the organized sections within the association—but the field's status has so improved that the likelihood of its being omitted from a future APSA "state-of-the-discipline" book seems small.

Of course, the story of the resurrection of public bureaucracy within the American Political Science Association does not tell the entire story of the field's fate within the discipline. Glancing at the recent programs of the regional political science associations reveals that public bureaucracy also has gained ground within them. A similar perusal of college and university catalogs would turn up a number of courses on the politics of bureaucracy offered by departments of political science. And articles on public bureaucracy now appear regularly in the broad range of political science journals. *Administration and Society* has been an especially important forum for research in public bureaucracy, and such new journals as *Governing* and the *Journal of Public Administration Research and Theory* have begun publication. Compiling a list of recent, significant contributions to the public bureaucracy literature would be a difficult task because the list would be so long. All in all, it appears that public bureaucracy has become an accepted specialization within political science.

Public Bureaucracy, Public Administration, and Beyond

Conspicuously absent from this chronicle is an account of public administration's relationship to public bureaucracy.[64] In addition, in order to avoid confusion, I have committed the sin of oversimplification by treating some individuals as only political scientists, when they may actually have been as much involved with public administration as with political science. Other prominent figures may have been ignored because I considered them to be practitioners of public administration rather than political science. I admit that placing a scholar in one discipline rather than another frequently was arbitrary. Making generalizations about a discipline as broad and large as public administration is risky, but I believe that, in general, the discipline has not taken public bureaucracy seriously. A thorough discussion of this judgment would require a chapter as long as the present one; the following comments are meant only to be suggestive.

During the 1939 meeting of the American Political Science Association, the American Society for Public Administration (ASPA) was formed and given the mission "to advance generally the science, process, and art of public administration." Rather than focusing on political analysis, most leaders of public administration have been interested in applied matters such as the following "three principal values" identified in an official ASPA history: improving the theory and practice of public administration, advocating professionalism in the public service, and developing a sense of community among practitioners and academicians in the discipline.[65]

Of course, a number of pieces of evidence may be cited to indicate that public administration *has* taken public bureaucracy seriously. For example, neither Leonard White nor Dwight Waldo dropped their interest in public bureaucracy while performing their roles as editors of the *Public Administration Review*. And ASPA has contributed to the study of public bureaucracy in a variety of ways during the past half-century—particularly through publishing articles from the field's perspective in the *PAR* and offering panels at conventions. One sustained program indicating the discipline's interest in public bureaucracy was the efforts during the 1960s of the Comparative Administration Group, led by Fred Riggs. And participants in the New Public Administration Movement certainly were champions of public bureaucracy.

Perhaps public administration's most important potential affinity with public bureaucracy has to do with the discipline's basic orientation. Whereas political science often has been society-oriented and has considered the state to be epiphenomenal, public administration usually has been state-centered and has considered the state to be autonomous. Although this assumption normally is left implicit, writers in public administration ordinarily assume that administrators have considerable opportunity to decide whether, when, and how to act. That administrative discretion involves the making of choices that properly should be called "political," however, was systematically ignored by public administration during the ascendancy of the doctrine of the politics–administration dichotomy. The political implications of many recommendations from scholars of public administration still are often neglected. Thus the potential relationship between public bureaucracy and public administration has not yet been fully realized, and its future seems uncertain.

An impediment to public bureaucracy research in public administration has been the murky status of scholars in the discipline. Many academicians appear to have felt under pressure to produce "useful" research and to stay away from projects that might cast doubt on the quest for scientific progress in administration by suggesting that the process of public administration really is about *politics*. As public administration becomes more professionalized—*vide* the increasing power of the National Association of Schools of Public Affairs and Administration to accredit degree programs—will scholars in the discipline feel that projects in public bureaucracy involving the study of "mere" politics might undermine their positions?

I believe that this possibility cannot be ignored, but that a counterforce also is emerging. The recent creation of many large schools and departments of public administration has greatly increased the numbers of people who study public organizations and are daily confronted with their essentially political natures. Naturally, many of these scholars are beginning to think about the phenomena from a political perspective; a great many of the members of the APSA Section on Public Administration are affiliated with schools or departments of public administration rather than political science.

All in all, I believe that public bureaucracy is developing as a significant new academic field—analogous to the field of organizational theory—that ignores arbitrary disciplinary boundaries and draws from a number of social science and applied social science fields.[66] Public bureaucracy is an "invisible college" that ignores institutional boundaries.[67] The strength of the college lies in the shared intellectual focus of its members. The following five chapters do not constitute a comprehensive survey of the state of public bureaucracy research, but they treat important themes of the field and exemplify its development.

Overview of Part One

In "A Legitimate Role for Bureaucracy in Democratic Governance," Gary L. Wamsley, Charles T. Goodsell, John A. Rohr, Orion White, and James Wolf argue in this "Blacksburg Manifesto" that the concept of "governance" has been avoided by American political scientists, who became fascinated with "politics" under the spell of pluralist thinking. Public administration theorists—influenced by pluralism by the politics–administration dichotomy and by scientific management notions— also have avoided "governance." These authors believe we have been left with two models of governance—the pluralist-democracy model and the administrative-efficiency model—but that a middle ground has emerged from the writings of the bureaucratic politics theorists and the complex organizational analysts.

Because Wamsley, Goodsell, Rohr, White, and Wolf believe that American cultural prejudice has hampered our ability to understand public bureaucracy, they attempt to develop a normative framework endorsing a bureaucratic role in governance. Their framework includes the following nine points: (1) We should place public bureaucracy in a broad political, economic, and historical perspective. (2) We need to clear out the pejorative, antibureaucratic underbrush so prevalent in our culture, and to recognize that public agencies and workers make positive contributions to American political life. (3) We should adopt value premises that assume that public administration is a social asset, that private management is normatively distinct from public administration, and that the "agency perspective" is a legitimate viewpoint from which to analyze public bureaucracies. (4) We ought to rescue the concept of the public interest from the positivist critique, which focuses on the *content* of particular policy situations, and focus instead on the concept as an idealized value, whose attainment may remain problematical. (5) We should attempt to clarify the extent to which a politics–administration dichotomy does or does not exist—understanding that the answer may depend on the level of abstraction chosen. (6) We should explore critically the relationship between capitalism, which has succeeded reasonably well in fulfilling the economic and the unconscious emotional needs of most individuals, and public administration, which has been used insufficiently as a vehicle to fulfill conscious, collective needs. (7) We must develop a more favorable interpretation of the public administration's constitutional role in which administrators are viewed as implementing a covenant between them and citizens to pursue the public interest. (8) We should recognize that public bureaucracy is a highly representative institution—even in comparison with elected institutions—and is, thus, highly legitimate. (9) We should reconceptualize the role of individual public servants so that they are expected to exercise discretion as trustees of the public interest rather than to pursue instrumentally the dictates of a narrow professionalism.

All in all, Wamsley, Goodsell, Rohr, White, and Wolf conclude that the failure to define a legitimate role for bureaucracy in the governance process is a major shortcoming of the American political system and believe that the normative framework they have set out could provide a structure for such a definition. They cite the political-cultural and institutional changes that allowed the judicial system to become an important, legitimate actor in the governance process as a possible precedent for the development of such a role for public administration.

The comparative outlook has much to offer both political science and public administration, as B. Guy Peters demonstrates in "Comparative Perspectives on Bureaucracy in the Policy Process." In addition, when attempting to answer such questions as "what is the state of public bureaucracy?" an exclusive focus on American institutions may lead to ethnocentric interpretations of the phenomena. Peters illustrates the importance of comparisons for building theory by examining the relationship between bureaucracy and five dependent variables. First, he focuses on personnel. In many countries, simply finding out how many people work for governmental bureaucracies is much less straightforward than one might expect. The bulk of the personnel literature focuses on the social backgrounds of top-level civil servants, usually from the "representative bureaucracy" perspective. Wide variations exist among countries in the extent to which key bureaucratic posts are held by an identifiable "power elite" that seems to represent and promote either its own interests or those of certain social classes or corporate bodies.

Second, Peters examines bureaucratic attitudes as a dependent variable. A growing body of comparative research has explored the attitudes of civil servants, sometimes in juxtaposition with those of such other elites as legislators and political executives. In general, the studies have examined various aspects of bureaucrats' role perceptions, including those about involvement in the policy-making process; research reveals that many bureaucrats in this country, as well as elsewhere, do not subscribe to the orthodox American doctrine that depicts them as neutral executors rather than makers of policy.

Third, Peters considers bureaucrats' behavior, which may not be congruent with their attitudes, as a dependent variable for comparative research. Three issues have provided a focus for this research: behavior toward politicians; behavior in managing the organization; and behavior toward clients. Frequently, models of bureaucrats' linkages with politicians—which range from the traditional American notion of a functional separation between policy making (by politicians) and "mere" implementation (by bureaucrats) to the radical notion of bureaucratic dominance of the policy process—are compared with actual behavior in various countries. Also, many studies have focused on Japanese management, mainly in the private sector; cross-cultural public management styles and techniques are important subjects for future comparative research. Finally, a new strand of the literature on bureaucratic behavior has begun to explore relations with clients. Perhaps the cross-cultural similarities in the tasks of service delivery will facilitate attempts to investigate the impact of such variables as social structure on public organizations' interactions with clients.

Fourth, Peters treats bureaucratic structure as a dependent variable for comparative analysis. Questions arise about the meaning of "public" as well as of "organizations." On the latter point, for example, an analysis that focused only on the highly formal structures characteristic of American public bureaucracy might ignore less differentiated structures (such as interagency committees) that may play key roles in other countries. Many of the issues that originally preoccupied organizational theorists are inevitably raised by attempts at structural analysis. For example, the degree of centralization of authority, which varies greatly between unitary and federal states, is an obvious focus for analysis. Little comparative research on population ecology models of public organizations, which have become popular among organizational theorists, has been conducted; but governmental reorganization has become a favorite topic. Most students of reorganization doubt its results are beneficial.

Fifth, Peters considers bureaucratic outcomes as a dependent variable for comparative analysis. Who benefits from the actions of agencies? Of course, policies may be *designed* to affect members of certain political parties, classes, or kinship groupings differently; through the service delivery process, these differential impacts also may originate lower in the organization. Both possibilities again raise the issue of representative bureaucracy: does it matter whether members of the affected groups are designing and administering the policies? How matters of these sorts are handled certainly may have repercussions for the legitimacy of the state. Also, the recent outpouring of (mainly American) literature on implementation is relevant to the study of comparative bureaucratic outputs. Peters is critical of this literature's naivete, its excessive pessimism, its mechanistic tendencies, and its normative conservatism, and does not believe it has made important theoretical contributions to the study of bureaucratic outcomes. All in all, Peters concludes that the literature on comparative public bureaucracy is underdeveloped and confused, but he is optimistic that the increasing focus on the concept of the state will restore public bureaucracy to an important position in the study of political systems.

Comparisons of the characteristics, as well as the relative virtues, of public and private organizations have long been the subject of debate in this country. Hal G. Rainey joins the controversy in "On the Uniqueness of Public Bureaucracies." In the history of organizational theory, Rainey identifies two more or less distinct strands of literature. The first, generic organizational theory, has been chiefly concerned with such structural matters as degrees of centralization and levels of hierarchy and with such processual ones as decision making and communication. Writers representing this strand have cast their theoretical nets widely to encompass organizational behavior, psychology, and environments, and they assume that their findings are applicable to all organizations—including governmental agencies. The second strand of literature views public organizations as being distinctive. Writers representing this strand have concentrated on the political environments of agencies and on the political roles both of bureaucrats and of their agencies. Evaluations of bureaucratic responsiveness and accountability are frequent. Some evaluations are mainly positive, while others are mainly negative.

Although the two strands of literature have been separate for the most part, Rainey describes a convergence in which scholars have begun to apply the empirical and conceptual insights of organizational theory to public bureaucracies, while conducting more rigorous analyses of their political aspects. An early exemplar of the convergence was Dahl and Lindblom's 1953 book *Politics, Economics, and Welfare*, which argued that governmental agencies differ from enterprises in significant respects. For examples: agencies get resources from budgetary appropriations, whereas enterprises depend on the market system; agencies frequently have intangible and multiple objectives, whereas enterprises must pay attention to the "bottom line"; agencies are subject to strict political-legal supervision on such matters as due process, whereas enterprises are much less accountable. A second early work illustrative of the convergence Rainey sees was *Inside Bureaucracy*, published by Downs in 1967, which presented a set of interrelated propositions that are generally compatible with the Dahl and Lindblom analysis. Downs extended the argument in important respects; for example, he asserted that in the absence of the market's constraints, public bureaucracies are affected by the various roles bureaucrats assume (such as "climber" or "conserver"), which results in swollen budgets and undue rigidity. Downs also included a chapter on the agency's "power setting" in which the relationships between the agency and such environmental actors as a sovereign, rivals, allies, beneficiaries, and regulators were identified.

Rainey also examines several more recent contributions to this species of literature—including those by Warwick, Meyer, Barton, Lynn, and Kaufman—which in various ways advanced the convergence he describes. The final component of the convergence that he discusses is a body of research and theory, developing over the last several decades but accelerating recently, that features controversies over whether public bureaucracies are distinctive from private ones. Rainey evaluates numerous studies that take different positions on the similarities and differences of public and private agencies on such dimensions as incentive structures, strategic decision processes, organizational structures, and work-related attitudes of employees and managers.

Although the concept of the state was banished from political science for most of the past half-century, the term recently has enjoyed a renaissance. In "Bureaucracy, Power, Policy, and the State," Bert Rockman links the recent expansion of the role of bureaucracy in modern governments with the literature that has begun to reconceptualize the idea of the state and explores the relationship of this discussion to the venerable concepts of power and policy. Important implications attend the definitions given to each term in the chapter's title. How we choose to conceive of the relationship between bureaucracy and the state in normative terms also is important. Those who adopt the Marxist assumption that bureaucrats pursue the illegitimate interests of the dominant class, for example, certainly will take a very different view from those who adopt the idealist assumption that bureaucrats strive to represent the public interest.

The literature on the concept of power in bureaucratic organizations has emphasized the supposed pathologies of bureaucratic power. For example, hierarchy is often depicted as causing distorted interorganizational communication and also as being undemocratic and alienating. Rigidity, inefficiency, and disintegration are said to be other significant bureaucratic dysfunctions. Furthermore, bureaucracies often are suspected of exercising their discretion so that particularism and dehumanization are more apparent than universalism and compassion in dealing with clients. Rockman also considers whether the administrative elite can be thought of as an autonomous group. Although debate rages about whether bureaucrats have become a separate class in many countries, the matter is hardly discussed in the United States where civil servants obviously are low in status and lack cohesion as a corporate entity; they cannot control entry to their positions and are viewed as highly dispensable by other political elites. Nonetheless, Rockman argues that the opportunity for making political choices necessarily arises out of the performance of administrative functions; he also identifies several aspects of the American context (e.g., the separation of powers, the multiple points of access to the policy process) that force our administrative elite to devote more attention to political considerations than their European colleagues. Whereas American bureaucrats frequently are relatively successful as administrative politicians in dealing with particular issues, elected officials increasingly have concentrated on manipulating the bureaucracy to ensure that, in general, it serves their partisan ends. As the process of politicization proceeds—through, for example, layering-in additional ranks of political appointees, who are given ever-greater authority—contentions that the bureaucracy behaves as an autonomous force seem less and less credible.

Finally, Rockman demonstrates that one's conception of bureaucracy's power is dependent upon one's image of the state: if one perceives of the state as being defined by central political actors seeking to uphold the public interest, then bureaucrats seem mainly to be servants of the state; if one sees the state as lacking a strong central core and dominated by subgovernments, then bureaucracy also will be weak at the center and strong at the bureau level; if one conceives of the state as being engaged in a rationalistic pursuit of technocratic imperatives rather than of the political good, then bureaucracy is likely to play an important role in making political decisions defined in terms of social engineering; if one visualizes the state as an object reacting and adapting to past acts, but restricted in its ability to initiate new programs, then central administrative institutions are likely to play key roles in managing those reactions. Thus, Rockman concludes, the analysis of bureaucratic power remains problematical. Bureaucracy's impact on policy resides in its institutional strengths, but its power always is variable and contingent upon a number of matters—especially upon the political linkages bureaucracy is able to forge with elected officials.

The ancient problem of governmental responsiveness has taken on an added dimension in our bureaucratic era. In "Explorations in Bureaucratic Responsiveness," Grace Hall Saltzstein contends that the newly formulated problem has become a formidable challenge for democratic governments. She finds that two perspectives on bureaucratic responsiveness may be differentiated. According to the most common perspective, bureaucracy should be responsive to the public, either directly or indirectly. Within the perspective, one school holds that bureaucracy ought to respond *indirectly* by complying with the wishes of elected officials, the only repositories of legitimate policy authority; another school holds that bureaucracy itself has a legitimate policy function and bureaucracy is allowed—even obligated—to respond *directly* to the public by making decisions, compromising, and bargaining. According to the second perspective, however, bureaucracy should be responsive to the state rather than to the public. Such standards as efficiency, effectiveness, and professionalism ought to be pursued by these politically neutral instruments of the state. Saltzstein points out that administrators who choose one perspective on responsiveness may behave quite differently from those who choose another.

Choosing a perspective on bureaucratic responsiveness is likely to reflect one's definition of the phenomenon, but Saltzstein indicates that a number of other definitional questions also arise. Simply saying, for example, that bureaucrats should be responsive to the public does not indicate *which* members of the public. Geographically, should bureaucrats respond to the interests of a particular suburb or to the possibly conflicting interests of a larger metropolitan area? Within a given community, to whose competing claims should bureaucrats be responsive: to those of the mass public, of elites, of organized groups of clients? Furthermore, choices must be made about whether responsiveness is owed only to the public's articulated demands, to public opinion, or to the public's needs— however the latter may be defined. Those who fear technocracy may believe that bureaucrats should be delegates, while those who have confidence in bureaucratic professionalization are likely to endorse the trustee role. Finally, is it enough to be responsive procedurally, for example, to allow input to the policy process, or must outcomes be congruent with the wishes of the designated group? Many of the same questions arise for those who believe bureaucrats should be responsive to the interests of the state. For example, where does the bureaucrat's duty lie when contradictory instructions are given by the congress and the president?

When Saltzstein analyzes the small body of research thus far conducted on bureaucratic responsiveness, she finds that virtually all of it employs a "consumer model" that focuses on responsiveness to the wishes of the public. Such alternative models as the "professional responsibility model" or the "neutral executor model"—both suggested by the earlier discussion—have as yet stimulated little research. Most of the empirical literature on bureaucratic responsiveness treats such topics as citizen participation, decentralization, service delivery systems, and representative bureaucracy. Close examination of the studies reveals that the following kinds of problems are frequently ignored: if bureaucratic responsiveness means that administrators' value preferences should match those of citizens, which levels of administrators and which citizens should be taken into account? In the absence of unambiguous survey data, how may the public's wishes be reliably ascertained? Is it reasonable to treat citizen dissatisfaction with governmental services as an index of bureaucratic responsiveness when the funding level for services has been set by politicians? What level of analysis should be chosen in evaluating bureaucratic responsiveness—a given target population, a subunit of the jurisdiction, or the jurisdiction as a whole? What conflicts may exist between bureaucrats' obligations to be responsive to citizens, to professional standards, and to elected officials? Saltzstein recommends that future research investigate the problems she has sketched and focus on such additional matters as the impact of citizens' perceptions about bureaucratic responsiveness on their willingness to support government in general.

Notes

1. "Americans Speak Out: On Inflation, Politicians, Bureaucracy: National Survey," *U.S. News and World Report* 81 (September 13, 1976): 41.

2. The survey, which was conducted by Louis Harris and Associates, is reported in U. S. Congress, Subcommittee on Intergovernmental Relations of the Senate Committee on Government Operations, *Confidence and Concern: Citizens View American Government, A Survey of Public Attitudes*, 93d Cong., 1st sess., 1973, Committee Print, p. 236. This document is cited below as Harris, *Confidence and Concern*.

3. Victor A. Thompson, *Modern Organization*, 2d ed. (University of Alabama Press, 1977), p. 24; Herbert Kaufman, "Fear of Bureaucracy: A Raging Pandemic," *Public Administration Review* 41 (January/February 1981): 1-9.

4. George Gallup, Jr., *The Gallup Poll: Public Opinion 1985* (Wilmington, DE: Scholarly Resources, Inc., 1985), p. 141.

5. Warren E. Miller and Santa Traugott, *American National Election Studies Data Sourcebook, 1952-1986* (Cambridge, MA: Harvard University Press, 1989), pp. 261-62.

6. See "The Role of Government: An Issue for 1988?" *Public Opinion* (March/April 1987): 24-29.

7. "Government's Role in Reshuffling Income," *U.S. News and World Report* 90 (March 2, 1981): 26.

8. Daniel Katz, Barbara Gutek, Robert L. Kahn, and Eugenia Barton, *Bureaucratic Encounters: A Pilot Study in the Evaluation of Government Services* (Ann Arbor: Survey Research Center, Institute for Social Research, University of Michigan, 1975), pp. 20-21, 64, 102. "Not ascertained" responses were deleted in figuring percentages.

9. Reported in Harris, *Confidence and Concern*, pp. 111, 288, 293. "Not ascertained" responses were deleted in figuring percentages. A strict comparison of the two polls' responses is impossible because, whereas the SRC question can be dichotomized into satisfied and dissatisfied categories, the Harris question had a middle category, "only somewhat satisfied."

10. A compendium of these studies is Charles T. Goodsell, *The Case for Bureaucracy: A Public Administration Polemic*, 2d ed. (Chatham, NJ: Chatham House, 1985), ch. 2.

11. *USA Today*, September 12, 1985.

12. Computed from Katz et al., *Bureaucratic Encounters*, pp. 121-24. The gap between evaluations of encounters with constraint agencies and general perceptions of governmental offices was much smaller than the gap reported above for service agencies. Much of the disparity surely must be attributed to the circumstance that questions were asked only about "problem" encounters with constraint agencies.

13. Ibid., p. 135.

14. Ibid., pp. 176-77.

15. Cited in Robert J. Wagman, column for Newspaper Enterprise Association, August 13, 1981.

16. Even Washington insider Gerald Ford got into the antibureaucratic spirit with the following promise—perhaps made in order to counter the appeal of his opponent, Jimmy Carter—delivered as Ford accepted the Republican Presidential nomination: "We will go on reducing the deadweight and the impudence of bureaucracy" (*New York Times*, August 19, 1976).

17. A marker in the development of this understanding was a 1977 column by Patrick J. Buchanan, who had served as a presidential speechwriter in the Nixon administration and would become Director of Communications in the Reagan administration ("GOP Must Come to Terms with Welfare State," column for Special Features Syndicate, December 2, 1977). After charting the "alarming" growth of government under Nixon and Ford, Buchanan asserted that they "presided over erection of the greatest welfare state in history." He then offered the following analysis for the next Republican presidential candidate: "The great Robert A. Taft is dead. The struggles for limited government in which he fought have been lost irretrievably. The American Welfare State is an established fact with which the traditional Republicans must make their separate peace. For there are literally tens of millions of Americans, veterans and retirees, willing to vote 'conservative,' who will never pull the lever for a candidate or party that threatens the federal lifeline upon which they have come to depend for survival."

18. Associated Press, October 2, 1981. Bureaucrats were one of Mr. Reagan's most favored targets. He was even willing to use American bureaucracy as a scapegoat in conducting public diplomacy with the Soviet Union. When asked at a news conference in Moscow whether the restrictions on emigration from the Soviet Union should be attributed to the Soviet bureaucracy or to governmental policy, he replied: ". . . I think one of the sins of government, and one with which we must deal and never have been able to be completely successful with, and this includes our own government, is that the bureaucracy, once created, has one fundamental rule above all others: preserve the bureaucracy. And I think that governments will always find that they are having to check on bureaucracy and make sure that it is not abiding by its own rules and taking the easiest course. And so, I wasn't picking on one government other than another." The president offered an anecdote in response to a follow-up question: "Maybe I should illustrate to you why I feel the way I do about bureaucracies. Once during the war I happened to be involved in a situation in which one level of the military wanted a warehouse full of filing cabinets, wanted permission to destroy the files so they could use those filing cases and they were able to prove that the documents had no historic value, they had no bearing on present-day government at all; they were just useless. And so the message went up through the ranks requesting permission to destroy these obsolete files. And then back down through the ranks from the top command, endorsed by each level of command, came the reply: Permission granted—provided copies were made of each file destroyed." When asked whether this response let Mr. Gorbachev off too easily, Mr. Reagan said: ". . . . No, but I just have to believe that in any government, some of us do find ourselves bound in by bureaucracy, and then sometimes you have to stomp your foot and say unmistakably, I

want it done. And then maybe you get through with it. But I have great confidence in his ability to do that" (reported in the *Washington Post*, June 2, 1988).

Another noteworthy example of bureaucratic scapegoating occurred during the 1988 presidential campaign when Republican vice presidential nominee Dan Quayle criticized the State Department for failing to "put American interests first" on trade issues. In responding to later questions, David Broder reported that Quayle "appeared to become concerned that his remarks might be seen as too critical of the Reagan administration. George P. Schultz, he said, is 'one of the best secretaries of state' in history, but 'there is a huge bureaucracy there,' whose members often 'have a fundamentally different idea of what makes America tick than the average man and woman' " (*Washington Post*, September 4, 1988).

19. See Robert N. Bellah, Richard Madsen, William M. Sullivan, Ann Swidler, and Steven M. Tipton, *Habits of the Heart: Individualism and Commitment in American Life* (Berkeley: University of California Press, 1985), chapter 6.

20. See, for example, Francis E. Rourke, *Bureaucracy, Politics, Public Policy*, 3d ed. (Boston: Little, Brown, 1984), ch. 3.

21. Although I prefer to use the rubric of "public bureaucracy"—because of the reasons discussed in the Introduction and because I think that creating this artificial field helps to cut through some historical confusions—I believe that a broad understanding of "public administration" also encompasses "public bureaucracy." Readers who find "bureaucracy" infelicitous and who define "public administration" broadly may make the appropriate substitution throughout.

22. *Proceedings of the American Political Science Association Held at Chicago, Ill.*, December 28–30, 1904, pp. 10-15 (hereafter cited as *Proceedings [1904]*).

23. Frank J. Goodnow, "The Work of the American Political Science Association," *Proceedings (1904)*, pp. 37-45.

24. Frank J. Goodnow, *Politics and Administration: A Study in Government* (New York: Russell and Russell, 1900), pp. 24 and 16.

25. Woodrow Wilson, "The Study of Administration," *Political Science Quarterly* 2 (June 1887): 212. The history of this article's scholarly impact is problematical. Paul Van Riper reports that it was hardly cited by others until after World War I and that it appeared to have no impact on the field until well after 1950: "The American Administrative State: Wilson and the Founders—An Unorthodox View," *Public Administration Review* 43 (November/December, 1983): 479.

26. Wilson, "Study of Administration," p. 213.

27. Ibid., p. 219.

28. Leonard D. White, *Introduction to the Study of Public Administration* (New York: Macmillan, 1926), p. 2.

29. Ibid., p. 4.

30. Ibid., p. 2.

31. Ibid., p. viii. See also White's innovative examination of the linkages between public opinion and bureaucracy, *The Prestige Value of Public Employment in Chicago: An Experimental Study* (Chicago: University of Chicago Press, 1929).

32. Full citations of these works follow: Carl J. Friedrich and Taylor Cole, *Responsible Bureaucracy: A Study of the Swiss Civil Service* (Cambridge, MA: Harvard University Press, 1932); Gabriel Almond and Harold D. Lasswell, "Aggressive Behavior by Clients toward Public Relief Administrators," *American Political Science Review* 28 (August 1934): 643-55; E. Pendleton Herring, *Public Administration and the Public Interest* (New York: McGraw-Hill, 1936); John M. Gaus, Leonard D. White, and Marshall Dimock, *The Frontiers of Public Administration* (Chicago: University of Chicago Press, 1936); V. O. Key, Jr., *The Administration of Federal Grants to States* (Chicago: Public Administration

Service, 1937); Carl J. Friedrich, "Public Policy and the Nature of Administrative Responsibility," *Public Policy* 1 (1940): 3-24; Herman Finer, "Administrative Responsibility in Democratic Government," *Public Administration Review* 1 (1941): 335-50; Robert E. Cushman, *The Independent Regulatory Agencies* (New York: (Oxford University Press, 1941); James W. Fesler, *The Independence of State Regulatory Agencies* (Chicago: Public Administration Service, 1942); Avery Leiserson, *Administrative Regulation: A Study in Representation of Interests* (Chicago: University of Chicago Press, 1942); J. Donald Kingsley, *Representative Bureaucracy: An Interpretation of the British Civil Service* (Yellow Springs, OH: Antioch Press, 1944); Lynton K. Caldwell, *The Administrative Theories of Hamilton and Jefferson: Their Contributions to Thought on Public Administration* (Chicago: University of Chicago Press, 1944); Paul H. Appleby, *Big Democracy* (New York: Alfred A. Knopf, 1944); Hebert A. Simon, *Administrative Behavior: A Study of Decision-Making Processes in Administrative Organizations* (New York: Macmillan, 1947); Robert A. Dahl, "The Science of Public Administration: Three Problems," *Public Administration Review* 7 (1947): 1-11; Dwight Waldo, *The Administrative State: A Study of the Political Theory of American Public Administration* (New York: Ronald Press, 1948); Norton E. Long, "Power and Administration," *Public Administration Review* 9 (1949): 257-64; Oliver Garceau, *The Public Library in the Political Process* (New York: Columbia University Press, 1949); Charles Hyneman, *Bureaucracy in a Democracy* (New York: Harper and Brothers, 1950); Herbert A. Simon, Donald W. Smithburg, and Victor A. Thompson, *Public Administration* (New York: Alfred A. Knopf, 1950).

33. V. O. Key, *Politics, Parties, and Pressure Groups* (New York: Thomas Y. Crowell, 1942), pp. 171-98; Charles E. Merriam, *Systematic Politics* (Chicago: University of Chicago Press, 1945), pp. 118-78.

34. Carl J. Friedrich, William C. Beyer, Sterling D. Spero, John F. Miller, George A. Graham, *Problems of the American Public Service: Five Monographs on Specific Aspects of Personnel Administration* (New York: Mc Graw-Hill, 1935), pp. 3-77.

35. Thomas S. Kuhn, *The Structure of Scientific Revolutions* (Chicago: University of Chicago Press, 1962).

36. Albert Somit and Joseph Tanenhaus, *The Development of American Political Science: From Burgess to Behavioralism* (Boston: Allyn and Bacon, 1967), pp. 177-79.

37. A leading compendium of early behavioral research was *Introductory Readings in Political Behavior*, ed. S. Sidney Ulmer (Chicago: Rand McNally, 1961). According to my count, fifteen of the book's forty-eight readings were concerned to an important degree with official or unofficial political institutions, but only three or four readings featured an examination of institutional members as actors or of institutions as behaving political entities. The remaining "institutional" studies treated such matters as the social backgrounds, the personality dimensions, the norms, and the roles of the institutional members.

38. Although behaviorally oriented studies of institutions were discouraged, they were never proscribed. And the victory of the "noninstitutional" approach to the study of institutions was never complete, not even for the areas where it was most prominent. For example, the approach to legislatures through role analysis held the behavioral high ground during the 1960s (see John C. Wahlke, Heinz Eulau, William Buchanan, and LeRoy C. Ferguson, *The Legislative System: Explorations in Legislative Behavior* [New York: John Wiley, 1962]), but distinguished work that viewed legislatures as behaving entities composed of behaving actors continued to be published (see Ralph K. Huitt, "Democratic Party Leadership in the Senate," *American Political Science Review* 60 [June 1961]: 333-44).

39. But sociologists were responsible for the bulk of the most significant writing during this period; see, for example, the references to Merton, Selznick, Bendix, Gould-

ner, Blau, and Eisenstadt in the Introduction, note 4. Most of the small number of writings on public bureaucracy by political scientists during this period appeared in monographs and textbooks, but see Matthew Holden, Jr., " 'Imperialism' in Bureaucracy," *American Political Science Review* 60 (December 1966): 943-51.

40. Herring, Key, Cole, Hyneman, and Friedrich also were identified—perhaps more prominently, in the minds of many scholars—with the broader field of American politics, with constitutional law, or with comparative politics.

41. Leiserson also belonged to the general field of American politics. In addition, the following presidents of the association during the decade between Friedrich and Leiserson had significant experience in public bureaucracy—usually at early stages in their careers—but were not popularly identified with the field: C. Herman Pritchett, David B. Truman, Robert A. Dahl, and Robert E. Lane.

42. The following study provided indirect evidence about the popularity of public bureaucracy during the time. According to an analysis of directories of the American Political Science Association conducted by Albert Somit and Joseph Tanenhaus, 35 percent of those listed identified themselves with the subfield of public administration in 1953; the proportion had dropped to 26 percent for the 1961 directory. Members could list as many as three fields for the directory; in 1963, when Somit and Tanenhaus asked a sample of association members to identify themselves with a *single* field, only 12 percent identified with public administration. But public administration was not the discipline's least prestigeous field: when the sample was asked to rank the fields in which the most and the least significant work was being done, public administration's ratio of positive-to-negative evaluations caused it to be ranked in the middle of seven fields; both public law and political theory received far more negative evaluations. See *American Political Science: A Profile of a Discipline* (New York: Atherton, 1964), pp. 52-56.

43. For a discussion and citation of his earlier works, see Harold D. Lasswell, "Policy Sciences," *International Encyclopedia of the Social Sciences,* vol. 12 (New York: Macmillan, 1968), pp. 181-89.

44. See Lewis A. Froman, Jr., "Public Policy," *International Encyclopedia of the Social Sciences,* vol. 13 (New York: Macmillan, 1968), pp. 204-8.

45. Theodore J. Lowi, "American Business, Public Policy, Case-Studies, and Political Theory," *World Politics* 16 (1964): 677-715.

46. David Easton, "The New Revolution in Political Science," *American Political Science Review* 63 (December 1969): 1052.

47. Nonetheless, many political scientists did become aware of the criticisms made of logical positivism by philosophers and other social scientists; see, for example, Eugene F. Miller, "Positivism, Historicism, and Political Inquiry," *American Political Science Review* 66 (September 1972): pp. 796-817; see also the responses in the same issue by David Braybrooke and Alexander Rosenberg, Richard S. Rudner, and Martin Landau.

48. Jeffrey L. Pressman and Aaron B. Wildavsky, *Implementation* (Berkeley: University of California Press, 1973). For a skeptical reaction to their contention (p. 166) that the book was the first "significant analytic work dealing with implementation," see Dwight Waldo, *The Enterprise of Public Administration: A Summary View* (Novato, CA: Chandler and Sharp), 1980, pp. 72-74.

49. A useful guide to the approach and to the expanding literature is Daniel A. Mazmanian and Paul A. Sabatier, *Implementation and Public Policy* (Glenview, IL.: Scott, Foresman, 1983).

50. This neglect may have a historical basis; early policy studies activists, many of whom felt intellectually superior to the practitioners of public administration, sought to separate themselves from those traditionalists. I am indebted to Todd La Porte for this observation.

51. Samuel P. Huntington, *Political Order in Changing Societies* (New Haven, CT: Yale University Press, 1969), p. 12; see also Samuel P. Huntington, "Political Development and Political Decay," *World Politics* 17 (April 1965): 386-430. Compare Huntington's approach with that of Nelson W. Polsby, "The Institutionalization of the U.S. House of Representatives," *American Political Science Review* 62 (March 1968): 144-68. Two sociologists, whose works were known to political scientists, helped stimulate this strand of literature: Philip Selznick, *Leadership in Administration: A Sociological Interpretation* (New York: Harper and Row, 1957); S.N. Eisenstadt, *Essays on Comparative Institutions* (New York: John Wiley, 1965). Among other political scientists making early contributions to this literature were Milton J. Esman and Hans C. Blaise, *Institution-Building Research: The Guiding Concepts* (Pittsburgh: University of Pittsburgh Graduate School of Public and International Affairs, 1966); Ralph Braibanti, "External Inducement of Political-Administrative Development: An Institutional Study," in *Political and Administrative Development*, ed. Braibanti (Durham, NC: Duke University Press, 1969), pp. 3-106.

52. Fred W. Riggs, "The Comparison of Whole Political Systems," in *The Methodology of Comparative Research*, ed. Robert T. Holt and John E. Turner (New York: Free Press, 1970), p. 77; the essay was originally written in 1966.

53. See, for example, Eric A. Nordlinger, *On the Autonomy of the Democratic State* (Cambridge, MA: Harvard University Press, 1981). Because a focus on the state points to the importance of public bureaucracies (see the quotations above from Goodnow), the resurgent literature on the state already has contributed to the resurrection of public bureaucracy within political science. I do not treat the new focus on the state as a principal contribution to public bureaucracy's resurrection because the two developments were more or less contemporaneous.

54. This certainly was true of an article I myself published on the subject in the mid-1970s; in attempting to justify my departure from orthodoxy, I took care to cite the authority of all of the distinguished authors mentioned above in note 51: Larry B. Hill, "Institutionalization, the Ombudsman, and Bureaucracy," *American Political Science Review* 68 (September 1974): 1075-85. Of course, exceptions to the generalization may be found. For example, in the early 1970s, James Q. Wilson (who was more interested in political analysis than in theoretical speculation, but who took what may be described as an institutional approach) conducted a broad-ranging study of interest groups in the tradition of V. O. Key: *Political Organizations* (New York: Basic Books, 1973). In addition, about a decade later, in arguing that "institutions have come to dominate the processes of interest representation in American national politics," Robert H. Salisbury viewed interest groups as behaving entities and, thus, offered what continued to be a revisionist interpretation. But he presented a straightforward explanation of the differences between mere groups and institutions without defensiveness: "Interest Representation: The Dominance of Institutions," *American Political Science Review* 78 (March 1984): 64.

55. *American Political Science Review* 78 (September 1984): 734-49. The passages quoted in the following list are from pp. 736-37.

56. Ibid., p. 738.

57. Ibid., p. 747.

58. See, for example, Rogers M. Smith, "Political Jurisprudence, the 'New Institutionalism,' and the Future of Public Law," *American Political Science Review* 82 (March 1988): 89-108.

59. Also, many of the policy organizations formed in recent years have become institutionalized—no pun intended—and are likely to be significant actors in academic life for years to come.

60. See *Political Science: The State of the Discipline*, ed. Ada W. Finifter (Washington, DC: American Political Science Association, 1983). In fairness, such sensitivity

seems overblown; the selection of topics and the identification of subfields probably reflected only the preferences of the program organizer.

61. I use the current section name, which was adopted at the 1984 annual meeting. The 1983 convention program listed the section as "Administration, Organizations and Executives"; the 1984 program listed the section as "Public Administration, Organizations, and Executives." These names also had been used earlier, when the group was included in the "Courtesy Listing of Unaffiliated Groups" at the back of the convention program.

62. Because I have been involved with the section's affairs, I cannot claim to be a disinterested observer of these developments. See Larry B. Hill, "The APSA's 'New' Section on Public Administration," *PS* 18 (Spring 1985): 274-78.

63. *PS* 20 (Summer 1987): 714. The following comment appeared in the Council Minutes concerning the creation of the lectureship: "The Council requested that the president be sensitive to the Public Administration Section's requests in selecting the members of the selection committee and in selecting the first lecture recipient" (*PS* 18 (Summer 1985): 702. President Wildavsky followed that request.

64. As mentioned on page 29, this account also omits any discussion of the treatment of public bureaucracy by several other social sciences and applied social sciences.

65. Darrell L. Pugh, *Looking Back—Moving Forward: A Half-Century Celebration of Public Administration and ASPA* (Washington, DC: American Society for Public Administration, 1988), 2-4.

66. Public bureaucracy's practitioners also belong to a number of professional associations in addition to the APSA and the ASPA, for example, the Academy of Management—Public Sector Section, the Operations Research Society of America, the Decision Science Institute, and the Institute of Management Sciences.

67. See Diana Crane, *Invisible Colleges: Diffusion of Knowledge in Scientific Communities* (Chicago: University of Chicago Press, 1972).

2

A Legitimate Role for Bureaucracy in Democratic Governance

Gary L. Wamsley, Charles T. Goodsell,
John A. Rohr, Orion White, and James Wolf

> *Government that is unlimited in scope but formless in action is government*
> *that cannot plan. Government that is formless in action and amoral in*
> *intention (i.e., ad hoc) is government that can neither plan nor achieve justice.*
> —Theodore J. Lowi, *The End of Liberalism*

> *Though we cannot acquiesce in the political heresy of the poet who says—*
> *"For forms of government let fools contest; what' er is best administered is*
> *best"—yet we may safely pronounce, that the true test of a good government*
> *is its aptitude and tendency to provide a good administration.*
> —Publius, *Federalist 68*

Most Americans are likely to find the title of this chapter disquieting at best and repugnant at worst. Others with a wry twist of mind may see the title as an extended oxymoron as in "greater Cleveland," "military justice," or "faculty salaries." Our purpose is to encourage serious reconsideration of the role of bureaucracy in the political system. Such a reconsideration of that role must begin with a new way of thinking about the public administration in America. Toward that end we will outline a normative framework for the development of a legitimate role in governance for the bureaucracy and the bureaucrat—or, as we prefer, for the public administration and the public administrator.

The Concept of "Governance" in American Political Discourse

In the popular jargon, American politicians are "elected," "win office," "serve," "represent," "hold office"; apparently they do just about everything but *govern*.

Curiously, many American political scientists also seem to have an aversion to the latter term: consider that *The American Political Dictionary* contains no reference to "govern" or "governance."[1] *Webster's* defines "govern" quite fully, however, as follows:

> [OF. governer, fr. L. gubernare to steer, govern fr. Gr Kybernan] 1. to direct and control; rule. 2. to regulate; restrain. 3. To be a rule of law for; to determine. Syn. Govern, rule means to exercise power or authority in controlling others. Govern connotes as its end a keeping in a straight course or smooth operation for the good of the individual and the whole.

The etymology of the word is fascinating. It comes from the Greek noun *Kybernatas* (Latin—gubernator), a helmsman. Plato gave us the apt metaphor of the "ship of state" in his *Republic*.[2] Both Plato and Aristotle were concerned with such fundamental questions as: "Who should govern?"; "What happens when one group governs rather than another?"; and "What qualities are essential in those who govern?"

American political scientists, who pride themselves on being part of an intellectual tradition reaching back to Plato and Aristotle, have had amazingly little to say about the phenomenon that was the central concern of those political philosophers. Perhaps this is because modern political science came into being just as pluralism became the dominant conception of the American political system. Thus, political science was, to use Lowi's harsh verb, "corrupted" by pluralism's intellectual weakness. Political science embraced "the myth of the automatic society granted us by an all-encompassing, ideally self-correcting, providentially automatic political process."[3] An automatic process may invite description and analysis of *politics* but it does not encourage the study of how politics is related to *governance*—after all, there is no need for governance in the automatic society.

As for public administration, governance was at least implied in Woodrow Wilson's complaint that it was becoming harder "to run a constitution than to frame one," but somehow the concept never went beyond implication with Wilson or most scholars of public administration who came after him.[4] Public administration was "corrupted" not only by pluralism but also by the politics–administration dichotomy and by scientific management.[5] In the automatic society, one need not "steer," "direct," "rule," or do any of the distasteful things denoted by the term governance; one need only manage, as in business. Wilson and Goodnow's creation of the politics–administration dichotomy fitted nicely with the shop-floor focus of Taylor's scientific management. The former assumed the ends would be "given," as in cabinet government with strong parties; the latter assumed the ends would be "given," as in loading pig iron. Since strong parties have not developed and government is not a shop floor, neither the politics–administration dichotomy nor scientific management have been of great utility to American public administration. Scholars of public administration have debunked the politics–administration dichotomy but have never found a suitable replacement for it as normative foundation. There has been little to fulfill that function but neutral competence—scientific management or administration committed to carrying out the "given" ends by the most efficient means. Public administrators in the field of action still make such a claim. What else can they do? There is no legitimacy for anything else but "management" in which the ends are presumed to be given. No one is "governing"—everyone is just "managing." The political system is on autopilot.

Two Competing Ideologies About Governance

As Douglas Yates points out, we have been left with two dominant and contradictory "models" of how our government should work and be structured[6]: the pluralist-democracy and the administrative-efficiency "models." Neither is closely attuned to the realities of the way our system actually functions; both are better described as tacit ideologies[7] that have become consensually validated doctrine. They have become a part of what Husserl referred to as the "natural attitude" and Schutz called "*Lebenswelt*" or "everyday life world."[8] From them, we have derived our conventional wisdom that guides our day-to-day behavior.

The two "models" are antithetical and exist in a state of tension. Efforts to enhance one diminish the other, and we unwittingly engage in this behavior on a regular basis. Although both contain important implications for governance, neither is very explicit on the subject.

The pluralist-democracy "model" assumes:

> 1. that there are multiple, diverse, and competing interest groups in the political process
> 2. that government should offer these groups multiple access points and means of participation
> 3. that government should have multiple and dispersed centers of power (powers are shared vertically and horizontally) to ensure that ambition counteracts ambition and a balance of power results
> 4. that American government and politics can, therefore, be best understood as a competition among minority interests
> 5. that "there is a high probability . . . that an 'active and legitimate group in the population can make itself heard effectively at some crucial stage in the process of decision' "[9]
> 6. that "the competition among governmental institutions and nongovernmental interest groups leads to bargaining and compromise and produces, it is hoped, a rough balance of power in the society"[10]

To Yates, the logic of the pluralist democracy "model" suggests a bureaucracy (and thus a mode of governance) that would: "(1) present multiple centers of power (by means of which concentrations of power would be checked), (2) facilitate the representation of interest groups by providing multiple points of access (especially to minority interests), (3) have strong elements of decentralization, (4) be internally competitive, (5) be open and participative, (6) produce widespread bargaining." In addition, the pattern sketched above is pervaded with a "far-reaching suspicion of power and especially of executive power."[11]

To be sure, the "model" of pluralist democracy would have been congenial to Madison, perhaps to Jefferson, and certainly to such contemporary students of politics as Robert Dahl.[12]

Yates, ascribing the following assumptions to the administrative efficiency "model," says:

> 1. that pluralist democracy has been subject to abuse and has failed to provide the appropriate basis for public decisions that are rational and value free
> 2. that the prime value in decision making should be efficiency—the greatest output at the least cost
> 3. that bureaucrats should be professionals, selected and promoted competitively on the basis of competence and merit
> 4. that merit and expertise are most effectively organized in a hierarchy with specialization of function and clearly delineated responsibilities and duties
> 5. that politics and administration and facts and values are and should be separable
> 6. that planning is essential to "good" public decisions and centralized fiscal management is essential to their effective and honest accomplishment
> 7. that a strong overall capability to coordinate and energize the parts of the system should be lodged in the elected chief executive, who represents the interests of all the people[13]

Although the administrative efficiency "model" has deep roots in American political culture (they can be traced back to Alexander Hamilton), it only reached full flower with the Brownlow Commission Report of 1937. This "model" draws upon, and indeed usually passes for, management theory, but it is in fact no less a manifestation of political theory and no less an ideology than the pluralist democracy "model." Like the latter, it has a derived conventional wisdom firmly entrenched.[14]

Two perennial questions, which may appear in many different guises, are raised by the "models." Is the pluralist-democracy "model," and its corollary implications for administration, adequate to meet the problems of a modern, industrialized, and complex society? Conversely, is the administrative-efficiency "model," with its emphasis on businesslike procedures and rational decision making, adequate to deal with the problems of administration in a *political* and *democratic* setting?

As long as our intellects are constrained by two so-called "models," which are in fact reflections of ideologies rather than descriptive or heuristic models, we are likely to keep asking these questions over and over and unlikely to generate the kind of thinking that is needed to address our problems. As long as these two "models" hold us captive, we can never really come to grips with the elemental problem of our contemporary political system, perhaps its Achilles heel—how to *govern* a political economy that requires a strong administrative system while providing for as much democracy and efficiency as possible.

The eternal questions of politics relate to governance—to the issues of how to "direct," "control," and "rule," and how to gain cooperation and compliance. Americans have been blessed (or cursed), however, with a providential history that frequently has enabled them to forget or ignore many of the gritty facts of governance. Because of our ever-expanding political economy, we have avoided the strife of a zero-sum society and, thus, have been allowed the luxury of ignoring the *first* part of Madison's famous dictum on government: "In having a government which is to be *administered* by men *over* men," Madison said, "the great difficulty lies in this: You must first enable the *government to control the people*; and in the next place, oblige it to control itself."[15] We have tended to focus upon only the latter part of Madison's charge "obliging [government] to control itself." Laymen can be excused for this oversight; students of politics and administration cannot. The unique angle that the American political system brings to questions of governance is how to "direct," "control," or "rule" in a system that was consciously designed first to establish a means of governance and then to constrain it. The pluralist-democracy "model" sidesteps this crucial question, and the administrative-efficiency "model" answers with the "imperial presidency." We assume that administration is not only part of politics but central to governance and believe that the sooner we recognize this, the sooner we can come to grips with the problems we face.

A Nascent Middle Ground between the Ideologies

It would be unfair to leave the impression that the thinking of students of political science and public administration has not moved beyond oversimplifications attendant either to the pluralist-democracy or to the administrative-efficiency "model." Most scholars are aware of devastating critiques that have made virtual strawmen of the two "models." No matter how much they are flailed and beaten, however, the "models" remain the battered-but-intact embodiments of conventional wisdom. Ideologies (or their derived conventional wisdom) do not normally lose their adherents abruptly. A single, devastating intellectual blow is unlikely to shatter these "models." The present effort is intended as a part of an incremental chipping and reshaping of the way we think about these issues. At the outset, it is appropriate to acknowledge the work of scholars in the middle ground between the two "models" described above.

As a result of works by the "bureaucratic politics" school of political science and by the complex organizational analysts of sociology, we know a good bit about the part bureaucracy plays in governance.[16] These two strands of literature have been competently reviewed elsewhere. We shall simply point to a few of the more important contributions from each strand. First, among political scientists, Paul Appleby was doing an excellent job of discrediting the politics–administration dichotomy and making the case that politics affected public administration in largely positive ways (assuring representation and responsiveness) at the very time when the administrative efficiency model was reaching its zenith.[17] Others, such as Avery Leiserson, at roughly the same time were showing how public administrators often balanced contending political impingements against one another to achieve a compromise akin to the public interest.[18] Many others contributed to a sizable literature that showed administration and politics were *not* as separable as Wilson and Goodnow had at first implied. Max Weber, Norton Long, Herbert Kaufman, James Q. Wilson, Louis Gawthrop, and Harold Seidman augmented our knowledge of bureaucratic politics in a host of ways.[19] Francis Rourke's writings in the 1960s and 1970s have done a great deal to spell out in an even-handed manner the skills and capabilities of bureaucrats in the policy process; he showed, for example, that bureaucracies not only are impinged upon by politics but that they manipulate their political environments.[20] Additionally, Herbert Simon's ideas about "bounded rationality" became very important in explaining the relationship of organizational processes to bureaucratic behavior and policy outcomes.[21] These relationships were particularly manifest in the work of Graham Allison, who drew on Simon for his organizational-process model, which he combined with a bureaucratic-politics model to analyze the Cuban Missile Crisis of 1962.[22]

Second, such complex organizational analysts as Merton and Blau have contributed a great deal through extending the discussion of Weber's ideas on bureaucracy.[23] Other noteworthy contributions from this school include Selznick's work on institutionalization; James Thompson's work on interaction between organizational technologies, their elites, and the organizational environment; and Kenneth Benson's writings about public organizations as parts of larger and quite complex networks of organizations.[24]

These valuable contributions to our knowledge of bureaucratic governance have taken us a considerable distance, but not far enough to alter ideologies and conventional wisdom. Our knowledge of bureaucratic governance remains largely disconnected and inert, we believe, for lack of normative content. The pluralist-democracy and the administrative-efficiency "models" hold all the normative ground, but we usually fail to recognize their normative content, which is masked by their positivist underpinnings.

Knowledge generated by studies of bureaucratic politics is useful to public administrators, but if a legitimate role is to be found for the public administration in governing modern America, something more will be required. That "something more" can come only from normative values that can give overarching direction to knowledge derived from description and analysis, and that can provide guidance for action; it cannot come from positivist social science. Furthermore, because public administration is not a discipline but an interdisciplinary field of action and study, stimuli for generating new knowledge are likely to come from the field of action. Knowledge and norms applied in a field of action to meet a pressing need have the best chance of making an impact on ideologies or conventional wisdom. In the generation and application of knowledge, public administration can probably find a better analog in engineering or medicine than in political science.

This brings us to the central purposes of this chapter: (1) confronting our ideological discomfort over governance and the legitimacy of bureaucracy in the governance process; and (2) outlining normative concepts appropriate to developing a legitimate role for bureaucracy (the public administration) and bureaucrats (the public administrators) in governance.

Considering the development of a legitimate role for bureaucracy in democratic governance requires us to confront several things:

1. Our resistance to the idea of governance; the notion of the automatic society has lost little of its appeal.

2. Our discomfort in admitting a legitimate role in governance for administrators.

3. The limitations both of the pluralistic democracy and the administrative-efficiency "models" in facing the crucial question of how to govern a bureaucratic republic with a reasonable degree of democracy and efficiency.

4. That our knowledge of "bureaucratic politics" and "organizational analysis" remains largely inert for lack of normative content.

If we cannot admit that bureaucracy has a role in governance, we remain, at worst, paralyzed between Yates's polar models or, at best, stalled in the potentially valuable but inchoate body of knowledge we call bureaucratic politics. We can develop neither new questions nor answers; nor can we contribute to the change of ideology and conventional wisdom or come to grips with the key problems of today. Serious consideration of a legitimate role for bureaucracy in governance unlocks the door to a host of new concepts and ways of perceiving things about both bureaucracy and democracy. Central to new perceptions is some kind of normative framework for the role of bureaucracy in governance. In the remainder of this chapter we shall attempt to develop such a framework.

A Normative Framework for a Bureaucratic Role in Governance

Developing a Broader Perspective

Public administration as a field of study and the discipline of political science have a responsibility to place bureaucracy in a broad political, economic, and historical perspective. But their literatures read as though bureaucracy were a genie loosed from a bottle as recently as the New Deal. Complex organizational theorists also have been generally ahistorical. Fortunately, works are now appearing to supplement Leonard White's classic exception to our dismal academic record.[25]

Most of the bureaucratic politics literature has been very narrowly framed so that it deals largely with relations between agencies and interest groups or the intergovernmental and intragovernmental struggles in an ahistorical context. We need to foster the understanding of bureaucracy's political and economic context more broadly defined.

At this stage in the development of the American political system we are still struggling to redefine our concepts of justice and equity. Government must and should play a role in our efforts to develop a uniquely American definition of these concepts.[26] Our economy has entered a stable, slow-growth stage of advanced capitalism in which we face fierce foreign competition with a transportation infrastructure that is deteriorating and a heavy industrial plant that is probably obsolete, but most certainly is overaged.[27] Compounding these problems, we are caught in what James O'Connor calls the "fiscal crisis of the state" in which we must sustain political legitimacy by funding a heavy burden of entitlements that hamper capital accumulation for private investment.[28] This political-economic context makes it difficult for the state to shrink and makes it impossible to refrain from intervention. It is this context that places bureaucracy in the eye of recurrent political storms, not some pernicious imperialism within bureaucracy itself. Both ends of the political spectrum want government (and thus bureaucracy) to intervene in matters that the political partisans or the interest groups deem important, while at the same time both rail against bureaucracy and "government intervention" in other matters. One faction may want intervention to "halt abortions," another to "foster choice" in decisions of human reproduction. One may want intervention in the form of tax credits but not in the form of regulation. Still another coalition of factions may be willing to see federal government manipulate grants to the states to raise the legal age for drinking but not to provide certain funds for community development.

As academics, we have failed in a fundamental way because we have not been critical enough of this political game, nor have we made clear some of its negative implications and the consequences for bureaucracy. The symptoms of Lowi's "interest group liberalism" are well known to all of us, but there is little evidence to indicate that we have taken his polemic seriously. We note his points without contesting them and then proceed to teach American politics and government and public administration just as we always have. Bureaucracy will continue to be the scapegoat for our problems until we conduct better research and teach what is taking place in our political system at the macro level of political economy. Candidates of both parties will continue to make attacks on bureaucracy the centerpieces of their campaigns only to find that this tactic, so useful in getting elected, becomes a self-inflicted wound in the subsequent struggle to govern. The gap between our system's need for effective governance and the capacity of our elected and administrative officials to provide it will continue to widen at an alarming rate. Public administration must take, and in fact is taking, the lead in breaking the bounds of positivism and turning to the works of such macrotheorists and political economists as Habermas, Miliband, and Poulantzis to gain a broader and more philosophically critical perspective on the role of the "state" (and thus of the public administration) in governance.[29]

Clearing out Mythological Underbrush

Academics, like journalists, delight in showing that "things are not what they seem." It is strange, therefore, that we have devoted little attention to examining the pejorative mythology that surrounds the public sector and public administrators. Instead, we, who are supposed to be able to achieve some detachment from our political culture, have added to its myths. How often do our general academic writings acknowledge research findings such as the following?

• Most clients of bureaucracy are not dissatisfied; in fact, the vast majority are very pleased with the services and treatment received.[30]

• The rate of productivity increase in the public sector is not clearly lower than in the private sector; public sector productivity is probably higher overall.[31]

• The federal government has not grown in number of employees since the early 1950s.[32]

• The bureaucracy is not a monolith; it is composed of many small and diverse bureaus and offices.[33]

• Public agencies stimulate and implement change; resistance to change is no more endemic to the organizations in the public sector than to the private ones.

• Studies have shown that the private sector is more top-heavy with administrative personnel than the public sector.[34]

• Waste and inefficiency are no more prevalent in the public sector than in the private; in the former, however, they are seen as draining the taxpayers' money, while in the latter we fail to see that the costs are passed on to us in the prices we pay as consumers.

Our purpose in analytically tackling antibureaucratic myths should not be to praise bureaucracy but simply to reveal alternative "facts" or interpretations.[35] While we are at it, we ought to reconsider terminology like "bureaucracy." It is, after all, a particular organizational form found not only in government but in private and third-sector organizations. We ought to focus on the functions of government agencies rather than organizational forms, and alter our terminology accordingly.

We need to invent language that is less pejorative and that can help shift our political rhetoric and dialogue into more productive channels. Both the rhetoric and the dialogue are still very negatively focused on *whether* or not government has any role in matters such as the revitalization of industry, the preservation of natural resources, and the maintenance of our place in a world economy. Since all segments of the political spectrum clearly intend that government have a role, debate and rhetoric ought to focus on "how?" and "what form is most effective?" Our political dialogue ought to focus on *how* (not whether) intentions and actions should be pursued through the public sector. *How* can the public administration act so as to be backed up by the authority and legitimacy of the state while at the same time being subject to its constraints? Academics have a responsibility to help clarify American political discourse by providing a better balance of "facts," offering clearer conceptions, and developing more accurate and less pejorative terminology.

Adopting Different Value Premises

Shifting the American political discourse by developing a legitimate role in governance for the public administration will depend heavily on producing analyses that would start with very different value assumptions than the ones currently used. The first value premise we should adopt is that the public administration—with the managerial skills that lie at its core and its experience in applying those skills in a political context—is a social asset. Most work done up to now has taken exactly the opposite value assumption: that bureaucracy is a problem, a threat, a concern, i.e., a social liability.

A second value premise we should adopt is that public administration has a distinctive character that sets it apart from private management.[36] A number of studies in recent years have aimed at empirically validating the difference between public administration and private management. The difference is difficult to validate empirically, for it is not merely structural or behavioral, but it lies in the perceptions of citizens and elites as to what is appropriate. The difference lies in the realm of norms, of "should" and "ought." Empirically proving public administration is different on some dimensions is largely beside the point.

The public administration has at its core generic management technologies that comprise its "administrative capacity." These are a vital part of public administration's expertise, and they closely resemble the technologies of management in the private sector. Nonetheless, Wallace Sayre puts it aptly when he says that business and public administration are alike in all unimportant respects.[37] For the public administration is more than generic management: it is the administration of public affairs in a political context. It is governance. As Carl Friedrich noted a half-century ago, administration is the core of modern government; administration involves an application of state power for what we hope are moral and humane ends, but always the possibility exists that it will be used otherwise.[38]

Since governance entails the state's rewarding and depriving in the name of society as a whole, and since politics includes the art of gaining acceptance for those allocations, administration is an inextricable part of both governance and politics. Because of its role in rewarding and depriving, distributing and redistributing, and regulating, and because it is the only set of institutions that can rightfully coerce to achieve society's ends, government is seldom viewed dispassionately. Rather it is, as Murray Edelman reminds us, an object against which the people displace fears, hopes, and anxieties.[39] As the action arm of government, the bureaucracy, or the public administration, is inescapably the target of this displacement. Therein lies the public administration's distinctive character. Its part in governance means that: (1) the public administrator must engage not in a struggle for markets and profits, but in a struggle with other actors in the political and governmental processes for jurisdiction, legitimacy, and resources; (2) those persons with whom he or she must interact possess distinctive perceptions, expectations, and levels of efficacy toward the public administration as the embodiment of state power; (3) the requisite skills and the perceived tasks of the public administration differ markedly from private sector management.[40] The latter differences are so great that a manager who is successful in one sector will not be as successful in another without displaying considerable adaptability.[41] To the extent that we fail to operate from the value assumption that the public administration is distinctive in character, we undercut any basis for a legitimate role for bureaucracy in governance. To that extent we erode governance. We have often done exactly that.

A third value premise we should adopt is that there are positive aspects to the "agency perspective." By agencies we refer to those institutions that have grown up in the executive branches at all levels of government and the independent regulatory commissions at the federal level and their state counterparts.[42] These agencies are organizational instruments of action in pursuit of public policy and the public interest. Until now, our value assumptions about agencies have been essentially negative. Agencies, the process of their institutionalization, and the roles and perceptions that institutionalization imparts to members have all been viewed as "parochial," "narrow," and "particularistic."[43] Thus, we recommend following Selznick's conception of institutions and institutionalization: he viewed the latter as a constructive social process and the former as social assets.[44]

A greater appreciation of the positive aspects of the "agency perspective" could be gained from conducting broad, institutional histories of agencies that feature their political economies. Viewed from a positive perspective, agencies are repositories of specialized knowledge and historical experience. Furthermore, agencies represent some degree of consensus as to the public interest relevant to a particular societal function. Indeed, the staffs of these agencies have been charged—often for generations—with acting in the public interest to execute the popular will in ways that sustain and nurture legitimacy. The "agency perspective" is thus based on many years of struggle within the larger political system and the limited-governance process to achieve some kind of consensus over specific aspects of public policy. This unique experience is worth far more than our value assumptions have allowed us to acknowledge.

This is not to say that the agencies have not been misdirected or misused by others, or that they have not operated at times in self-serving ways. Surely, agencies have contributed at times to the centrifugal pressures in American government. But the dangers of parochialism are endemic to all organizations, and they are, in the final analysis, perversions of the "agency perspective" advocated here. Viewed positively, the "agency perspective" provides public administrators with a "center of gravity," or a "gyroscope," as they go about their duties; the perspective provides a foundation from which agencies may build a concern for broader public principles and values, i.e., a concern for the public interest.

Most recently, the public administration and the "agency perspective" have been eroded by a policy or program perspective featuring an excessive focus on output that lacks a balancing concern for the longer-term public good. The assumption that program outputs and the public good are synonymous has gone largely unchallenged. In fact, they are often not synonymous at all. A park service, for example, can process an increased number of visitors through facilities that are being overloaded and allowed to decay through lack of maintenance. Thus, an agency may be increasingly "responsive" to immediate pressures while it is simultaneously irresponsible with regard to the public interest. One of the characteristics of the "agency perspective" and of the public administration, therefore, should be a prudent and reasoned attention to agency performance— attention that gives consideration both to the short- *and* the long-run consequences, attention that uses qualitative as well as quantitative measures, and attention that rejects "the bottom line" as a slogan necessarily synonymous with good public administration.

While both public policy analysis and program evaluations, used wisely, can be valuable in carrying out public affairs and in measuring agency performance, such techniques should not become ends in themselves. Simplistic use and clever abuse must be constantly guarded against. When agencies use policy analysis, program evaluation, and decision sciences, these techniques should be subordinated to an "agency perspective" and to the agency's core management processes. Too often, these techniques have been allowed to intrude upon this perspective and these processes, and the results have been detrimental both to good public administration and to good policy and program analysis.

Other influences responsible for eroding the "agency perspective" came from humanistic psychology and from a variety of cultural dynamics during the 1960s. Both of these forces denigrated the role of authority in the administrative process. The adolescent texture of the 1960s' cultural upheaval wore heavily on our traditional concepts of authority within agencies. In retrospect, it is time to correct the misconceptions that arose from the debate between organization theory's traditionalists and humanists on this issue.

First, it should be said that the traditional point of view was inadequate to the extent that it sought to base obedience to authority purely on the principle of deference, and depicted managerial authority as a tool upon which managers could rely to improve performance (the "shape up or ship out" position). The traditional viewpoint was useful, however, in depicting the human situation as one requiring authority to check our sometimes capricious tendencies. Particularly, the traditional view is useful in emphasizing that the experience of having encounters with authority is an essential part of the maturation process, not only in adolescence but throughout life—both for superiors and subordinates.

By the same token, the humanists were misguided in carrying their attack on authority to the point of denying that it plays a needed role in institutional life and claiming that it can be replaced completely by processes of participation. They were providing a helpful corrective to the traditional view, however, by calling for more openness in the use of authority and for the establishment of a greater degree of mutual confidence within organizations. As humanists, however, they forgot that to live with and under authority is part of being human.[45]

We can distill from this debate the lesson that authority is not as useful as various "humanistic" communication devices for improving performance in administration, but that authority is essential for dealing effectively with the intractable problem of compliance on issues wherein reasonable persons can disagree. These issues of compliance are central both to the personal development of administrators and the people they manage, as well as the effectiveness of agencies in implementing public policies and programs. In sum, the message here is that the vitality of the "agency perspective," the health of the public administration, and the self-concept of the public administrator hinge upon our return to a fuller appreciation of the positive role of authority in administration.

In sum, the "agency perspective" is one that deserves greater legitimacy than it has received from our scholarship to date. To a considerable degree, the legitimacy for the role of the public administration in the governance process lies with the "agency perspective," which provides a historic, organic, and constitutional legitimacy deserving of illumination.

Rescuing the Concept of the Public Interest from Positivism

Our use of the term "public interest" may make some political scientists and students of public administration wince. We have been so negatively conditioned by the positivist critique of the public interest that we have all but consigned it to the conceptual dustbin.[46] Yet rescuing the concept is central to developing a legitimate role for the public administration in governance. The contention that public administration has a legitimate role in governance must rest on more than competence to manage in a political context. The contention must also rest upon a claim of competence directed toward the maintenance of (a) the "agency perspective," as discussed above; (b) the constitutional governance process, as discussed below; and (c) *the broadest possible public interest*, which we shall take up now.

Although we acknowledge the difficulties of precisely defining the public interest's contents, we are struck by the irony of the situation in which many social scientists who claim to be concerned with behavior are willing to ignore the fact that the "public interest" has a day-to-day impact upon the behavior of hundreds of thousands of public administrators. Caught, as public administrators are, in the struggle of conflicting interests, they understand intuitively that conflict frequently is rooted in competing notions of the public interest. Even though some public administrators may use the concept cynically or self-servingly, and despite our problems in defining its specific content, the "public interest" is a living, behavioral reality.

The positivist approach has been to ask, "What is the public interest in terms of the *content* of given policy situations?" This question may never be answered. But if we shift our perspective from specific content to an idealized value, the problem of defining the public interest is no longer insoluble. In our interpretation, the "public interest" refers to taking on several habits of mind in making decisions: attempting to deal with the *multiple* ramifications of an issue rather than only a select few; seeking to incorporate the *long-range* view into deliberations rather than concentrating on short-term results; considering the competing demands of *all* of the substantially affected parties, rather than catering only to the demands of the most powerful, articulate, and ubiquitous; and proceeding equipped with *more* knowledge and information rather than less. Admitting that "the public interest" is problematic is not to say that it is meaningless.

Although this type of definition will not satisfy those accustomed to posing the issue in content-specific terms, defining it as value to be sought but never quite attained is not that unusual—either as practical guidepost or positive symbol. The democrat endorses majoritarianism; the civil libertarian extols due process, and the lawyer cherishes an adversarial legal process. We recommend approaching the public interest in the same spirit. Even the strongest opponent of the public interest concept, the economic conservative, is committed to an idealized value—the competitive market. Because this definition of the public interest does not provide us with policy "answers," it invites the charge that the public administrator who lays claim to protecting the public interest is merely insisting on his agency's definition of what is "right." Yet the same should be said of all actors in the political process; there are subjective elements in any argument about which choice is "right." Many of those involved in the Watergate affair, for example, were certain that the public interest was embodied in the president's position. While we feel that conceiving of the public interest as a value provides the soundest grounding for the concept, we would not preclude other approaches. We wish to remain open to the idea that the public interest's content, however elusive and problematic, might yet to some degree be definable. But our emphasis is on an idealized value: we assume that when an institutionalized tradition exists to pursue that value and to nurture a process emphasizing the relatively comprehensive, long-term, deliberative, and informed efforts essential to the search for the public interest, the chances increase that action will follow in accord with these values. Whatever the weaknesses of the public administration, it provides more of an institutionalized tradition of this kind than may be found among many of the other actors in the political process. Certainly, it does so more than the political parties, the interest groups, or the mass media.

Reexamining the Politics–Administration Dichotomy

Finding a legitimate role for the public administration in governance also may depend on scholars reaching a new point of resolution of the venerable question of whether there is a politics–administration dichotomy. First, we must acknowledge that public administration theory detoured sharply into an intellectual cul de sac when some of us followed Herbert Simon's attempt to establish a fact–value dichotomy.[47] We also erred in following too closely the organizational sociologists in their relatively narrow quest to understand complex organizations. Both efforts led us astray from the important debate over a politics–administration dichotomy that had been carried on by Wilson, Goodnow, Gaus,[48] White, Appleby, Waldo, and others. Our temporary obsession with behavioralism and our attempts to stay in step with political science, which was in the heat of its own behavioral fad, delayed our moving on to a clearer resolution of the politics–administration dichotomy. Organizational sociology and business administration were of course, never interested in questions of governance; as political science drifted further and further from such concerns, public administration was pulled with it.

The distinction between politics and administration must be understood on three different levels. First, at the highest level, speaking descriptively and conceptually, no dichotomy exists. At this highest level of abstraction, public administration is an integral part of the governance and the political processes. At a second, less abstract level of meaning, however, a considerable distinction, if not a dichotomy, does exist. Persons in the governance and political processes seek to maintain a distinction between roles, behavior, situations, and phenomena that are political, and those that are administrative. Sometimes the distinction is made self-servingly or even cynically, but it is made nonetheless. To ignore it is to ignore the empirical reality of the behavioral phenomena we label public administration.

Finally, at a third level of meaning, speaking prescriptively to persons involved in politics and governing, we feel we should acknowledge, elucidate, and extend the distinction between politics and administration. We need to help clarify and nurture the distinction between political and administrative roles and develop better understandings of how they interact in the process of governing. At this third level of meaning, making the distinction between politics and administration is crucial if the public administration's role in governance is to be accepted as legitimate.

Exploring Critically the Relationship
between Capitalism and Bureaucracy

In *The Administrative State*, Dwight Waldo questioned whether the rationalistic mentality reflected in the literature of public administration could sufficiently comprehend what he called the "imponderable emotional substructure" of society.[49] His point seems to have been that this aspect of social life had to be adequately understood if general social health were to be ensured. We suggest, further, that the public administration, which naturally emphasizes rationality and structure, must find ways not only of understanding but also of relating to that emotional substructure. We feel that the basis for that relationship ought to be built upon critical reflexivity. We must turn to macro theorists and political economists to help us both describe and understand the relationship that exists between the public administration and capitalism.

In our view, social health, like individual health, depends upon the existence of a reflexive relationship between the emotional substructure or unconscious and the conscious side of the human process.[50] This reflexive relationship requires, on the one hand, a relative openness to the designs of the unconscious that emerge in ambition, pursuit of personal agendas, risk, and adventure. On the other hand, it also requires that these possibly selfish designs of the unconscious be juxtaposed with collective needs and with the needs for introspection, judgment, and moral reasoning applied to matters affecting others. In the case of the United States, it seems that the institutional form of capitalism has well provided for one half of the reflexivity equation. The genius of the market is that it can so quickly and easily give expression to the emergent needs, tendencies, and tastes that are constantly forming in the collective unconscious. This aspect of capitalism leads advocates of laissez faire to equate it with freedom. In this sense at least, suppression of the emotional substructure is hardly a problem in capitalist society. Growth and development—stemming from unconscious impulses, whether economic, social, or psychological—can take place in a relatively unimpeded fashion for most of our people, with the exception perhaps of a disturbingly persistent "underclass."[51]

But capitalism has been notably less successful in filling in the other side of the critical reflexivity equation. The marketplace can so facilitate the expression of the unconscious or emotional substructure that it can overwhelm the conscious side of society. As wants are expressed and satisfied with increasing speed and facility, a point can be reached where new wants are created by the process itself.[52] Gratification divorced from substance becomes the motivating orientation of individuals and eventually of society itself. When this happens, societal bearings are lost, both moral and practical points of reference become obscure, and the public standards essential for the exercise of collective human discretion fail us.[53]

Hence, the market is a necessary but not in itself sufficient device for maintaining our social well-being. Public authority, expressed through stable institutions of the public administration, is essential as a cooling, containing, and directing foil to the capitalist marketplace. Such institutions must represent the collective consciousness of our society and serve as the vehicle for efforts to bring to bear knowledge, reason, and moral judgment both on our problems and the design of our future. Capitalism has been helpful in releasing the energy required to move our societal ship, but it cannot by itself provide adequate navigation, e.g., governance. For this, we must look to the public administration, under the captaincy of our political institutions.

Developing a More Favorable Interpretation of the Public Administration's Constitutional Role

Our political rhetoric, symbols, and dialogue are badly out of synchronization with our "enacted constitution" or at least with a Federalist interpretation of it. For that interpretation encouraged and anticipated the public administration and its role in governance.[54] Unfortunately, existing public administration and political theory is distressingly weak on this point, and scholars of public administration have themselves forgotten or failed to grasp it. Instead, both scholars and practitioners have sought simply to emphasize nonpartisan instrumentalism and to emulate the management practices of business. Valuable though a claim of nonpartisan instrumentalism was in the emergence of the public administration at the turn of the century, it is neither well grounded in the Constitution nor adequate to the demands for governance in the late twentieth century. To some extent explicitly, and to a greater extent implicitly as well as through historic practice, the Constitution has assigned a more demanding and significant role to the public administration.

We have all known since our first civics class that the Constitution is designed to preserve freedom by dividing power, but we do not always connect that profound truth with the political circumstances of public administrators. In the never-ending battle between the chief executive, the legislature, and the courts, the public administration is a "free fire zone" and the public administrators serve as targets of opportunity for the combatants.

When we assert that the Constitution, or at least a Federalist interpretation of it, anticipated the public administration, do we mean that the framers thought of it in the bleak metaphors of war used above? Assuredly not. With the possible exception of Alexander Hamilton at his most prescient, they did not foresee the public administration of today any more than they could have foreseen the myriad changes in other institutions that have come to pass.[55] But the history of the earliest days of the Republic and indeed the actions of some of the framers themselves show that as soon as the constitutional drama began to unfold, the public administrators were the persons in no man's land who were left with ambiguities and a discretion that was viewed on the one hand as a threat to them (and to others), and on the other as a challenging opportunity to keep the constitutional process from becoming a stalemate in which the public interest would be the ultimate casualty.

Like other institutions and actors in our system, the public administration and public administrators must adapt and carve out new roles within the framework of our historic constitutional system. This constitutionally derived ambiguity and discretion, however, will always cause problems for any attempt to define a legitimate role in governance for the public administration. Therefore, the public administration must always act within the constraints imposed by its origin in covenant, a covenant reaffirmed in the Constitution, in such laws as the Pendelton Act, and in other historic events. The word "covenant" has sacral overtones that are appropriate for our purposes. Its secular usage preserves its fundamental sense of a solemn agreement on obligations between parties. "Covenant" seems to capture the way the public administration needs to perceive itself and to be perceived by others: a solemn agreement between public administrators and the citizens they serve; an agreement to serve the public with competence directed toward the public interest and the maintenance of a democratic process of governance; competence constrained by the vitality of the constitutional heritage, the law, and our common history as a people.

Scholars and practitioners of public administration should, therefore, be much more concerned with the public administration's historical and constitutional development. They must recognize that the public administration is scarcely worse off than other institutions in our system in terms of having its functions and role only vaguely spelled out in the written Constitution. These functions and roles must be worked out creatively within a broader constitution that consists of implied powers, dialogue, practice, and court opinions.

Reconciling the Public Administration with the Concept of Representation

If the public administration asserts its claim to be a legitimate participant in the governance process, it can contribute to the correction of a major problem in the Constitution: the unsatisfactory resolution of the issue of representation. This problem was the centerpiece of George Mason's brilliant argument against ratification and was a source of embarrassment to such staunch Federalists as Washington and Hamilton. Both friends and foes of the Constitution wondered how the 65 members of the House of Representatives would represent more than 3 million people; today, we ask how 435 members can represent a nation of 250 million people? Pluralist theory and the bureaucratic-politics school of thought have suggested that the competition among interest groups is the best assurance of representation of all the people and that the public interest emerges as the vector sum of all the interest-group pressures. The administrative-efficiency "model" pins all its hopes on the plebiscitary chief executive as "representative of all the people." While such claims are not without merit, they have never been persuasively demonstrated and have been subjected to devastating criticism. Clearly, not all citizens and interests are represented by the Congress, the interest groups, or the president.

In light of this constitutional problem, the public administration as an institution of government has as valid a claim to being as representative of the people in both a sociological and functional sense as a federal judge appointed for life, a freshman congressman narrowly elected by a small percentage of the citizens in southeast Nebraska, or a senator from Rhode Island. For that matter, the public administration may be quite representative of the people as a whole as compared with other political institutions. For example, in 1980, a president elected by a coalition of voting blocs and interest groups claimed a victory based on receiving less than 51 percent of the popular vote from less than 30 percent of the eligible voters; this was approximately 19 percent of the total populace. Why have we assumed that representation is something that only can be found in elected officials?

The popular will does not reside solely in elected officials but in a constitutional order that incorporates a remarkable variety of legitimate titles to participate in governance. The public administration, created by statutes and based on this constitutional order, holds one of these titles. Its role in governance, therefore, is not merely to be responsive to a legislative body, an elected chief executive, or the courts. Our tradition and our constitution give none of these institutions such power or sovereignty. If we take the larger "enacted constitution" as our guide, the public administration is subservient to no single branch, but rather is responsible to all. Like all other institutions, the public administration must share in governing wisely, but it can be said to have a special trusteeship role for the maintenance of *constitutional order* that the framers of the Constitution intended as an expression of the will of the people.[56]

Reconceptualizing the Public Administrator's Role

We also need to concern ourselves with developing the role of the individual public administrator. Initially, public administrators take an oath to uphold the Constitution of the United States—not the whims of the powerful. This oath should initiate them into a community created by that Constitution and should oblige them to know and support constitutional principles that affect their official spheres of public service. When law empowers rather than commands, i.e., when it confers discretion upon administrators instead of issuing specific orders to them, the administrators' oath should oblige them to exercise their discretion in a manner that is informed and guided by broad constitutional values as well as by more immediate, short-term considerations. This constitutionally bounded discretion is their "license" to participate in governance.

Much of the public administrators' loss of transcendent vision has been

brought on by their concern for professional status. Both scholars and practitioners of public administration have sought this, and both have paid a heavy price
for adopting too slavishly the trappings of science believed essential to a claim of
expertise. A focus on the *means* of governance as in management science, systems analysis, Planning Programming Budgeting System, and program evaluation is important to a claim of expertise. But when we focus on these means to
the exclusion of claims of transcendent purposes and moral commitment to
community building, or to the enhancement of freedom and dignity and the
improvement of the quality of citizens' lives, we erode the legitimacy of the
public administration and reduce the public administrator to being a member of
just one more profession or interest group. In such cases, we have let our vision
slip from transcendent purposes and moral commitment to a narrow focus on the
application of "value-neutral" instrumentalism. This development has cost our
political system dearly. Whether the public administrator is a member of a profession is not important; rather, it is important that the public administrator acts
in a professional manner in the sense of displaying a concern for the development of competence and standards within the context of a search for the broadest
possible definition of the public interest and the maintenance of the constitutional order. To act in a professional manner, then, is to use expertise and
competence toward these ends.

As scholars of public administration, we need to nurture the trustee role in our
writing and teaching. As a trustee, the public administrator must be urged to look
beyond the political pressures of the day and to adopt a self-image that goes
beyond mere instrumentalism. A trustee is more than the "artful dodger" implied
by the bureaucratic-politics literature, more than the referee of interest groups
implied by the pluralist-democracy "model," and more than the robot-like instrument implied by the administrative-efficiency "model." As a trustee, he or she
should strive for a role that is "critically conscious," that is purposive in pursuit
of the public interest, that maintains the democratic governance process, and that
is conscious of the occasional need to accommodate powerful forces through a
prudent temporary retreat, when necessary, from the broadest possible definition
of the public interest. Progress toward both the "agency perspective" and the
broader public interest may not always be steady.

The public administrator must be steadfast and persistent, heeding Hamlet's
advice to play to the judicious few, rather than to the vociferous many or the
powerful few, but the judicious few need not be a closed, elite group. The
possibility that the judicious few might become the judicious many is, after all,
an article of democratic faith. The duty of the public administrator is to expand
the ranks of the judicious few by stimulating reasoned debate on the meaning of
the public interest.

Much also has been written about making the bureaucrat responsive and
responsible.[57] The public administrator must, indeed, act responsibly, which
means being responsive to constitutionally and legally valid orders that are spe-

cific. Responsiveness also means being attuned to the agency's clientele. The responsiveness of the public administrator to clients or elected officials should be neither "seismographic," nor that of a "hired lackey," nor even that of a "faithful servant." Nor should the public administrator's responsiveness be simply that of a tactical, organizational politician working between and among the forces resulting from interest group pressures. More is required: the public administrator can only be responsible in the highest sense of the word if his or her responsiveness is that of a trustee of the "agency's perspective," the broader public interest, and the constitutional heritage.

In their role as trustees, public administrators may have to incline their agencies' responsiveness toward the president at one point and toward Congress at another, or at other times toward the courts, clients, or interest groups—whichever of these is likely to serve the long-term public interest as viewed from the "agency perspective." Less often, the public administrators may have to act on behalf of a public interest that is defined more broadly than the "agency perspective." We refer to those relatively rare occasions when they must help preserve the very process of democratic governance itself, as did some officials in the Watergate crisis. This means, in essence, that the public administrators may have to play the role of balance wheel in the constitutional order, using their statutory powers and professional expertise to favor whichever participant in the constitutional process needs their help at a given time to preserve the purposes of the Constitution itself.

Inevitably, some will view the public administration merely as a means to status and power, and others will pervert their duty into a sinecure. In spite of the failings of some, in spite of its erosion by careerism and the fragmenting pressures of specialization, and in spite of its current detractors, the public administration has been and remains a vocation given meaning in the service of a "cause."[58] In the everyday words of public administration, this cause is characterized as being a "civil servant," "career executive," or "public employee." If a self-conscious shift in American political discourse can be made, we feel that the sense of a calling will grow among public administrators. More of them will live "for" it as a "cause," and fewer will live "off" it from less noble impulses.

Certainly, the founders of the republic viewed public service as a "calling" and as a trusteeship; so did the idealistic reformers who came later in our history: the Populists, the Progressives, and the New Dealers. If we have not yet lost that vision, it clearly is in grave peril. As scholars, we have an obligation to help in its preservation and future development.

Other attitudes and mindsets on the part of both scholars and practitioners are important to a professionalism that is centered on trusteeship. Neither scholars nor practitioners like to admit that assumptions about human nature affect our scholarship or practice, but they do—and do so fundamentally. We, therefore, are going to be so bold as to prescribe an assumption. We feel our assumption should be that the human condition can be improved, though never perfected.

Public administrators should be able to educate and encourage work toward the amelioration of societal problems without expecting quick, cheap, ideal, or permanent solutions. The public administrator should understand that some problems can best be alleviated by outcomes of the market or the use of marketlike devices, while others can best be met by some form of indirect altering of incentives[59] or by direct state intervention. The "answers" to problems should not be preordained, but always subjected to critical analysis. If there is any preordained wisdom, it is that maximum effect at least cost is usually obtained whenever we can manage to follow James Madison's advice and let self-interest do the work of virtue.[60]

Those of us who are active in public administration as a field of study ought actively to pursue and develop our knowledge of policy problems, the alternative means of ameliorating them, and the related effects of each alternative. While public administrators must be responsive to ideological or party-based views of elected officials on social problems, they must also provide sound analysis and feasible options based on their special competence. Thus, the public administrator, whether in the field of study or of action, should be both an analyst and an educator. He or she must work for the long-term education of elected officials, other actors in the governance process, and citizens at large on matters of public interest. He or she must assume that this will often be a thankless and arduous task.

The public administrator, whether scholar or practitioner, should be committed to (1) praxis—critically conscious action or pursuit of goals; and (2) reflectiveness—thoughtful and critical assessment of action taken, in order to learn from experience. Both praxis and reflectiveness are essential to a role that directs its competence toward the kind of transcendent purposes we have outlined. Both set public administration as a field of study apart from traditional academic disciplines. Both also are essential to the day-to-day goals of practitioners in serving the public with grace and dignity—of respecting the public, while at the same time respecting one's self and one's peers.

Conclusion

One of our purposes has been to get the reader to confront the fact that the concept of governance itself is difficult for Americans to face. But the situation in which we have politics without governance is so serious that it is approaching the point of becoming a terminal disease for our system. A basic symptom of the disease is the lack of a legitimate role for bureaucracy (or, as we prefer, the public administration) in governance.

What about the oft-mentioned concerns that bureaucracy (the public administration) is already too powerful and that legitimating it will only enhance this power? We do not dismiss these valid concerns, but they are valid for any institution or set of actors in our political system. We have suggested, however, that the so-called "bureaucracy problem" is not that at all. The phenomena referred to under that rubric represent, instead, a systemic problem at the level of political economy and, more specifically, a problem in political discourse that is self-serving in the short run for political elites, but in the long run is disastrous for the governance of our system. Even if we grant the validity of some concerns about bureaucratic power, however, the answer lies not in wishing bureaucracy away or continuing to deny it legitimacy. Bureaucracy will not go away, and—more important—the most significant constraints for an institution are those imposed by legitimate role expectations, expectations the actors have of their own roles and the expectations of others. Restraint is imposed not only by adversarial power; equally important is the restraint imposed by positive role expectations. The normative framework we have proposed above for both scholars and practitioners of public administration is intended to help nurture and develop desirable role expectations.

The emergence of judges and courts as legitimate and valued actors and institutions in the governance process ("of" but not "in" politics) can serve as an analog for the development of the public administration. In the evolution of the English political system, judges began as agents of the king, traveling the realm, settling disputes in his name. Their work might best be looked upon as an early form of nation building. Their reputation for fairness fixed in the public mind a well-founded belief in the superiority of royal justice over the justice administered in the courts of the barons. These royal judges developed the common law—a law that was universalistic or "common" throughout the realm and of a higher quality than the particularistic law of the feudal manors.[61] Eventually, these royal officers developed distinctive symbols, rituals, a language, a way of reasoning (i.e., *stare decisis*), and a claim to expertise and legitimacy that gave them a role distinct from the king's—one that would lead them to use the law and their claim to be its legitimate interpreters to stand in opposition (but a loyal opposition) to the king. This development was taken even further on this side of the Atlantic when Chief Justice Marshall's adroit handling of *Marbury* v. *Madison* established the basis of the Supreme Court's claim to judicial review of the constitutionality of acts of Congress. Finally, the courts in general and judges in particular have worked out a well-defined and well-bounded role in the political and governance process that finds its most manifest expression in the doctrine of "judicial restraint."

Like the judicial system, the public administration needs to assert its propriety and legitimacy as an institution. The value of the "agency perspective" and the legitimacy of the public administrator as an actor in the governing process need recognition and acceptance. That legitimacy rests upon competence directed to the maintenance of the "agency perspective" and to the broadest possible understanding of the public interest and the constitutional governance process.

If this sense of legitimacy is achieved, civilian public administrators, like judges before them or like their military colleagues today, conceivably could question a directive of their political superiors and have the question regarded as a sober second thought rather than as an act of bureaucratic sabotage. When such acceptance can occur, the public administration, the public administrator, and our political system will have come of age.

Here we speak not only of practitioners of public administration, but also of scholars of the field, who have a role in establishing such legitimacy. As a field of study with strong ties to a profession (the primary degree offered is professional), scholars of public administration must face the fact that they are not simply members of an academic discipline. They also are a part of an enterprise that is much larger, more complex, and with some distinct responsibilities for the outcomes of the governance process.

Notes

The authorship of this chapter is equally shared with Goodsell, Rohr, White, and Wolf; Wamsley's name appears first simply because he was assigned the task of compiling and editing. We thank Richard Green, doctoral candidate at the Center for Public Administration and Policy at Virginia Polytechnic Institute and State University, for his invaluable criticism and assistance in preparing this paper. Many of the ideas presented in this chapter are summarized in "The Public Administration and the Governance Process: Refocusing the American Dialogue," in *A Centennial History of the American Administrative State*, ed. Ralph Clark Chandler (New York: Free Press, 1987), pp. 291–317.

1. Jack C. Plano, R.E. Riggs, and H.S. Rabin, *The Dictionary of Political Analysis*, 2d ed. (Santa Barbara, CA: ABC-CLIO, 1982). Under the "G's" in the *Dictionary of Political Analysis*, one finds such interesting entries as "group," "game theory," "generalization," and "Guttman Scale," but nothing for "govern." Walter J. Raymond's *Dictionary of Politics* (Lawrenceville, VA: Brunswick, 1980) also has no entry for governance. The only political dictionary we could find that came close to defining govern or governance was *A Dictionary of Political Thought*. We find it interesting that this book was edited by Britisher Roger Scruton assisted by a British panel. It is perhaps a final irony that only one member of the panel taught government. The latter book defines "government" as "the exercise of influence and control, through law and coercion, over a particular group of people, formed into a state" (p. 189).

2. Plato, "The Republic," in *Dialogues of Plato*, Jowett trans. (New York: Pocket Books, 1950).

3. Theodore Lowi, *The End of Liberalism: The Second Republic of the United States*, 2d ed. (New York: W.W. Norton, 1979).

4. Woodrow Wilson, "The Study of Administration," *Political Science Quarterly* 2 (June 1998): 200.

5. Frank J. Goodnow, *Politics and Administration: A Study in Government* (New York: Russell and Russell, 1900, reissued 1967); Luther Gulick and L. Urwick, eds., *Papers on the Science of Administration* (New York: Institute of Public Administration, 1937); Frederick W. Taylor, *Principles of Scientific Management* (New York: Harper and Row, 1911); The President's Committee on Administrative Management, *Report of the Committee* (Washington, DC: Government Printing Office, 1937).

6. Douglas Yates, *Bureaucratic Democracy: The Search for Democracy and Efficiency in American Government* (Cambridge, MA: Harvard University Press, 1982), pp. 9–10. We prefer to use the term "model" more stringently than Yates does. We use it to

refer to logically related and stable propositions suggesting causal relations. Thus, we have placed "model" in quotation marks throughout to show that we differ with Yates's use. For a discussion of models and theories, see George J. Graham, *Methodological Foundations for Political Analysis* (Waltham, MA: Xerox College Pub., 1971).

7. Michael Urban, *The Ideology of Administration: American and Soviet Cases* (Albany: State University of New York Press, 1982); Dwight Waldo, *The Administrative State: A Study of the Political Theory of American Public Administration* (New York: Ronald Press, 1948).

8. Edmund Husserl, *Cartesian Meditations: An Introduction to Phenomenology*, trans. David Carr (Evanston, IL.: Northwestern University Press, 1960); Alfred Schutz, *The Phenomenology of the Social World*, trans. G. Walsh and F. Lehnert, (Evanston, IL: Northwestern University Press, 1967); Alfred Schutz, *Collected Papers*, vol 1., ed. M. Natanson (The Hague: Martinus Nijhoff, 1962).

9. Robert A. Dahl, *A Preface to Democratic Theory* (Chicago: University of Chicago Press, 1956), p. 145; cited in Yates, *Bureaucratic Democracy*, p. 5.

10. Yates, *Bureaucratic Democracy*, pp. 12–13.

11. Ibid., p. 13.

12. Dahl, *Preface to Democratic Theory*.

13. Yates, *Bureaucratic Democracy*, pp. 20–30.

14. It was, of course, John K. Galbraith who gave us the concept of conventional wisdom (*The Affluent Society* [Cambridge, MA: Riverside Press, 1958]); J. Pfiffner and R. Presthus, *Public Administration*, 5th ed.(New York: Ronald Press, 1967).

15. James Madison, Federalist 51 from *The Federalist*, edited with introduction and notes by Jacob E. Cooke (Middletown, CT: Wesleyan University Press, 1961), p. 349.

16. Some would include contributions from such public choice theorists as William Niskanen, Anthony Downs, and Gordon Tullock. Their inclusion is an arguable point that need not be taken up here.

17. Paul H. Appleby, *Big Democracy* (New York: Russell and Russell, 1945, reissued 1970).

18. Avery Leiserson, *Administrative Regulation: A Study in Representation of Interests* (Chicago: University of Chicago Press, 1942).

19. H.H. Gerth and C. Wright Mills, *From Max Weber: Essays in Sociology* (New York: Oxford University Press, 1946); Norton Long, "Power and Administration," *Public Administration Review* 9 (1949): 257–64; Herbert Kaufman, *The Forest Ranger* (Baltimore: Johns Hopkins University Press, 1960); James Q. Wilson, "The Bureaucracy Problem," *The Public Interest* 6 (Winter 1967): 3–9; Louis C. Gawthrop, *The Administrative Process and Democratic Theory* (New York: Houghton Mifflin, 1970); Harold Seidman, *Politics, Position and Power* (New York: Oxford University Press, 1970).

20. Francis E. Rourke, *Bureaucratic Power in National Politics* (Boston: Little, Brown, 1965); Francis E. Rourke, *Bureaucracy, Politics and Public Policy* (Boston: Little, Brown, 1969).

21. Herbert Simon, *Administrative Behavior: A Study of Decision-Making Process in Administrative Organization* (New York: Free Press, 1945).

22. Graham T. Allison, *Essence of Decision: Explaining the Cuban Missile Crisis* (Boston: Little, Brown, 1971).

23. Robert K. Merton, "Bureaucratic Structure and Personality," *Social Forces* 23 (1945): 405–15; Peter Blau, *The Dynamics of Bureaucracy* (Chicago: University of Chicago Press, 1955); Peter Blau, *Bureaucracy in Modern Society* (New York: Random House, 1956).

24. Phillip Selznick, *Leadership in Administration: A Sociological Interpretation* (Evanston, IL: Row, Peterson, 1957); James D. Thompson, *Organizations in Action: Social*

Science Bases of Administrative Theory (New York: McGraw-Hill, 1967); Kenneth J. Benson, "The Interorganizational Network as a Political-Economy," *Administrative Science Quarterly* 20 (June 1975): 229–49.

25. Leonard D. White, *The Federalists: A Study in Administrative History* (New York: Macmillan, 1948). Leonard D. White, *The Jeffersonians* (New York: Macmillan, 1951); Leonard D. White, *The Jacksonians* (New York: Macmillan, 1954). Leonard D. White, *The Republican Era: A Study in Administrative History, 1869–1901* (New York: Macmillan, 1958); Michael Nelson, "A Short, Ironic History of American National Bureaucracy," *The Journal of Politics* 44 (1982): 747–78; William A. Niskanen, *Bureaucracy and Representative Government* (Chicago: Aldine Atherton, 1971); Vincent Ostrum, *The Intellectual Crisis in American Public Administration* (University: University of Alabama Press, 1971); John A. Rohr, "Public Administration and the Constitutional Bicentennial: An Essay on Research," *International Journal of Public Administration* 4 (November 1982): 349–80; Stephen Skowronek, *Building a New American State: The Expansion of National Administrative Capacities, 1877–1920* (Cambridge: Cambridge University Press, 1982); Barry Karl, *The Uneasy State: The United States from 1915 to 1945* (Chicago: University of Chicago Press, 1983); Barry Karl, *Executive Reorganization and Reform in the New Deal* (Chicago: University of Chicago Press, 1963; Midway reprint 1979); Peter H. Irons, *The New Deal Lawyers* (Princeton, NJ: Princeton University Press, 1982); Frederick C. Mosher, *Democracy and the Public Service* (New York: Oxford University Press, 1968); Malcolm J. Rohrbaugh, *The Land Office Business: The Settlement and Administration of American Public Lands 1789 - 1837* (New York: Oxford University Press, 1968); Matthew A. Crenson, *The Federal Machine: Beginnings of Bureaucracy in Jacksonian America* (Baltimore: Johns Hopkins University Press, 1975).

26. Rowland A. Egger, "The Period of Crisis—1933–1945." Paper prepared for the Annual Conference of the National Association of Schools of Public Affairs and Administration, May 2–5, 1974, Syracuse, NY.

27. Lester Thurow, *Zero Sum Society: Distribution and the Possibilities for Economic Change* (New York: Basic Books, 1980); Gordon Tullock, *The Politics of Bureaucracy* (Washington, DC: Public Affairs Press, 1965).

28. James O'Connor, *The Fiscal Crisis of the State* (New York: St. Martin's Press, 1973).

29. Jurgen Habermas, *Legitimation Crisis* (Boston: Beacon Press, 1973); Madison, Hamilton, and Jay, *The Federalist Papers*, intro. by Clinton Rossiter (New York: New American Library, 1961); R. Miliband, *Marxism and Politics* (London: Oxford University Press, 1977); R. Miliband, *The State in Capitalist Society* (New York: Basic Books, 1973); N. Poulantzas, *Political Power and Social Classes* (London: Oxford University Press, 1973); N. Poulantzas, *Fascism and Dictatorship* (London: Oxford University Press, 1973); H.G. Rainey, R.W. Backoff, and C.H. Levine, "Comparing Public and Private Organizations," *Public Administration Review* 36 (1976): 233–44.

30. Charles T. Goodsell, *The Case for Bureaucracy: A Public Administration Polemic* (Chatham, NJ: Chatham House, 1983), ch. 2.

31. Ibid., p. 53.

32. Ibid., pp. 119–20.

33. Ibid., pp. 110–16.

34. Ibid., pp. 52–53.

35. In using the term "facts," we do not assume any strict fact–value dichotomy or objective reality that can be made "known" to all. Rather, the kinds of "facts" in need of explication are those described by Lon L. Fuller as "moral facts." "They lie not in behavior patterns, but in attitudes and conceptions of rightness, in the obscure taboos and hidden reciprocities which permeate business and social relations." This kind of "knowl-

edge" is interpretive, fluid, and rich in meaning (*The Law in Quest of Itself* [Boston: Beacon Press, 1940, p. 65]).

36. C. Argyris, *The Applicability of Organizational Sociology* (London: Cambridge University Press, 1972); B. Buchanan, "Red-tape and the Service Ethic: Some Unexpected Differences between Public and Private Managers," *Administration and Society* 6 (1975): 422–44; B. Buchanan, "Government Managers, Business Executives, and Organizational Commitment," *Public Administration Review* 34 (1974): 339–47; R.A. Dahl and C.E. Lindblom, *Politics, Economics, and Welfare* (Chicago: University of Chicago Press, 1953); C.E. Lindblom, *Politics and Markets* (New York: Basic Books, 1977); M.W. Meyer, *Change in Public Bureaucracies* (London: Cambridge University Press, 1979); H.G. Rainey, "Public Agencies and Private Firms: Incentive Structures, Goals, and Individual Roles," *Administration and Society* 15 (1983): 207–42; H.G. Rainey, R.W. Backoff, and C.H. Levine, "Comparing Public and Private Organizations," *Public Administration Review* 36 (1976): 233–44; J.L. Perry and K.L. Kraemer, *Public Management: Public and Private Perspectives* (Palo Alto, CA: Mayfield, 1983); D.S. Pugh, D.J. Hickson, C.R. Hinings and C. Turner, "The Context of Organization Structures," *Administrative Science Quarterly* 14 (1969): 91–114.

37. There seems to be no doubt that Sayre said this or words to this effect. According to Dwight Waldo, however, neither he nor anyone he knows has found it in print.

38. Carl Friedrich, "Public Policy and the Nature of Administrative Responsibility," in *Public Policy I*, ed. C.J. Friedrich and E.S. Mason (Cambridge, MA: Harvard University Press, 1940).

39. Murray Edelman, *The Symbolic Uses of Politics* (Urbana, IL: University of Ilinois Press, 1964).

40. Gary L. Wamsley and Mayer M. Zald, *The Political Economy of Public Organizations* (Lexington, MA: D.C. Heath, 1973), pp. 5–10.

41. Allison, *Essence of Decision*; Michael W. Blumenthal, "Candid Reflections of a Businessman in Washington," in Perry and Kraemer, eds., *Public Management: Public and Private Perspectives*, pp. 22–23.

42. This, of course, arbitrarily excludes the General Accounting Office. It is supposedly an instrument of Congress, but the GAO could just as well be counted as an agency as the term is defined here.

43. Gary L. Wamsley and Lester Salamon, "Federal Bureaucracy: Responsive to Whom?" in *Government vs. People*, ed. Leroy Rieslbach (Bloomington, IN: Indiana University Press, 1975), pp. 151–88; Karl E. Weick, *The Social Psychology of Organizing*, 2d ed. (Reading, MA: Addison-Wesley, 1979).

44. Selznick, *Leadership in Administration*.

45. Yves Simon, *The Philosophy of Democratic Governance* (Chicago: University of Chicago Press, 1951).

46. Glendon Schubert, *The Public Interest* (New York: Free Press of Glencoe, 1960).

47. Simon, *Administrative Behavior*, pp. 45–60.

48. J.M. Gaus, *Reflections on Public Administration* (University: University of Alabama Press, 1947); May, *Courage to Create*; Goodnow, *Politics and Administration*.

49. Waldo, *The Administrative State*.

50. V.W. Odajnyk, *Jung and Politics* (New York: New York University Press, 1976).

51. "A Permanent Black Underclass," *U.S. News and World Report*, March 3, 1986, pp. 20–22.

52. Galbraith, *Affluent Society*.

53. Robert N. Bellah, R. Madsen, W.M. Sullivan, A. Swidler, and S.M. Tipton, *Habits of the Heart* (Berkeley: University of California Press, 1985).

54. John A. Rohr, "Professionalism, Legitimacy and the Constitution," *Public Administration Quarterly* 8 (Winter 1985): 401–18.

55. Richard T. Green, "Oracle at Weehawken: Alexander Hamilton and the Development of the Administrative State" (Ph.D. dissertation, Virginia Polytechnic Institute and State University, 1986).

56. For further development of this kind of thought, see John S. Rohr, *To Run a Constitution: The Legitimacy of the Administrative State* (Lawrence: University of Kansas Press, 1985), ch. 6.

57. Herman Finer, "Better Government Personnel," *Political Science Quarterly* 51 (December 1936): 569–699; Herman Finer, "Administrative Responsibility in Democratic Government." *Public Administrative Review* 1 (Summer 1941): 335–50; Carl Friedrich, "Public Policy and the Nature of Administrative Responsibility," in Friedrich and Mason, eds., *Public Policy I*.

58. Weber, "Politics as a Vocation," in Gerth and Mills, eds., *From Max Weber*, 77–128.

59. Lindblom, *Politics and Markets*; Charles L. Schultze, *Public Use of Private Interest* (Washington, DC: Brookings Institution, 1977); Roger Scruton, *A Dictionary of Political Thought* (London: MacMillan, 1982).

60. James Madison, *Federalist 10 and 51, The Federalist*, 1961.

61. J.A.C. Grant, *The Anglo-American Legal System* (Los Angeles: Students' Cooperative Store, University of California, 1947); F.W. Maitland and F.C. Montague, *A Sketch of English Legal History*, ed. James F. Colby (New York: G.P. Putnam's Sons, 1915).

3

Comparative Perspectives on Bureaucracy in the Policy Process

B. Guy Peters

This chapter assesses where the study of comparative public administration now stands as a component of the study of both political science and public administration. Furthermore, I shall make suggestions, which I hope will be seen as constructive, about where the study of comparative public administration ought to go in order to become a more vital component of those two scholarly fields.

The differentiation between political science and public administration is not a dominant theme of this chapter, but instances in which the scholarly concerns of the two "disciplines" diverge are explored. In general, this chapter is written mainly from the perspective of a political scientist and policy scientist who is interested in administrators as one of the many sets of important actors in the policy-making process than from the perspective of the management scientist who is mainly concerned about the operations of public organizations. My perspective is that of one who is mainly interested in research *on* organizations rather than research *in* organizations.[1] A major focus is on the role of comparative administration for theory construction both in comparative politics and in the study of comparative policy making more generally. I shall deal with public administration not as the "mere" application of the laws but as an increasingly vital component of the policy-making process.

The Importance of Comparison for Theory Development

In some ways, the need to write a chapter on *comparative* public administration represents the incomplete conquest of political science and public administration by those concerned with the development of social theory. It is almost trite to argue that theory in the social sciences proceeds largely by comparison or by the development of abstract concepts, such as Weber's ideal types, against which to compare elements of the real world. To think about comparative public administration as somehow distinct from public administration in general or, indeed, to think of comparative politics as distinct from the study of politics more generally is to be trapped in the "stamps, flags, and coins" school of comparative politics and comparative administration. Some critics have regarded comparative public administration as a series of excursions into the exotica of world political systems by those who intend only to describe different administrative systems and to develop a repertoire of amusing field stories. A study of much of the literature in comparative administration, which has been descriptive and country based rather than broadly analytic and comparative, would justify such a critical view.[2]

A decade ago, Fred Riggs predicted, however, that "inevitably a new framework for 'comparative' administration will evolve—not as a 'subfield' but as the master field within which 'American public administration' will be a subfield."[3] Although the prediction was—at least—premature, this outcome would certainly represent the greatest opportunity for theoretical development.

In making a plea for effective comparison and more explicit theory construction, I emphasize that comparison need not simply be across geographical entities. In studying public administration, as well as in studying other political institutions, it is equally useful to make comparisons across time.[4] Some very important insights into the nature of public bureaucracy have been gained from studying bureaucracies at earlier stages of development within now-existing political subsystems.[5] Of course, such analysis needs to be done within the context of an analytic framework that provides some meaning to the compilation of historical data. I argue that public bureaucracies are especially suited to this type of informed historical analysis because they have been identifiable institutions longer than most other institutions associated with contemporary governments (especially contemporary democratic governments), and they continue to perform functions that they have performed historically, while adding new functions and perhaps gaining new importance in public policy making.[6] Thus, we have a set of structures that have been identifiable for a long period of time and that we can then examine in terms of their roles and behavior within the context of the process of governing. Possibly we can determine such matters as how much variance (to use statistical language for research that actually would be qualitative) could be explained by national attributes, how much by level of development, or how much by the climate of ideas of the time. The results might provide some insight into the problems of studying contemporary bureaucracies created by diffusion and "Galton's problem."[7] The plea for comparative analysis across time is hardly novel, but arguing for more explicit comparative analysis of institutions over time is perhaps somewhat more novel.

A large body of literature—both popular and scholarly—has emerged that argues that bureaucracy has become the dominant institution in many contemporary political systems.[8] Leaving aside the accuracy of these claims, we might ask what it is about bureaucracy that apparently makes it capable of extending its powers during the contemporary period; this question is especially pressing because in many countries questions about the power of large institutions over members of society and specifically about the role of government, are increasingly being asked. Furthermore, is there *a* bureaucracy in most societies, or simply a collection of many bureaucracies? Perhaps developing a better conceptualization of the nature of governmental institutions in general and then applying that framework to the study of public bureaucracies and other institutions, such as legislatures and political executives, would be an appropriate undertaking. A plea for a "new structuralism" will be elaborated at the end of the chapter.

Having mentioned some of the substantive questions that must be considered when studying comparative public bureaucracy, some more conceptual and methodological issues will play a prominent role in the following discussion. The two sets of issues are not, of course, always separable. To a great extent, theoretical concerns help to guide the selection of substantive concerns, just as the array of substantive concerns mentioned briefly above guide the development of appropriate concepts and theories to describe the field.

In order to develop a more theoretically useful approach to comparative public bureaucracy, we need to have a clearer idea about what it is that we want to explain. At least five alternative dependent variables, each of which has distinctive implications for the type of research strategy that would be adopted and for the methodological tools that would be required in the development of the theory, might be used. These possible dependent variables are given the following labels: bureaucratic personnel; bureaucratic attitudes; bureaucratic behavior; bureaucratic structure; and bureaucratic outcomes. This is hardly a surprising list, but it is important to understand what is implied by the selection of one or another of the variables as the major focus for inquiry. Of course, each of these possible dependent variables, or actually *sets* of dependent variables, may serve as an independent variable for an analysis of one or more of the other dependent variables.

Bureaucratic Personnel as a Dependent Variable

The first thing we may wish to explain about administrative systems is the number and nature of the personnel who inhabit them. Finding out the numbers of persons employed by government may seem an extremely simple task, but carrying out this task in a rigorous manner is by no means easy.[9] In fact, relatively few *directly comparable* data on public employment are available, especially for Third World countries. In a period of public concern about "big government," determining the relative size of the public bureaucracy is important for understanding the administrative capacity of government and for understanding the relationship between the state and society.[10] In addition, some approaches to policy making have stressed the central role of the bureaucracy in developing and diffusing ideas.[11]

The attempt to determine how many people work for government raises an important question that will be discussed further in examining the structures of government. This question is the basic matter of just what is a government organization.[12] Most studies of public bureaucracy have concentrated on the upper echelons of the civil service and have tended to count as public employees primarily white-collar civil servants.[13] However, given the industrial functions of many governments and the tendency to hive-off industrial operations into semi-autonomous organizations, this approach may understate the true size of public employment.[14] In addition, there are numerous quasi-official bodies in almost every country, as well as "private" employment generated by government activities, that make the definition of a "public employee" more than a simple matter.[15]

Finally, when information on bureaucratic size is combined with information about the pay and perquisites of governmental employees, some insight into the place of the public service in society can be gained and the extent to which it is an elite body can be evaluated. For example, in many Third World countries, the average wage of a central governmental employee is much greater than the average per capita income; central governmental workers earn more than fifteen times the average income in Burundi and almost ten times the average income in Senegal.[16] On the other hand, in some industrialized countries (e.g., Austria), the average central government wage is only very slightly greater than the average income. Although compiling such data will not provide definitive answers, the data would be useful for gaining a general understanding of the probable position of the civil service in the society.

An examination of the literature on the *nature* of government personnel reveals that much of it falls under the rubric of "representative bureaucracy."[17] In general, this literature has looked at the social backgrounds—parental social class, education, race, sex, language, etc.—of civil servants and other elites. The vast majority of these studies have concentrated on the recruitment to the senior, "decision-making posts" in the civil service rather than on recruitment to the entire civil service, and they have tended to find that the top posts are primarily filled by well-educated males from middle-class backgrounds within the dominant social groupings in society. Quite rightly, the majority of the literature does not attribute the prevalence of this demographic profile to overt discrimination by those making selections for the civil service so much as to general social patterns in most societies: middle-class children have been more likely to receive the type of education necessary to fill posts in the senior civil service, and relatively few women have—until recently—worked outside the home.

Analysts appear to have selected the social background characteristics of civil service personnel as a dependent variable for three main reasons. First, understanding the characteristics of a powerful social grouping seems intrinsically interesting to those of a certain sociological nature. Second, such investigations may have a normative purpose. Perhaps authors attempt to demonstrate patterns of domination by certain social groupings over others and thereby to raise questions about desirable social change.[18] Such investigations might, of course, produce rather different findings if the entire civil service were investigated, rather than only the top echelons. While "decision-making posts" may well be crucial to the formulation of policy, the delivery of policies through the lower echelons of the civil service may be as important to citizens; thus, the gender, language, or race of the civil servant involved in policy delivery is an appropriate target of analysis.[19]

The third reason analysts have studied representativeness in the recruitment of civil servants is the most important one: there is a presumed connection between the social backgrounds of civil servants and their attitudes and behavior in government. This was the purpose that motivated Kingsley, who feared that a British civil service recruited almost exclusively from the middle classes, Clarendon Schools, and Oxbridge would find it difficult to implement the socialist program of a Labour government in postwar Britain. If this presumption were correct, then having knowledge about the social characteristics of the civil service would allow one to eliminate some of the other more difficult and expensive research options mentioned below. The trouble is, however, that a strong linkage between social background and attitudes and behavior does not appear to exist. Putnam refers to the hypothesized linkage as "plausible, but ambiguous and unsubstantiated."[20] In the empirical work of the Comparative Elites Project little evidence was found that the social backgrounds of civil servants influenced the ideologies, although a degree of linkage between the variables was found for politicians.[21] Apparently, the ideology and the behavior of civil servants are as much a product of their career and adult socialization as of their social origins. The Comparative Elites Project also found a stronger relationship between the nature of the organization in which civil servants worked and their attitudes than between their social origins and their attitudes. The absence of relationships between social origins and attitudes is especially pronounced when factors such as social class are considered; the relationship appears somewhat stronger when less mutable factors such as race or sex are considered. Nonetheless, in European countries some relationship does appear to exist between the type of education received and the performance of the bureaucracy in certain important economic development roles.[22]

Thus, research into the social origins of civil servants is inherently interesting and may be important for understanding the degree of representation that important collectivities in the society have achieved. But such research appears to be less useful for explaining the attitudes or behavior of civil servants in their official roles; apparently, attitudes and behavior are more closely related to later training, experiences, and job socialization than to social background.

Finally, the personnel of the senior civil service may be an important consideration in the study of comparative administration to the extent that they constitute an identifiable "power elite" within government and the society.[23] As indicated below, the structure of some political systems, such as in France and in Japan, allows the civil service to develop into such an elite.[24] In a behavioral sense, the relative autonomy of such an elite would allow them to exercise governance in a manner not allowed other civil servants who may be more bound by values and by a mechanism forcing greater public accountability.

Bureaucratic Attitudes as a Dependent Variable

A substantial amount of research into the attitudes of public administrators in a number of countries has been conducted. The most notable work of this sort has been done by the members of the Comparative Elites Project.[25] Other significant pieces of work using attitudes as the principal dependent variable are several studies examining and comparing the patterns of attitudes held by public officials and by members of the public.[26] Finally, Colin Campbell and his colleagues have produced a substantial body of literature comparing the perceived roles of civil servants and political executives in the United States, the United Kingdom, and Canada.[27] The concerns of this latter body of work extend beyond expressed attitudes of civil servants, however, to an examination of their actual performance in office and to the linkage between the civil servants' role definitions and their behavior.

What kinds of bureaucratic attitudes have been probed? The largest single body of this literature focuses on the civil servants' self-definition of their tasks. For example, in the Aberbach, Putnam, and Rockman study, civil servants were classified into one of nine role types based upon their answers to questions about how they viewed their jobs.[28] In Sweden, Anton used rather similar types of characteristics in order to develop his model of the "soft activist" in Swedish administration.[29] The Norwegian Power Project has produced several interesting volumes discussing the perceived role of civil servants in that country's policy making.[30] Finally, Muramatsu and Krauss have looked at the perceived roles of Japanese bureaucrats and their relationship with political leaders.[31] These works all share an underlying concern about the self-perceived role of civil servants in the policy-making process. Role perceptions obviously may vary widely, as Putnam's contrast between "classical bureaucrats" and "political bureaucrats" indicates.[32]

As bureaucrats attempt to define their roles, they necessarily develop perceptions about the proper relationships between them and their nominal political masters. The Comparative Elites Project, and the majority of the other research in this area, addressed this issue by interviewing both sides of the relationship and judging the degree of conformity between the official and the perceived roles. While this research method does illuminate interesting similarities and differences in role perceptions, it is perhaps questionable, given the normative biases surrounding the role of bureaucrats in policy making, whether the answers provided will fully describe the actual patterns of interaction in policy making. This is especially true because the norms about bureaucratic abstinence from making policy decisions tend to be more firmly entrenched in some societies than in others (leaving aside the differences in the degree to which civil servants actually do participate in policy making).[33]

Some important problems arise in the use of attitudes as a dependent variable in studying comparative administration. For example, although senior civil servants have been willing to be interviewed at length by scholars, they are generally unwilling to submit to the types of closed-ended questionnaires commonly used in attitudinal measurement. Thus, the assessment of attitudes usually depends upon coding responses to open-ended questions and then constructing attitudinal dimensions. Even though the studies cited above have exercised great care in coding and in checking for obvious problems, such as the cross-cultural relevance of their questions, some doubts about the seemingly "hard" attitudinal evidence always exist. Of course, if attempts at formal measurement were not made, attitudinal studies would be open to the criticism that they were little more than a new version of journalism and inside-dopesterism that really offered little to a theoretical understanding of what happens in government.

Bureaucratic Behavior as a Dependent Variable

Bureaucratic behavior is an extremely difficult dependent variable to utilize, especially when one is dealing with senior civil servants. Much of their work goes on in private and, especially in countries such as the United Kingdom where strong norms about secrecy and privacy exist, extracting reliable information on behavior may be difficult. Nonetheless, a number of interesting studies of the behavior of civil servants in decision-making roles have been conducted— notably the Heclo and Wildavsky study of that (presumably) most secretive of all institutions, the British Treasury.[34] Rather than being comparative, however, this body of literature consists mainly of studies of decision making within a single country and often of studies of a single decision; a major exception to this rule is Colin Campbell's study of elite decision making in the United States, the United Kingdom, and Canada.[35] Thus, it is often up to the reader to place the results of these inquiries into a broader theoretical and comparative context. Although those who conduct case studies of individual bureaucracies or decisions would be likely to have considerable insight into the particular countries they study, matched case studies of similar problems in different countries that clearly focused on comparison and explanation would be useful. Several projects now under way hold the promise for producing more directly comparable information about bureaucratic behavior.[36]

Although conducting an analysis of senior civil servants' behavior using the research methods of modern political science is a difficult undertaking, one strategy that has proved successful is to examine their *reported* behavior, either while they were in office or after they left. Much of this evidence has been anecdotal (sometimes it comes from self-serving memoirs), but some systematic attempts at analyzing reported behavior have been made. For example, Kvavik, and Johansen and Kristensen, among others, have done extensive analyses of the reported behavior of Scandinavian civil servants, especially as they deal with interest-group representatives.[37] Suleiman collected similar information for French civil servants.[38] Less systematically, Gordon, Christoph, and others have examined the behavior of British civil servants with respect to organized interests.[39] Heclo examined the behavior of political executives and civil servants within the "government of strangers" he found to exist in Washington, while Kaufman went one better and actually observed the behavior of senior civil servants as they went about their daily tasks.[40] Unfortunately, these interesting and important studies of bureaucratic behavior lack the comparative dimension, which is crucial for theoretical development.

One means of coming to grips with bureaucratic behavior is to analyze it using Mohr's terms of "reflexive" and "purposive" behavior.[41] Reflexive behavior is directed toward other members of the administrative structure or at political executives, while purposive behavior is directed toward clients or toward the actual taking of decisions. Thus, reflexive behavior involves the search for political and managerial power within the public bureaucracy, while purposive behavior is behavior more manifestly directed toward the ostensible purposes of that bureaucracy. Of course, in many practical situations the separation of these two forms of behavior may be academic in the worst sense of that word, but separating the two elements does appear to be analytically worthwhile.

One of the principal issues concerning the reflexive behavior of civil servants is their relationship to their nominal political masters. As noted above, this issue has been the subject of a great deal of attitudinal investigation, as well as a great deal of discussion in both governmental and academic circles. "Who Governs?" is a question with a long and honorable history that is still far from being answered with respect to the relationship between the civil service and political executives.[42]

One means of assessing that relationship is to develop various models and examine how closely the behavior of civil servants approximates behavior that would be predicted or described by the model. Aberbach, Putnam, and Rockman developed four "images" of this relationship in their work on senior civil servants in Western Europe.[43] These images were developed more with a mind to analysis of attitudinal data, but they have obvious utility for analyzing the behavior of civil servants. The first image is the always convenient strawman of the politics–administration dichotomy. The second, called "Facts/Interest," assumes that both politicians and civil servants participate in politics, but that each makes a distinctive contribution: the civil servant brings facts, while the politician assesses those facts in light of political interests. The third image, "Energy/Equilibrium," assumes that both politicians and civil servants have political interests;

they differ in that politicians may articulate broad policy interests while the civil servant is more concerned with narrow, clientele-based interests. Finally, in the "Pure Hybrid" image, the politician and the bureaucrat are seen as having very similar roles as the separation between politics and administration breaks down in contemporary democracies.

I have argued elsewhere that there are in fact five ways to conceptualize the relationship between civil servants and politicians.[44] The first is—as Aberbach, Putnam, and Rockman indicated—the conventional Wilsonian/Weberian model of the separation of politics and administration. The second is termed "village life," a phrase used by Heclo and Wildavsky to describe life in the British civil service.[45] In this model, senior civil servants and politicians are seen as having rather similar values and goals, the most important being the smooth functioning of government. The third model, called "functional village life," assumes that, rather than having integration across the whole range of public values, civil servants and their political masters are more likely to be functionally integrated, much as the "iron triangle" and the "picket fence" literatures in the United States depict the policy process.[46] This is very similar to Olsen's discussion of civil servants playing on "different teams" in policy making, not as components of an integrated force in opposition to politicians but rather as representatives of the interests of their particular functional area.[47] The fourth model, "adversarial politics" assumes that politicians and civil servants are contenders in a power struggle over the control of public policy making. It further assumes that this adversarial relationship may be overt, rather than a simple fact of life arising from mutual concerns over policy. The final model further assumes that the civil service has, in fact, won, and that there is an "Administrative State" in which civil servants actually, if not visibly, control policy.

Olsen also discusses a number of possible models of relationships between civil servants and their political masters in the context of Norwegian politics.[48] These range from the conventional hierarchical model with the political leaders as dominant to social elite models to bureaucratic dominance. As noted above, however, he finds that the functional model, similar to the "functional village life" model described above, is best suited for describing Norwegian politics. In other societies, however, different models might be more appropriate.

Both the Aberbach, Putnam, and Rockman scheme and my earlier scheme have their strengths and weaknesses, and one may argue about whether either scheme actually presents accurate descriptions of the relationships between civil servants and politicians in particular countries. The models do serve, however, as a starting point for empirical inquiry. Evidence can be marshalled to support each of the models—including even the policy–administration dichotomy. Of course, important differences may be detected between countries in the extent to which any of these would be considered applicable, e.g., the functional village life model appears to apply particularly well in the United States. Thus, the models may serve as a good starting point for truly comparative analyses of the behavior of senior civil servants as they explicitly or implicitly vie for power with political leaders.

Perhaps not surprisingly, some of the most formalized discussions of bureaucratic behavior relative to other political actors have been produced by economists who seek to apply their models of utility-maximizing behavior to public bureaucracies.[49] These models assume that bureaucrats will attempt to maximize the size of their bureaus as well as to create as many personal perquisites as possible. While this model has been critiqued any number of times, it may have some relevance for empirical, comparative research.[50] For example, Hood, Huby, and Dunsire have attempted (with disappointing results) to apply the model to departments in British central government.[51] Would the model fit, however, in an administrative system less centralized than the British, such as the United States (for which it was developed) or Sweden? Some preliminary analysis indicates that it would not.[52] In addition, are there extensions and improvements of the simple utility maximization model that would make it more generally applicable? It is tempting to scoff at the seeming naivete of some of the economic models, but they can be rigorously tested (even if many economists would not do so), whereas the more verbal models of political science and public administration are more difficult to test.

The other important aspect of reflexive behavior in the study of public bureaucracy is management. Undertaking a thorough review of the management literature as it relates to comparative politics is beyond the scope of this chapter. But—as the current fascination with Japanese management indicates—management practices vary cross-culturally in important ways.[53] Unfortunately, relatively little research exists specifying the relationship between factors that we would normally think of as independent variables and management styles.[54] It is perhaps here where the study of comparative politics and the study of public administration have their greatest disjuncture. This is simply because the practical bent of management studies views managerial techniques as ways of producing desired behavior within a single social and cultural context; such studies tend not to look at the broader social patterns that may influence the selection of managerial tools, although increasing concern is expressed about the degree to which management styles can be transported across cultural boundaries.

When we think about the purposive behavior of public bureaucrats, two important aspects of that behavior come to mind. One is the decision-making behavior of civil servants, especially as it is embedded in the context of broader public policy making. The second is the relationship between civil servants and their clients. It may be difficult to separate some aspects of these behaviors from the "reflexive" behavior discussed above, but the effort does appear to be worthwhile.

While the study of the recruitment of civil servants has concentrated on the upper echelons, there appears to be some potential utility in concentrating on the lower echelons when studying bureaucratic behavior. The role of the senior civil servant is constrained by the particular political and social mores of the service and the relationship with the political masters, but the tasks given to the lower echelons of the civil service may be more similar across cultures. Thus, we may be more able to assess the impact of cultural and social variables on behavior at the lower levels. This is especially true of the relationship between clients and civil servants in different social and political settings. Some research has already been conducted that shows substantial differences in interactions.[55] In one extremely interesting piece of research, Goodsell examines patterns of performance in the post offices of the United States and Costa Rica, attempting to see what effects differences in cultures—especially the "legalism" of the culture—would have on the performance of the same task and also on the patterns of interaction within the organization.[56] This type of work seems likely to reproduce more fruitful results about the impact of some of the usual independent variables—social structure, culture, etc.—than the traditional work concentrating on the peaks of power.

Bureaucratic Structure as a Dependent Variable

The structure of administrative systems is the most frequently manipulated and perhaps the least understood aspect of public administration.[57] Since time immemorial, whenever politicians could find nothing else to do in order to try to demonstrate their concern about public problems, they have reorganized the bureaucracy. In addition, the study of formal structures in government was where comparative administration and, indeed, comparative politics began. This scholarly and political activity has not, however, left us very much in the way of usable theory for designing public organizations at the micro level or for designing systems of organizations at the macro level. That sweeping dismissal of a great deal of previous work requires some explanation.

At the micro level, a number of studies have attempted to relate the task environment of public organization to their internal structure. These studies have been quite prominent in the United Kingdom, where a number of investigators have discussed factors such as "political salience," accountability, and uncertainty as independent variables to explain the internal structure of public organizations.[58] Perhaps the most complete analysis of the structures of governmental organizations was conducted by Hood and Dunsire, who gathered data on eighteen structural variables for sixty-nine bodies identified as "departments" in British government.[59] Using these data, they were able to develop imaginative, if not always clearly useful, portraits of those governmental departments. The faces of these departments constitute something of a rogues gallery, but the analysis should be seen as breaking new ground in the analysis of the structure of government. Furthermore, given the greater access to information in some other countries, their analysis could be usefully replicated and extended for comparative purposes.

In the above paragraph, the word departments was placed in quotation marks. This was done because the important structural question that must be answered in the study of comparative public administration is "Just what constitutes a public organization?" There are really two questions here. The first is: "What is a *public* organization?" This has obvious empirical relevance, since any attempt to enumerate and analyze the structure of government at the macro level will require some operational definition of the boundaries of the system. Thus, various attempts at classification of organizations in the United States and elsewhere have attempted to identify organizations that may not be thought to be public in the usual sense of public organizations, but that do indeed perform as public organizations.[60] The development and utilization of fringe bodies in government may also have normative significance because such bodies may have more limited accountability than do traditional public agencies.[61] Thus, our inquiry into the comparative study of public administration must perform the "simple" task of defining just what we are talking about.

The second question implied in "What is a public organization?" is identifying what *organization* means in this context. Studying the public bureaucracy of the Untied States is, in comparative terms, quite easy because of identifiable organizations established by some legal or administrative act with budget and personnel attached to them. Nonetheless, attempting to assess the organization of the Office of the Secretary of Defense, for example, involves acts of faith as to what an organization or an organizational component is. In many European countries, and indeed in most of the world, the structure of government below the department level is fluid and rarely articulated to the degree found in the United States (contrast, for example, the British *Civil Service Yearbook* with the *United States Government Manual*). In addition, beyond the identifiable structures are the interdepartmental committees, the interministerial committees, etc., that are so important for sorting out the details of policy when organizations (inevitably) overlap. Are these entities organizations? If so, how do we include them in our model of government and administrative accountability? Finally, as those interested in implementation have pointed out so well (see below), the important thing in government may not be *the* organization, but sets of organizations that somehow are involved in delivering services. While the students of implementation have made progress in identifying and conceptualizing such systems, more comparative research and theorizing is necessary before the place of these organizational systems can be adequately understood.

When we begin defining systems of organizations existing in government, we encounter some of the same difficulties encountered when discussing individual organizations. Language about "decentralization" and "deconcentration" has been around for a number of years, but such terms have rarely been effectively operationalized for dealing with systems of organizations.[62] More recently, scholars interested in interorganizational politics, especially as it affects implementation, have made strides in conceptualizing patterns of interaction among public organizations, but have been less successful in actually defining the nature of the networks. Several dimensions, some of which appear close to the old "classical organization theory," come to mind when one begins to think about the organization of the machinery of government.[63] The first would be the degree of decentralization of authority within the major units of government, which will be called departments for the time being. Clearly, there is a difference between a system such as the United States where the real action in government is at the subdepartmental (agency) level and a system such as the United Kingdom where the major activity occurs in the department. Furthermore, an administrative system such as that of Germany, which relegates much of implementation to subnational governments, disperses administrative power, whereas a system such as the unitary one of the United Kingdom concentrates power, at least, relatively speaking.[64] Such structural differences have importance for the location of power and authority and also for the coordination and the effectiveness of governmental programs.[65]

One of the interesting manifestations of structural change in many industrialized democracies has been the tendency to create specialized organizations to meet a specific policy need. Some of these may be temporary while others may be permanent. For example, in France (administrations de mission) and in Germany (Projektgruppen), nominally temporary organizations were established to meet temporary administrative needs, and most were then disbanded.[66] On the other hand, in the United Kingdom and the Netherlands, the creation of many new agencies will create much more specialized organizations than the former ministries to implement programs. Although the reasons behind these changes are numerous, one of the most common has been the desire to enforce accountability for a program and to make each organization something like a "profit center" in a private business.

Related to the point about coordination is a concern about—dare we say it?—the administrative span of control and the size of government organizations. Going back to such early studies as the Haldane and the Brownlow Commissions in the United Kingdom and the United States, respectively, concern has been expressed about just how much should be included within the purview of a single organization. These concerns are reflected in the changes that have occurred in the organization of British government during the 1960s and the 1970s.[67] At times, "super-ministries" were created in order to try to bring together all organizations in government working on a problem, e.g., the Department of Trade and Industry. At other times, various bodies have been "hived-off" to create smaller and presumably more accountable bodies. The major organizational considerations appear to have been reducing friction between organizations and thereby improving coordination under a single organization, or improving accountability and management by delegation and the creation of smaller units. Not surprisingly, there appears to have been an oscillation between these two approaches to organization in almost all governments.

Related to the structure of authority within government is the concern about the degree to which central agencies can effectively control the line agencies of government. This concern is partly a rearticulation of the old chestnut about staff and line, but it is important for understanding how policies may get made and implemented. There are also considerable differences in the degree to which central agencies have been developed and the latitude with which they can function.[68]

Especially at the macro level, studies of public bureaucracies seemingly have not kept pace with the development of organizational theory in other disciplines. With all the concern about the "growth of government" and the supposedly burgeoning bureaucracies in most developed countries, little attention has been paid to the various population ecology models of organizations that have been developed in organizational sociology.[69] While these models are subject to the criticism of being excessively mechanistic in treating the development of organizational populations, they do have some potential utility in describing how the organizational population in the public sector changes or how change is resisted. For example, Kaufman found that governmental organizations at the U.S. federal level were largely immortal, while Nystrom and Starbuck, using a very different sample and definition of organizational "death," found that the death rate in the federal bureaucracy resembled quite closely the death rate in private sector organizations.[70] What is most interesting is that nearly all of the change that occurs actually represents replacement of organizations within established "niches," as opposed to the creation of new niches by legislative or executive action.[71] Those two types of change have very different implications for the nature of emerging governmental structures and are related to questions of agenda building at the broadest possible level.[72] For example, the expansion of the public sector may arise from the expansion of existing organizations or from the replacement of older organizations with larger ones performing approximately the same functions, much in the manner described by Niskanen.[73] Such a situation would be very different from one in which government is expanding by adding new functions and creating entirely new organizations to fulfill them; for example, the Advisory Commission on Intergovernmental Relations described growth in the U.S. federal government as occurring according to the later model and fueled by aggressive policy entrepreneurs. Of course, some of both types of change have been occurring, but it is important to look at the balance of change.

In the prescriptive literature about organization and reorganization, there is a great deal more literature that explains why reforms take place and what the pitfalls and problems of reorganization are than there are studies that relate needs for improved or even different performance to specific organizational change.[74] Leemans, in what remains perhaps the most comprehensive theoretical statement about reorganization, spends most of his effort explaining how a reform is likely to occur.[75] Similarly, Grafton develops a model to explain the creation of new organizations and the reorganization of existing ones at the federal level in the

United States that should have applicability in other settings.[76] On the other hand, March and Olsen point to the underlying premises of reorganizations and their general lack of predictability.[77] Writers such as Miles and Kaufman have written interesting and important pieces directed at the frequently naive politicians who believe that reorganization is a solution to their problems.[78] Another variety of naivete assumes that the solution to all of government's problems is to adopt the practices of the private sector. This assumption was to some degree evident in the transplanting of the Planning Programming Budgeting System and the Zero-Based Budgeting System into the public sector and is seen in a more explicit form in efforts such as the Grace Commission or the Rayner exercises to "reform" government.[79]

Initiatives such as the Grace Commission and its analog in Canada illuminate the fundamental weakness of the reorganization and reform literature.[80] Naive attempts to make the public sector more like the private sector indicate a failure to understand the setting in which any proposed structural or procedural changes would have to be implemented. Thus, until we have a better understanding of the statics of public sector organization, any attempts at manipulating its dynamics are likely to be unsuccessful. As Salamon, who participated in a major reorganization exercise, has noted, the goals of the exercise must be specified; within the context of most government reorganizations, the goals of improving economy and efficiency may be impossible to attain.[81]

Bureaucratic Outcomes as a Dependent Variable

The final dependent variable in the study of comparative public administration is what happens at the end of the administrative process. This variable can be conceptualized in at least two different ways. The first is the Lasswellian version in which the question becomes: who gets what as a result of the behavior of bureaucrats and the structuring of the state? The second is now commonly referred to as the question of implementation: given a set of policy intentions, how closely does the policy as it is put into effect conform to those intentions?[82]

The Lasswellian question, as it relates to public administration, is quite close to the question discussed above about the relationship between civil servants and their clients. As mentioned above, while so much ink has been spilled on the impact of senior civil servants on policy, a great deal of the outcome of the policy process is determined by the relationship between the lowest ranks of the civil service and their clients. This is true in a material sense in that we know that clients may be treated differently depending upon their social class, race, sex, or whatever. Furthermore, the degree of variation in the receipt of benefits also varies across countries depending upon the degree of institutionalization of certain bureaucratic norms about universalistic criteria.[83] Those norms, in turn, may be related to the degree of fragmentation in the society along class or ethnic lines.

As important as the differences in the receipt of benefits are to their client, the relationship between citizen and civil servant (in a broad sense including policemen, teachers, etc.) may also have a normative significance in the context of the preservation of the legitimacy of the state. *How* the citizen receives the benefit is consequential as well as *whether* he or she receives the benefit. Thus, the question of representative bureaucracy may take on a new significance. As noted above, most studies of representative bureaucracy have concentrated on the presumed "decision-making" positions in the bureaucracy. It may be that the lower echelons, which are actually in day-to-day contact with citizens, are, however, the levels where the representativeness of the bureaucracy is more important. The good news—for those interested in system maintenance—is that those levels do indeed tend to be more representative of the population as a whole.

The second possible meaning of outcomes in comparative public administration can be seen as traveling under the now famous banner of "implementation." Students of implementation have made a very important contribution to the study of public administration, both comparatively and within the context of individual nations. This contribution has been of two sorts. The first is in reminding the naive policy maker or academic that things do, in fact, go wrong, and often go wrong badly.[84] The cause of policies going astray may well be in the administrative structures that were intended to put them into effect. Thus, more careful attention must be paid to the design of the organizations (or sets of organizations) that will be responsible for the implementation of policy. This can be seen as the "top-down" view of the contribution of implementation studies to the study of public administration.[85]

The other major contribution of the implementation approach has been to recognize, from the "bottom-up" perspective, that the organizational networks responsible for delivering policies and programs are complex, are often uncoordinated, and are composed of many organizations rather than "single, lonely organizations."[86] We noted previously, when discussing the structures of government, that it is important to recognize and include this complexity and absence (or possible absence) of hierarchical control in models of administration. Furthermore, this provides those who devise implementation systems for programs, at least, a place to start when attempting to create the mechanisms necessary for success.

Nonetheless, the implementation "movement" in public administration does not appear to have made the type of progress that is often claimed for it. This lamentation upon implementation is driven by two fundamental concerns. The first is the question of the theoretical content of the concept of implementation.[87] At its most basic level, the idea of implementation studies may simply alert us to things that good managers have known all along; things simply do not always work out the way they are intended. The humorous literature on this subject (both Parkinson and Murphy as examples) may go as far in identifying the problems with implementation as a great deal of the scholarly literature. The original Pressman and Wildavsky analysis did do a great deal in alerting us to the pitfalls of naive policy making in an era in which it was still common to think that governments could and should do anything they wished with little fuss or bother.[88] It is interesting, however, that the Pressman and Wildavsky framework itself can be shown to be overly pessimistic and in its own way somewhat naive in assuming that policy makers have only a single course of action that they can follow in order to achieve their ends, and further that they would give up after trying very little in the way of strategic or political maneuvering.[89] Thus, while it is useful to be reminded of the difficulties associated with getting what one wants from the policy making process, it could be argued that the implementation approach has injected an excessive amount of cynicism and pessimism. Also, although it was designed in part to demonstrate the political problems associated with pushing a program through, it has emerged as a somewhat mechanistic approach to policy. For example, in Mazmanian and Sabatier's conceptual framework for the implementation process, the characteristics of the "sovereign," and particularly the manipulable characteristics of the sovereign, have rather little attention devoted to them, as compared to some of the characteristics of target populations and structural constraints.[90] Thus, concentrating on the manipulable characteristics of the policy-making and implementation system seems advisable rather than merely describing the problems that the policy maker is facing. In his more recent work on "advocacy coalitions," Sabatier has emphasized even more the manipulable aspects of policy making, and the need for active intervention to produce desired policy outcomes.[91]

Equally important normative questions are involved with the implementation approach, especially because it may be taken to extremes. A very conservative assumption seems sometimes to be built in that defines *good* policy as policy that can be implemented, and assumes that by "backward mapping" we can make good policies.[92] This implies the acceptance of much of the status quo in policy making and assumes that policies that do not upset the status quo may be preferable to those that are more likely to present difficulties in implementation. This conservatism may be as much about the *methods* that will be used to implement the policy as the actual content of the policy, e.g., the utilization of social insurance for social and health problems rather than more direct redistributive mechanisms. In either case, the utilization of an implementation approach as the guide for policy design may tend to undermine the rest of the policy process and to place the goals of getting something done ahead of the more appropriate goals of getting the right thing (be it in terms of goals or means of attaining goals) done.[93]

Summary and Conclusions

I hope that by examining alternative dependent variables this chapter has to some degree illuminated the current state of play in the comparative study of public bureaucracy. Unfortunately, the picture that emerges is a rather confusing one. Many things must be explained, and what may appear as a dependent variable in one analysis soon reappears as an independent variable in another. In fact, the use of the language of variables and variance in this chapter may place too "scientific" a cast on a field that has not really gotten to the point of developing many of the scientific trappings of other fields in political science. That having been said, however, there does appear to be a very important place for the study of public bureaucracy, and especially the comparative study of public bureaucracy, in the direction in which much contemporary work in political science is now going.

I refer, of course, to the burgeoning interest in the role of the "State."[94] While to date much of this literature seems to use the state as a shibboleth, these developments are important for returning the study of public bureaucracy to a central place in the study of political systems. Whereas the behavioral analysis of politics and policy making tended to have little place for structural factors or for institutions, the burgeoning concern about the State places structural features in a central position in understanding how policies emerge and how government governs. This does not imply a return to old-style structural analysis—or description—of administrative systems, but it does imply a definite concern with structural elements in government.

What appears to be required, therefore, is the development of a theory, or set of theories, about the structure of government and the impact of structures on the performance of political systems. Structure is commonly used as a dependent variable in the study of public administration, but it should perhaps be even more central—especially if "state-centric" theories are to be an important element of the future of political science. Obviously, structural elements would be important as independent variables to explain factors such as the "autonomy" of the state and the ability of the state to influence economic and social conditions. Such a theoretical approach to state structure would have to include a number of elements, including factors such as internal controls within the state structure, relationships between those in government and key actors in the society, and relationships among principal elements within the state structure itself. I hope that at least the rudiments of such a theoretical approach will be one result of the newly organized International Political Science Association Working Group on the Structure and Organization of Government (SOG). As is traditional, therefore, I end with pleas for additional research and high hopes for the future.

Notes

1. John Kimberly, "Issues in the Design of Longitudinal Organizational Research," *Sociological Methods and Research* 4 (1976): 321-47.
2. On the one hand, see F.F. Ridley, *Government and Administration in Western Europe* (Oxford: Martin Robertson, 1979); K.K. Tummala, *Administrative Systems*

Abroad (Washington, DC: University Press of America, 1982). On the other hand, see Edward C. Page, *Political Authority and Bureaucratic Power* (Knoxville: University of Tennessee Press, 1984); B. Guy Peters, *The Politics of Bureaucracy*, 3d ed. (New York: Longman, 1989); B. Guy Peters, *Comparative Public Administration: Problems of Theory and Method* (Tuscaloosa: University of Alabama Press, 1988).

3. Fred W. Riggs, "The Group and the Movement: Notes on Comparative Development Administration," *Public Administration Review* 36 (1976): 641-45.

4. Roger Benjamin, "The Historical Nature of Social Science Knowledge: The Case of Comparative Political Inquiry," in *Strategies of Political Inquiry*, ed. Elinor Ostrom (Beverly Hills, CA: Sage, 1982), pp. 69–88.

5. S.N. Eisenstadt, *The Political Systems of Empires* (New York: Free Press, 1963); K.A. Wittfogel, *Oriental Despotism* (New Haven, CT: Yale University Press, 1957); Richard Chapman, *Administrative Leadership* (London: George Allen and Unwin, 1984); John A. Armstrong, *The European Administrative Elite* (Princeton, NJ: Princeton University Press, 1973); Henry Parris, *Constitutional Bureaucracy* (London: George Allen and Unwin, 1969).

6. Andre Molitor, "L'Histoire de l'Administration: Introduction," *International Review of Administrative Sciences* 49 (1983): 1-3.

7. David Klingman, "Temporal and Spatial Diffusion in Comparative Analysis of Social Change," *American Political Science Review* 74 (1980): 123-37.

8. Peter Kellner and Lord Crowther-Hunt, *The Civil Service* (London: Macdonald, 1980); Hugo Young and Anne Sloman, *No, Minister* (London: BBC, 1982); Herbert Kaufman, "Fear of Bureaucracy: A Raging Pandemic," *Public Administration Review* 41 (1982): 1-9; Kenneth Lieberthal and Michael Oksenberg, *Policymaking in China* (Princeton, NJ: Princeton University Press, 1988).

9. Richard Rose (with Edward Page, Richard Parry, B. Guy Peters, Andrea Cendali Pigmatelli, and Klaus-Dieter Schmidt), *Public Employment in Western Democracies* (Cambridge: Cambridge University Press, 1985); Dora Orlansky, "Public Employment in Argentina and the United States," unpublished paper, Department of Political Science, University of Pittsburgh, 1990.

10. B. Guy Peters and Martin O. Heisler, "Thinking about Public Sector Growth," in *Why Governments Grow*, ed. Charles L. Taylor (Beverly Hills, CA: Sage, 1983), pp. 177–98; Richard Rose, "Disaggregating the Concept of Government," ibid., pp. 157–76.

11. Hugh Heclo, *Modern Social Politics in Britain and Sweden* (New Haven, CT: Yale University Press, 1974); Robert Reich, *The Power of Public Ideas* (Cambridge, MA: Harvard University Press, 1988).

12. Lloyd Musolf and Harold Seidman, "The Blurred Boundaries of Public Administration," *Public Administration Review* 40 (1980): 124-30; Christopher Hood and Gunnar Folke Schuppert, *Delivering Public Services in Western Europe* (London: Sage, 1988).

13. Charles Debbasch, *La Function Publique en Europe* (Paris: CNRS, 1981).

14. Lennart Waara, *Den Stätliga Företagssektorns Expansion* (Stockholm: Liber, 1980).

15. B. Guy Peters, "Providing Public Services: The Public and Private Employment Mix," in *The Private Exercise of Public Functions*, ed. Dennis L. Thompson (Lexington, MA: D.C. Heath, 1989), pp. 105–26.

16. Peter S. Heller and Alan A. Tait, *Government Employment and Pay: Some International Comparisons* (Washington, DC: International Monetary Fund, 1983); J.-M. Duffau, "Les Remunérations Principals dans la Fonction Publique," *Revue Française d'Administration Publique* 28 (1983): 75-87.

17. J. Donald Kingsley, *Representative Bureaucracy* (Yellow Springs, OH: Antioch Press, 1944); Kenneth J. Meier, "Representative Bureaucracy: A Comparative Assess-

ment," *American Political Science Review* 69 (1975): 526-42; A. Gboyega, "The Federal Character, or the Attempt to Create Representative Bureaucracies in Nigeria," *International Review of Administrative Sciences* 50 (1984): 17-24.

18. Samuel Krislov and David H. Rosenbloom, *Representative Bureaucracy and the American Political System* (New York: Praeger, 1981); M.L. Herrman, et al., *Frauen im Öffentlichen Dienst* (Bonn: Verlag Neue Gesellschaft, 1983).

19. Charles Goodsell, *The Case For Bureaucracy*, 2d ed. (Chatham, NJ: Chatham House, 1985).

20. Robert P. Putnam, *The Comparative Study of Political Elites* (Englewood Cliffs, NJ: Prentice-Hall, 1976), p. 44.

21. Joel D. Aberbach, Robert D. Putnam, and Bert A. Rockman, *Bureaucrats and Politicians in Western Democracies* (Cambridge, MA; Harvard University Press, 1981); Hans-Ulrich Derlien, "Repercussions of Government Change on the Career Civil Service in West Germany: The Cases of 1969 and 1982," *Governance* 1 (1988): 50-78.

22. John A. Armstrong, *The European Administrative Elite* (Princeton, NJ: Princeton University Press, 1973).

23. Mattei Dogan, ed., *The Mandarins of Western Europe* (New York: John Wiley, 1975).

24. Ezra N. Suleiman, *Politics, Power and Bureaucracy in France* (Princeton, NJ: Princeton University Press, 1974); Pierre Birnbaum, *Les Sommets de l'Etat* (Paris: Editions de Seuil, 1977); Thierry Pfister, *La République des Fonctionnaires* (Paris: Albin Michel, 1988).

25. Aberbach, Putnam, and Rockman, *Bureaucrats and Politicians*; Anders Mellbourn, *Byrakratins ansikten* (Stockholm: Liber, 1979); Samuel J. Eldersveld, Jan Kooiman, and Theo van der Tak, *Elite Images in Dutch Politics* (Ann Arbor, MI: University of Michigan Press, 1981); the second wave of this study, being conducted in the later 1980s and early 1990s, will expand the coverage of countries as well as provide a longitudinal data base for analysis.

26. David Nachmias and David H. Rosenbloom, *Bureaucratic Culture: Citizens and Administrators in Israel* (New York: St. Martin's, 1978); Samuel J. Eldersveld, V. Jagganadham and A.P. Barnabas, *The Citizen and the Administrator in a Developing Democracy* (Glenview, IL: Scott, Foresman, 1968).

27. Colin Campbell and George Szablowski, *The Superbureaucrats: Structure and Behaviour in Central Agencies* (Toronto: Macmillan, 1979); Colin Campbell, *Governments under Stress: Political Executives and Key Bureaucrats in Washington, London, and Ottawa* (Toronto: University of Toronto Press, 1983).

28. Aberbach, Putnam, and Rockman, *Bureaucrats and Politicians*.

29. Thomas J. Anton, *Administered Politics: Elite Political Culture in Sweden* (Boston: Martinus Nijhoff, 1980).

30. Johan P. Olsen, *Organized Democracy* (Oslo: Universitetsforlaget, 1983); Per Laegreid and Johan P. Olsen, *Byråkrati og Beslutningar* (Oslo: Universitetsforlaget, 1979).

31. Michio Muramatsu and Ellis S. Krauss, "Bureaucrats and Politicians in Policymaking: The Case of Japan," *American Political Science Review* 78 (1984): 126-46.

32. Robert D. Putnam, "The Political Attitudes of Senior Civil Servants in Western Europe: A Preliminary Report," *British Journal of Political Science* 3 (1973): 257-90.

33. Ezra N. Suleiman, ed., *Bureaucrats and Policy Making* (New York: Holmes and Meier, 1984).

34. Hugh Heclo and Aaron Wildavsky, *The Private Government of Public Money* (Berkeley: University of California Press, 1974). For an insider's view, see Sir Leo Pliatzky, *Treasury under Mrs. Thatcher* (Oxford: Basil Blackwell, 1989).

35. Campbell and Szablowski, *Superbureaucrats*; Campbell, *Governments under Stress*.

36. Joel D. Aberbach and Bert A. Rockman, "Government Responses to Budget Scarcity: The United States," *Policy Studies Journal* 13 (1985): 494-505; Norman C. Thomas, "Policy Responses to Economic Stress and Decline in the Anglo-American Democracies," in *Organizing Governance, Governing Organizations,* ed. Colin Campbell and B. Guy Peters (Pittsburgh: University of Pittsburgh Press, 1988), pp. 239–63; F. F. Ridley, ed., *Policies and Politics in Western Europe* (London: Croom Helm, 1984).

37. Robert B. Kvavik, *Interest Groups in Norwegian Politics* (Oslo: Universitetsforlaget, 1978); L.N. Johansen and Ole P. Kristensen, "Corporatist Traits in Denmark, 1946-76," in *Patterns of Corporatist Policymaking,* ed. Gerhard Lehmbruch and Phillipe Schmitter (Beverly Hills, CA: Sage, 1982), pp. 189–218; M. Michilletti, "Interest Groups in Post-Industrial Sweden," in *Interest Groups in Post-Industrial Democracies,* ed. C.S. Thomas (London: Unwin Hyman, forthcoming).

38. Suleiman, *Politics, Power, and Bureaucracy.*

39. Michael R. Gordon, "Civil Servants, Politicians, and Parties: Shortcomings in the British Policy Process," *Comparative Politics* 4 (1971): 29-58; James B. Christoph, "Higher Civil Servants and the Politics of Conservatism in Great Britain" in Dogan, ed., *Mandarins,* pp. 25–62; A. G. Jordan and Jeremy J. Richardson, "The British Policy Style, or the Logic of Negotiation," *Policy Styles in Western Europe,* ed. Jeremy J. Richardson (London: George Allen and Unwin, 1982), pp. 80–110.

40. Hugh Heclo, *A Government of Strangers* (Washington, DC: Brookings Institution, 1978); Herbert Kaufman, *The Administrative Behavior of Federal Bureau Chiefs* (Washington, DC: Brookings Institution, 1981).

41. Lawrence B. Mohr, "The Concept of Organizational Goal," *American Political Science Review* 67 (1973): 470-81.

42. Geoffrey Hawker, "Who's Master, Who's Servant?," *Reforming Bureaucracy* (Sidney: George Allen and Unwin, 1981).

43. Aberbach, Putnam, and Rockman, *Bureaucrats and Politicians,* pp. 4-21.

44. B. Guy Peters, "The Relationship between Civil Servants and Political Executives," in *Bureaucracy and Public Resource Allocation,* ed. Jan-Erik Lane (London: Sage, 1986), pp. 255–82.

45. Heclo and Wildavsky, *Private Government.*

46. A. Grant Jordan, "Iron Triangles, Woolly Corporatism, or Elastic Nets: Images of the Policy Process," *Journal of Public Policy* 1 (1981): 95-124.

47. Olsen, *Organized Democracy.*

48. Ibid.

49. William Niskanen, *Bureaucracy and Representative Government* (Chicago: Aldine/Atherton, 1971); Albert Breton and Richard Wintrobe, "The Equilibrium Size of a Budget-Maximizing Bureau," *Journal of Political Economy* 83 (1975):195-207.

50. Maurice Kogan, *Comment on Niskanen's Bureaucracy: Servant or Master?* (London: Institute of Economic Affairs, 1973); Peter M. Jackson, *The Political Economy of Bureaucracy* (Oxford: Philip Alan, 1982), pp. 131-35.

51. Christopher Hood, Meg Huby, and Andrew Dunsire, "Bureaucrats and Budgeting Benefits: How Do British Central Government Departments Measure Up?," *Journal of Public Policy* 4 (1984):163-80.

52. B. Guy Peters, "The European Bureaucrat," in *The Budget Maximizing Bureaucrat,* ed. André Blais and Stephané Dion (Pittsburgh: University of Pittsburgh Press, 1991), pp. 295–350.

53. William G. Ouchi, *Theory Z: How American Businessmen Can Meet the Japanese Challenge* (Reading, MA: Addison-Wesley, 1981).

54. But see L.L. Roos and N.P. Roos, *Managers of Modernization* (Cambridge, MA: Harvard University Press, 1971); Mason Haire, Edward E. Ghiselli, and L.W. Porter, *Managerial Thinking: An International Study* (New York: John Wiley, 1966); Mu-Eun Bae, "Comparative Management Study: Convergence vs. Divergence," *Pacific Focus* 5 (1990): 115-28.

55. Charles Goodsell, ed., *The Public Encounter* (Bloomington, IN: University of Indiana Press, 1981); Elihu Katz and S.N. Eisenstadt, "Some Sociological Observations on the Response of Israeli Organization to New Immigrants," *Administrative Science Quarterly* 5 (1960):113-33; Jeffrey M. Prottas, *People Processing: The Street-Level Bureaucrat in Public Service Bureaucracies* (Lexington, MA: Lexington Books, 1979).

56. Charles T. Goodsell, "An Empirical Test of 'Legalism' in Administration," *Journal of the Developing Areas* 10 (1976): 485-94.

57. James G. March and Johan P. Olsen, "What Administrative Reorganization Tells Us about Governing," *American Political Science Review* 77 (1983): 281-96; see also James G. March and Johan P. Olsen, *Rediscovering Institutions: Organizational Factors in Political Life* (New York: Free Press, 1989).

58. Royston Greenwood, C.R. Hinnings, and S. Ranson, "Contingency Theory and the Organization of Local Authorities I: Differentiation and Integration," and "Contingency Theory and the Organization of Local Authorities II: Contingencies and Structures," *Public Administration* 53 (1975): 1-23, 169-90; Royston Greenwood and C.R. Hinnings, "Contingency Theories and Public Bureaucracies," *Policy and Politics* 5 (1976): 159-80.

59. Christopher Hood and Andrew Dunsire, *Bureaumetrics: The Quantitative Comparison of British Central Government Agencies* (University: University of Alabama Press, 1981).

60. Anthony Barker, *Quangos in Britain* (London: Macmillan, 1982); Ira Sharkansky, *Wither the States?* (Chatham, NJ: Chatham House, 1979).

61. D.C. Hague and Bruce L.R. Smith, *The Dilemma of Accountability in Modern Government* (London: Macmillan, 1971); Hood and Schuppert, *Delivering Public Services*.

62. Paul Meyer, *Administrative Organization: A Comparative Study of the Organization of Public Administration* (London: Stevens, 1957).

63. Christopher Pollitt, *Manipulating the Machine: Changing the Pattern of Ministerial Departments, 1960-1983* (London: George Allen and Unwin, 1984); R.A. Chapman and J.R. Greenaway, *The Dynamics of Administrative Reform* (London: Croom Helm, 1980).

64. J.J. Hesse, *Politikverflechtung im Föderativen Staat* (Baden-Baden: Nomos, Verlag, 1978); K. König, H.J. Van Oertzen, and F. Wagener, *Öffentliche Verwaltung in der Bundesrepublik Deutschland* (Baden-Baden: Nomos, 1981).

65. Brian W. Hogwood and Michael Keating, *Regional Government in England* (Oxford: Oxford University Press, 1982).

66. J. Rigaud and X. Delcros, *Les Institutions Administrative Françaises, les Structures* (Paris: Presses de la Fondation National de Sciences Politiques, 1984).

67. Pollitt, *Manipulating the Machine*; D.W. Chester and F.M.G. Willson, *The Organization of British Central Government, 1914-1964*, 2d ed. (London: George Allen and Unwin, 1968).

68. Campbell and Szablowski, *Superbureaucrats*; Peter A. Hall, "Policy Innovation and the Structure of the State: The Politics-Administration Nexus in France and Britain," *The Annals* 466 (1983): 43-60.

69. Howard E. Aldrich, *Organizations and Environments* (Englewood Cliffs, NJ: Prentice-Hall, 1979); M. Hannan and J. Freeman, "The Population Ecology Model of

Organizations," *American Journal of Sociology* 82 (1977): 929-64; J.V. Singh and C.J. Lumsden, "Theory and Research in Organizational Ecology, *Annual Review of Sociology* 16 (1990): 161-95.

70. Herbert Kaufman, *Are Government Organizations Immortal?* (Washington, DC: Brookings Institution, 1976); P. Nystrom and W. Starbuck, *Handbook of Organizational Design* (New York: Oxford University Press, 1981).

71. B. Guy Peters and Brian W. Hogwood, "Births, Deaths and Metamorphoses in the U.S. Federal Bureaucracy, 1933-83," *American Review of Public Administration* 18 (1988):119-33.

72. B. Guy Peters and Brian W. Hogwood, "In Search of the Issue-Attention Cycle," *Journal of Politics* 47 (1985): 239-53.

73. Brian W. Hogwood and B. Guy Peters, *Policy Dynamics* (New York: St. Martin's, 1983).

74. Gerald E. Caiden and Heinrich Seidentopf, *Strategies for Administrative Reform* (Lexington, MA: Lexington Books, 1982); Mohammed M. Khan, *Bureaucratic Self-Preservation* (Dacca: University of Dacca, 1980); Hans-Ulrich Derlien, "Regierungsorganisation—Institutionelle Restriktion des Regierens?," in *Regieren in der Bundesrepublik I*, ed. Hans-Hermann Hartwich and Gottrik Wewer (Opladen: Leske and Budrich, 1990), pp. 80–96.

75. Arne F. Leemans, *The Management of Change in Government* (The Hague: Martinus Nijhoff, 1976).

76. Carl Grafton, "Response to Change: The Creation and Reorganization of Federal Agencies," in *Problems of Administrative Reform*, ed. Robert Miewald and Michael Steinman (Chicago: Nelson Hall, 1984), pp. 25–46.

77. March and Olsen, *Rediscovering Institutions*.

78. Rufus E. Miles, Jr.,"Considerations for a President Bent on Reorganization," *Public Administration Review* 40 (1980):155-62; Herbert Kaufman, "Reflections on Administrative Reorganization," in *Setting National Priorities: The 1978 Budget*, ed. Joseph Pechman (Washington, DC: Brookings Institution, 1977), pp. 391–418.

79. President's Private Sector Survey on Cost Control (The Grace Commission), *Report to the President* (Washington, DC: Government Printing Office, 1984); N. Warner, "Raynerism in Practice: Anatomy of a Rayner Scrutiny," *Public Administration* 62 (1984): 7-22.

80. V.S. Wilson, "What Legacy? The Nielsen Task Force Program Review," in *How Ottawa Spends, 1988/89: The Conservatives Heading into the Stretch*, ed. K.A. Graham (Ottawa: Carleton University Press, 1988), pp. 23–48.

81. Lester M. Salamon, "The Question of Goals," in *Federal Reorganization: What We Have Learned*, ed. Peter Szanton (Chatham, NJ: Chatham House, 1981), pp. 58–84.

82. Jan-Erik Lane, "The Concept of Implementation," *Statsventenskaplig Tidskrift* 86 (1982): 17-40.

83. Fred W. Riggs, *Administration in Developing Countries: The Theory of Prismatic Society* (Boston: Houghton Mifflin, 1964); E.J. Schumacher, *Politics, Bureaucracy and Rural Development in Senegal* (Berkeley: University of California Press, 1975).

84. William S. Pierce, *Bureaucratic Failure and Public Expenditure* (New York: Academic Press, 1981)

85. Chris Ham and Michael Hill, *The Policy Process in the Modern Capitalist State* (Brighton, UK: Wheatsheaf, 1984); Brian W. Hogwood and Lewis A. Gunn, *Policy Analysis for the Real World* (Oxford: Oxford University Press, 1984); E.O. Laumann and D. Knoke, *The Organizational State: Social Change in National Policy Domains* (Madison: University of Wisconsin Press, 1987).

86. Kenneth Hanf and Fritz W. Scharpf, eds., *Interorganizational Policymaking: Lim-*

its to Coordination and Central Control (Beverly Hills, CA: Sage, 1978); Bennie Hjern and David Porter, "Implementation Structures: A New Unit of Administrative Analysis," *Organization Studies* 2 (1981): 211-24; Kenneth Hanf, "Regulatory Structures: Enforcement as Implementation," *European Journal of Political Research* 10 (1982): 159-72.

87. Lane, "Concept of Implementation," Andrew Dunsire, *Implementation in a Bureaucracy* (New York: St. Martin's, 1978); Susan Barrett and Colin Fudge, *Policy and Action* (London: Methuen 1981).

88. Jeffrey L. Pressman and Aaron Wildavsky, *Implementation*, 3d ed. (Berkeley: University of California Press, 1984).

89. Elizabeth R. Bowen, "The Pressman-Wildavsky Paradox: Four Addenda or Why Models Based on Probability Theory Can Predict Implementation Successes and Suggest Useful Tactical Advice to Implementors," *Journal of Public Policy* 2 (1982): 1-22. But see, in response to Bowen, Ernest R. Alexander, "Improbable Implementation: The Pressman-Wildavsky Paradox Revisited," *Journal of Public Policy* 9 (1989): 451-65.

90. David A. Mazmanian and Paul A. Sabatier, *Implementation and Public Policy* (Glenview, IL: Scott, Foresman, 1983).

91. Paul Sabatier, "An Advocacy Coalition Framework of Policy Change and the Role of Policy-Oriented Learning Therein," *Policy Sciences* 21 (1988): 129-68.

92. Richard F. Elmore, "Backward Mapping: Implementation Research and Policy Decisions," *Political Science Quarterly* 94 (1980): 601-16.

93. John Dryzek, "Don't Toss Coins into Garbage Cans: A Prologue to Policy Design," *Journal of Public Policy* 3 (1983): 345-68.

94. B. Guy Peters and James F. Hollifield, eds., *The State and Public Policy* (Boulder, CO: Westview, 1992).

4

On the Uniqueness of
Public Bureaucracies

Hal G. Rainey

One of the most important issues for contemporary social theory and institutional design is concerned with the relative virtues of governmentally controlled decision and allocation processes as compared with more decentralized processes.[1] A major question within this broad issue is whether organizations under a high degree of governmental direction differ from those under less governmental direction. I shall review here a set of books and articles that assert that they do differ and shall summarize a growing body of pertinent research. Although the assertion that public and private organizations differ is a venerable one, the sizable literature on the subject in the United States has usually treated the assertion implicitly rather than explicitly. Toward the end of the 1970s, however, a number of authors from diverse backgrounds began calling for more direct attention to analysis of the supposed distinctiveness of public organizations. Many of these authors, who apparently were often unaware of each other's work, also argued that concepts and techniques from generic organizational theory should be applied to the analysis of governmental bureaucracies.

These authors generally agreed that a literature in political science and economics offered elaborate depictions of public bureaucracies, but the literature placed primary emphasis on the bureaucracies' role in external political processes and relied mainly on descriptive case studies and anecdotes. Frequently espousing the methodological approaches predominant in generic organizational theory during the 1960s and the 1970s, these scholars differed from the organizational theorists by asserting that public agencies possess certain unique attributes arising mainly from the absence of economic markets for their outputs and from

111

their political accountability. These assertions, which have important implications for both theory and institutional design, require clarification and substantiation. After reviewing key contributions to this literature, I shall describe research developments on the distinctiveness of public bureaucracies and their differences from other types of organizations, especially private firms. I shall also give examples of the approaches that researchers have followed in analyzing this issue, as well as examples of some of the streams of research on particular dimensions of public bureaucracies.

Defining the Disciplinary Categories: Generic Organizational Theory and the Public Bureaucracy Literature

Since both the generic organizational theory and the public bureaucracy streams of literature could be treated as parts of the vast literature on organizations, the categories must be clarified. By "generic organizational theory," I mean the part of the social scientific literature on organizations sometimes called "functional organizational theory,"[2] and, more specifically, the recent work on organizational structure and process culminating in contingency theory.[3] Beginning with the work of Max Weber and running through the Administrative Management School up through James Thompson, Herbert Simon, and other recent theorists, these writers have been particularly concerned with the determinants of organizational management, structure, and process—much more so than have writers on the public bureaucracy. For example, organizational theorists developed concepts that concern relatively enduring internal properties of organizations—usually called organizational structure—such as centralization, formalization (extensiveness of rules and procedures), complexity (number of hierarchical levels, subunits, and specializations), and standardization. In addition, these theorists have been concerned with more fluid processes, such as decision making, change and innovation, growth, and communication. They have devoted extensive attention to the determinants of these aspects of structure and process. For example, contingency theorists have argued that organizations adapt their internal structures and processes to such contingencies as organizational size, organizational technology or task characteristics, and environmental uncertainty. I also include in this category of generic organizational theory the body of work often called organizational behavior, or organizational psychology, covering such topics as worker motivation and satisfaction, leadership behavior and effectiveness, and numerous related topics focusing on groups and individuals within organizations.

Until the last decade or so, this generic organizational theory literature has been heavily empirical and logical-positivist in its epistemology. Researchers emphasized the importance of explicitly defining and measuring concepts and testing the relations among them through data gathering and statistical tests. These procedures were typical of those used by the social sciences in general during the 1960s and the 1970s. Generic organizational theorists sought concepts and models that could supposedly be applied generally to all organizations. For example, scholars advancing theories of work motivation have always treated their theories as applicable across organizational settings and types. Furthermore, the influential studies published by Peter Blau and his colleagues on organizational size were conducted in governmental agencies, but the conclusions were stated generally, as if they were to apply to all types of organizations.[4] When organizational researchers following this tradition have sought to develop taxonomies of organizations, they have often rejected such distinctions as public–private and profit–nonprofit as misleading colloquial oversimplifications, or at least as too limited for a general typology of organizations.[5]

On the other hand, a smaller stream of literature on public bureaucracies treats them as a distinct category among organizations. This literature mainly emphasizes the political and legal setting of the governmental bureaucracy and the roles of bureaucrats and their agencies in the political system.[6] Authors in this group certainly examine structure and behavior within the bureaucracies, but the work on those topics has been much less intensive than that in the organizational theory group.[7] The writers on public bureaucracy also strongly favor case and anecdotal description; empirical data-gathering projects are relatively rare in the genre.[8] Observations such as these about the public bureaucracy literature are common in the references reviewed below, many of which call for more application of organizational theorists' concepts and procedures in the analysis of public bureaucracies.

Toward Convergence: Organizational Analysis in Public Agencies

Around 1980, a number of books appeared, calling for more attention to the managerial and the organizational dimensions of public bureaucracies, but also for analysis of the influence on those dimensions of the distinctive contexts of public bureaucracies. The authors of these works vary among themselves, but tend to express the following perspective: organizational theory has a better-developed empirical and conceptual tradition than the public bureaucracy literature, and it has better-developed concepts and procedures for the analysis of internal management, structures, and processes. Organizational theorists have paid insufficient attention, however, to the political and governmental influences on organizations. The public bureaucracy literature has more carefully considered such influences, but has provided less clear analysis of the above-mentioned internal impacts, because the stream of literature has been primarily anecdotal and discursively descriptive. Applying the concepts and procedures of organizational analysis, paying special attention to political and governmental influences, would improve the analysis of public bureaucracies. Along with other contributions that cannot be covered here, these books fed a growing trend toward integrating the organizational theory and the bureaucratic politics literatures.

Precursors: Dahl and Lindblom and Downs

Some of the books reviewed below actually draw on a perspective on public bureaucracy that has been prevalent for years. For example, a view of governmental bureaucracy as rigid and rule-bound because of the concomitant absence of economic markets and presence of political constraints dates back at least to the writings of classical conservative economists. In the mid-1950s, Robert Dahl and Charles Lindblom provided a clear statement of this position in their analysis of alternatives for the organization of political economies.[9] They observed that nations choose among variants of two fundamental modes of decision and allocation: activities can be directed through a politically constituted hierarchy or through relatively decentralized, autonomous organizational forms controlled by the price system, or economic markets. All nations obviously employ complex admixtures of these modes, such as governmental regulation of private firms and governmental ownership of industrial organizations. Nonetheless, one can distinguish organizational forms at the two extremes, which Dahl and Lindblom called "agencies" and "enterprises."

Although Dahl and Lindblom noted such general similarities between agencies and enterprises as internal hierarchy and bureaucratic form,[10] they also noted differences, which they saw as quite significant for institutional design. Agencies, they said, are more subject to such disabilities of bureaucracy as red tape, rigidity, and timidity, owing to the external hierarchical controls imposed upon them. Since agencies obtain revenues through budget appropriations and are not subject to the automatic penalties and rewards of the price system, they show weaker tendencies toward cost reduction. Because enterprises will be unable to resolve various failures of the economic markets—including externalities, demands for public goods, factor immobilities, and perceived needs for income redistribution—many of these kinds of problems will be assigned to agencies. Agencies are often given relatively intangible objectives; deprived of market indicators; and placed under political and institutional requirements for accountability, due process, and equity. In addition, agencies typically have a greater diversity of missions than enterprises, and they have fewer objective tests of achievement in product or service. Therefore, agencies emphasize control and evaluation on the basis of procedures followed. This view of the basic differences between public and private organizations has been very widely espoused in the literature up through the recent references listed below.

A similar but much more explicit and elaborate treatment appeared in the late 1960s in Anthony Downs's *Inside Bureaucracy*.[11] This book became the most widely cited single reference in the public bureaucracy literature, and was particularly influential on the very recent references reviewed below—apparently, in part, because it was unusual within that genre. In a field dominated by case description, Downs presented a systematic set of propositions about bureaucratic motivations and behaviors and about the environments, territoriality, internal structures, communications, control, change, and decision-making processes of bureaus.

Much of Downs's analysis of these dimensions was akin to generic organizational theory in that he cited common organizational properties as causal factors. For example, he posited that the extent of hierarchy is determined by the need for coordination and conflict resolution, which is in turn influenced primarily by the large scale and the internal diversity of bureaus. The extensiveness of formal rules is determined by the routineness of functions and the length of time a function has been performed. Downs analyzed communications problems largely by reference to Tullock's arguments about information distortion in hierarchies, implying that the number of levels of hierarchy is the primary determinant. Control problems in bureaus arise, he said, primarily as a result of the variance of goals among internal actors and authority leakage down the hierarchy.

Yet, like Dahl and Lindblom, Downs attached major significance to the absence of economic markets for agency outputs and to the accompanying political and institutional controls on the public bureaucracy. He treated the absence of voluntary markets for outputs as the primary defining characteristic of bureaus and, together with the political environment, as a major influence on their internal properties. The very existence of bureaus, he argued, is explained by the need to provide goods and services that economic markets do not adequately provide. His "Law of Hierarchy" stated that the "coordination of large-scale activities without markets requires a hierarchical authority structure."[12] Bureaus make extensive use of formal rules, Downs said, because they have no direct measure of outputs, because they need rules to control spending, because they need to ensure equal treatment of clients, and because rules are efficient means of controlling large-scale activities.[13] Owing to the absence of market information and the presence of political oversight institutions, superiors in bureaus require many more reports than they can possibly read; they decide which ones to read by attempting to discern which issues are most likely to result in external criticism. He noted that "external monitors" play a role in the control process.[14]

Downs also related the nonmarket, service-oriented nature of bureau functions to the motives and behaviors of bureaucrats and, in turn, to a "rigidity cycle" for bureaus.[15] Some officials allegedly display mixed motives and serve the public interest as well as their self-interests; others are purely self-interested and seek either to climb in the hierarchy or conserve their positions in it. In the absence of markets, he argued, all of these types of motivation together cause undue growth and rigidity in public agencies: "climbers" push for more, "conservers" try to hold what they have, and even those with public service motives need bigger budgets and organizations to pursue their goals. The hierarchical structures are stifling and create pressures to become a conserver. Thus, idealism and altruism flag even among the mixed-motive types of agencies. Larger, older bureaus tend to fill up with conservers and become rigid.

As for the political environment, Downs devoted a brief chapter to the agency's "power setting," which consists of a sovereign, rivals, beneficiaries and sufferers, regulators, suppliers, and allies. Beyond simply sketching out these components, Downs noted only that they should be used in classifying bureaus. He also noted briefly that the social functions of a bureau can be located at various points in "policy space" (which they may share with other bureaus engaged in similar functions), and he sketched the tendencies of bureaus to defend their territories.[16]

Downs's analysis oversimplified in many ways. His spare outline of the political environment, for example, was not as rich and informative as the treatment in some of the other literature accused in the references below of being too discursive and anecdotal. Furthermore, he analyzed hierarchy and control by reference to internal diversity, without explicitly considering the role of the pluralistic political environment in enlarging that diversity. Nevertheless, his combination of conceptual explicitness, internal organizational analysis, and attention to political and nonmarket environments has been very appealing to many recent authors who seek to extend this work.

Warwick: A Theory of Public Bureaucracy

Donald Warwick mounted one of the first explicit challenges both to the organizational theory and the public bureaucracy research.[17] He complained that the previous literature on public bureaucracy had been largely descriptive and anecdotal, without explicit conceptual frameworks. The more conceptually explicit and empirically based work in organizational theory, on the other hand, had ignored the distinctive attributes of public agencies, such as the political influences on them.[18]

Warwick actually provided another case study, however. He described an effort at administrative streamlining in the State Department. One division attempted to implement a management-by-objectives process and to eliminate a number of layers of hierarchy. The effort proved unsuccessful, and the levels of hierarchy were regenerated. Warwick concluded that the environments of public agencies interact with internal forces to create particularly elaborate hierarchies, rules, and clearance requirements that remain quite resistant to change. One cannot adequately analyze public agencies, then, without paying much more attention to their political and institutional environments than organizational theory provided at that time.[19] In particular, Warwick cited Blau's studies of organizational size and structure, noted above, as an example of organizational theorists' inattention to the political environments of public bureaucracies.

Warwick did not provide a conceptually explicit model or theory, and much of his analysis appears to weave together points from previous writers on public bureaucracy, particularly Downs. Warwick's power-setting diagram resembles Downs's with some concepts from organizational theory added. He quotes with approval Downs's Law of Hierarchy, and generally paints a highly similar picture of the public bureaucracy.

Yet Warwick fleshed out Downs's framework in a number of important ways and justified his claim that he added to the organizational theory literature as it applies to public agencies. At that time, organizational theorists heavily emphasized the influence on organizational structures of such contingencies as size, technology, and environmental uncertainty. Warwick stressed the obvious point that external entities empowered to control an agency often directly specify structure from the outside. Congress may do so by statute, and such monitoring agencies as the Government Accounting Office may directly impose reporting and record-keeping requirements. Certain rules, such as civil service and purchasing regulations, are imposed "systemwide" across all agencies within a governmental jurisdiction.[20] Warwick also addressed the less formal influences on agency structure and process described by the public bureaucracy literature. Legislators, other components of the executive branch, and constituent and interest groups can exert pressure for or against structural change. In doing so, he observed, they display a "managerial orthodoxy" that emphasizes the importance of maintaining clear hierarchical lines of authority and accountability.[21]

These environmental influences also interact with internal contingencies in ways that lead to more complex rules and hierarchy. Linkages with other agencies that have overlapping roles in policies and programs aggravate the coordination problems, which creates pressures for hierarchy and rules. In addition, political appointees at the tops of agencies find it hard to control lower levels. Their formal authority over structural and personnel changes is sharply limited, and subordinates can resist their authority by forming alliances with legislators and constituents, resulting in "power leaks."[22] Also contributing to this concern with controlling lower levels is the desire to avoid adverse political reactions (by the media, legislators, and interest groups) to the actions of a subordinate or subunit. Especially since performance criteria remain relatively unclear, these problems cause higher-level officials to try to control lower levels through the proliferation of rules and specified procedures. Higher officials heavily emphasize the importance of retaining hierarchical authorization of actions and maintaining multiple levels of review of lower-level decisions. The same forces cause subordinates to be receptive to rules and hierarchy because they provide direction and security within the context of the environmental pressures and the vague performance criteria.

These conditions make for elaborate, rigid structures and procedures, and efforts at change are further inhibited by short-term orientations among congressmen and political executives. Career officials have learned to "sit tight" and wait out change efforts, especially since agency incentive systems tend to emphasize security.[23] Existing arrangements can be frozen by statute or by opposition from interest groups and legislative committees that virtually own an agency. Warwick cited all these factors in interpreting the failure of the reforms at State. He painted a picture of public bureaucracies quite similar to that of Downs, but much richer in its observations about the internal influences of the external political and institutional environment.

Meyer: Change in Public Bureaucracies

Four years after Warwick's book was published, Marshall Meyer reported a study of structural change in city, county, and state finance agencies.[24] Using a quantitative and qualitative analysis of longitudinal data, Meyer concluded that the agencies face complex environmental pressures for change. For example, rapid changes in electronic data-processing (EDP) technology forced decisions as to whether finance agencies should handle data-processing functions. These pressures sometimes caused EDP subunits to be split away and assigned elsewhere, thus resulting in structural changes—changes in the number of agency subunits. Some agencies averted these pressures, however, through "claims to domain" (simply put, the extent to which an agency has a focused, consistent claim concerning its proper scope of activity), and through the political stability of the agency head (a civil servant or politically elected head, rather than an appointee). Meyer also reported data showing that agency personnel rules have been influenced by federal efforts to propagate merit systems across this century.[25]

Meyer's conclusions differed in some ways from those of Downs and Warwick. He argued that public agencies do not show marked resistance to change, but actually remain particularly open to environmental pressures for change. He suggested that emphasis on rule enforcement in public agencies comes not from caution but from a strong concern with fairness and impartiality.[26] In other ways, however, his conclusions resembled those of Downs and Warwick. He emphasized the role of the political environment in shaping the structure of public agencies:

> A characteristic of bureaucracies . . . is that most decisions result from administrative or political judgments rather than technological imperatives. For this reason, contrary to stereotypes, bureaus tend to be very open and vulnerable to their immediate environments. . . . Increasing bureaucratization of public agencies through additional rules and layers of hierarchy results in part from their openness to their environments.[27]

Meyer's data actually showed that the hierarchical levels in the agencies he studied remained remarkably stable amid other changes and environmental pressures—a finding consistent with Warwick's observations. Meyer cited Downs in concluding that because public bureaucracies do work for which there is no market alternative, public administrators have no choice other than to emphasize simple hierarchy in organizational structure. Public agencies tend to adopt Weberian bureaucratic structures, heavily emphasizing rule compliance and evaluating performance in terms of conformity with higher authority. Claims to domain and leadership are important in large part because of the absence of clear information from economic markets.[28] Meyer showed no awareness of Warwick's book and apparently arrived at his conclusions independently. Like Warwick, he criticized the divergence between the public bureaucracy and the organizational theory literatures, arguing that organizational theorists had ignored the distinction between public agencies and profit-oriented firms in a way that had led to overgeneralization in their field.[29]

The Linkage to Public Management

In an article on bureaucratic reform published in 1980, Allen Barton offered a brief set of propositions about bureaucratic maladies very similar to the perspectives described above.[30] He argued that the absence of market-based performance measures, the history of patronage and corruption, and the power of organized special interests cause public bureaucracies to have rigid rules imposed on them and to have weak employee rewards, penalties, and professional service norms. Public bureaucracies, therefore, tend toward inefficiency, lack of innovation, and unresponsiveness to public wants. As oversimplified as this framework is, it succinctly crystallized some of the central tenets of this stream of literature (Barton, too, cites Downs). His framework also emphasized, moreover, the relevance of this issue to administrative reform and improved management of the public bureaucracy.

Several other works echoed this call for more attention to management and organizational analysis in public bureaucracies in various ways. In addition to the calls for more organizational analysis and an increasing concern with the performance of the public bureaucracy, more and more writers emphasized public sector management. This discussion was fueled by a conviction akin to the one expressed in calls for more public sector organizational theory: the general management literature was inattentive to the public sector, while the literature on public administration needed more work on actual managerial procedures and functions.[31]

Lynn: Managing the Public's Business

Among those working on this public management topic, Laurence Lynn contributed an analysis of the work of the high-level federal executive.[32] He, too, emphasized the complex political and institutional interventions that severely complicate administrative processes within agencies. The same processes that impose enormous responsibilities on these executives also create "centrifugal forces" that dilute their authority to carry them out. Their agencies are often "sprawling agglomerations" of bureaus and programs over which Congress, the White House, the courts, and interest groups struggle for control. Congress and the courts have increasingly prescribed internal organization and management. Together, these forces create a system of "management without managers."[33]

To avoid political embarrassment and impotence, the executive must master immensely complex policy issues. Objectives and criteria remain elusive. Congress assigns tasks for which the technology is vague or nonexistent and may avoid clarification of objectives in the interests of reaching a compromise. In trying to achieve the assigned tasks under strong accountability pressures, executives face a problem of "inevitable bureaucracy"—trying to tighten accountability and efficiency at lower levels unavoidably increases rules and red tape. Amid these and other constraints, such as a press corps that knows or cares little about substantive issues in policy and administration, little incentive exists for conscientious executive performance. Low-keyed, substantive approaches are penalized in favor of political style.[34]

While purporting to emphasize management, Lynn's analysis reflects the problem he laments. In his discussion of the public executive's role, he actually places much more emphasis on involvement in the policy process than on managing the organization. This illustrates the difficulty cited by Lynn and others—that top officials become preoccupied with high-level policy and inattentive to internal management. This suggests a reason for the divergence between the organizational theory and the public bureaucracy studies that these authors address. In a context in which major public policy issues are being fought out by powerful forces, internal organizational matters can appear trivial to both public executives and political scientists inclined to study the bureaucracy. Whatever the reasons for the divergence, Lynn, like the others, emphasized the need to resolve it.

Kaufman: The Administrative Behavior of Federal Bureau Chiefs

In justifying his intensive observations of the work of six federal bureau chiefs, Herbert Kaufman also noted the surprising scarcity of research on the actual activities of public managers.[35] Many of his conclusions, published in 1981, resembled those of the other works reviewed above, particularly those concerning the external constraints of the governmental setting and the related internal procedural complexities. He found that Congress exerts a much stronger influence on the bureau chiefs than their department heads exert on them. Kaufman noted that bureau chiefs must constantly monitor interest groups and the media; agencies' information-scanning activities place a heavy emphasis on avoiding political embarrassment. Also, he identified many administrative constraints—complex signature rules, extensive directives, regularities of the budgetary process, cross-cutting agency jurisdictions—as well as interventions by Congress, oversight agencies, and the White House.

Kaufman's careful analysis of actual behaviors also provided a counterpoint for this literature. He emphasized that much of what these managers did resembled the work involved in running any large organization. Managers devoted a great deal of time to making decisions, to motivating and communicating with their work forces, to setting the tone for the bureau, and so on. Perhaps the most frequent assertion in the public bureaucracy literature concerns the greater vagueness of performance criteria in the absence of economic markets, yet Kaufman showed that these managers sometimes dealt with objectives as clear as those in any management setting—for example, board feet of lumber sold. Thus, while Kaufman's treatment generally agreed with that of the other writers under review, it also forced some important questions. For example, is preoccupation with external policy processes a function of organizational level? Kaufman's bureau chiefs were below the departmental level, which appears to be the focus of Lynn's discussion. In addition, does the widespread assertion about public agencies having vague goals need to be clarified? More generally, could it be that some of the purported distinctiveness of public bureaucracies is overblown by the other authors?

The British Are Coming: A Similar
Theme from across the Atlantic

Also during this period British authors independently joined this stream of work on the distinctiveness of public bureaucracies. In 1981, two books appeared out of Great Britain that made similar observations about the state of the literature. The authors argued that organizational theory had ignored public organizations, while the public bureaucracy literature had been too discursive and anecdotal.

D.C. Pitt and B.C. Smith argued that the contingency theories then predominant in organizational analysis failed to consider adequately the political processes in organizational environments and the normative issues inherent in performance criteria for government agencies.[36] Rather than condemning organizational theory, however, they called for more of it. Complaining that the public administration literature had been too concerned with legal analysis instead of behavioral analysis, they sought to illustrate how organizational theory might be usefully applied to governmental departments. The environmental influences on governmental departments that Pitt and Smith found most important were the values imposed by external institutions. These values included accountability, efficiency, legality, consultation, fairness, and reasonableness. Furthermore, they pointed out that one must examine the resultant influence on rules and procedures in the departments, and pointed out that such factors had been omitted in discussions of organizational environments in contingency theories, which at that time were stressing environmental flux and uncertainty. Yet Pitt and Smith also illustrated the application of concepts from organizational theory, such as organizational technology, to the analysis of public bureaucracy.[37]

Christopher Hood and Andrew Dunsire voiced a very similar criticism of organizational theory and the research on public bureaucracy in reporting their elaborate effort to construct an empirical taxonomy of British central governmental agencies.[38] They complained that empirical studies of the internal structures and processes of governmental departments were virtually nonexistent and that most governmental reform efforts as well as university teaching on the topic relied on historical and case descriptive accounts. Yet they also argued that many governmental reform efforts blithely assumed that business management techniques apply readily to government agencies. The analysis of public agencies, they said, requires paying attention to distinctive political and institutional dimensions. In their study, they used archival data to develop measures of dimensions of agencies' internal structure, of their political and budgetary environments, and of their task characteristics, and to analyze the relations among the dimensions. Using statistical clustering techniques, they attempted to group the agencies in an inductive taxonomy.

In discussing challenges in research on public agencies and in constructing measures of the political environment, Hood and Dunsire emphasized many points similar to those emphasized by the group of authors already described. For example, they argued that the problem of identifying the units of analysis—the entities as the organizations to be analyzed—is particularly acute in the public sector, where each organizational entity is embedded in overarching units. Many large agencies in Britain and the United States are designed in holding-company fashion. A number of diverse subunits are commonly grouped into one of the sprawling agglomerations to which Lynn referred, and many of these subunits have considerable functional and political autonomy. Also, Hood and Dunsire reported an interesting effort to devise a measure of the political salience of agencies based on evidence of legislative attention to the agency. As did Pitt and Smith, Hood and Dunsire also attempted to deal with the complex problem of separating the effects of organizational task from the effects of the political environment: at what point is internal structure shaped by demands of the work itself, and at what point is it shaped by external political interventions? Their work did not conclusively resolve this issue, but it considerably advanced Downs's rough assertion that the two factors determine bureaucratic structure and process.[39]

While both sets of authors staunchly advocated organizational analysis, Pitt and Smith and Hood and Dunsire also insisted that the public bureaucracies have unique characteristics. Both books described problems that have occurred in British administrative reform efforts owing to a lack of adequate organizational analysis and to the adoption of facile assumptions about the applicability of business management techniques. Thus, they joined the group of authors arguing persuasively that political actors and institutions heavily influence the management and the organization of the public bureaucracy.

The Growing Body of Evidence

These authors have reached a consensus on the general distinctiveness of the public bureaucracy, some disagreements among them notwithstanding, and subsequent studies have substantiated and advanced their general conclusions.[40] Their consensus extended a decades-old, but often implicit, perspective in the

writing on public bureaucracies by calling for more explicit analysis of managerial issues and internal organizational dimensions after the pattern of organizational theory, but with attention to the significance of political environments long
recognized in the public bureaucracy literature. Some elements of the consensus
on the general distinctiveness of public bureaucracies are carried in the cultures
of the United States and other industrialized democracies. These ideas are shared
by respondents to opinion surveys, majorities of whom report their belief that
public agencies perform less efficiently than private firms.[41] During the last
decade, the perception that public organizations operate differently, and less
efficiently than private ones, also fueled the movement demanding the privatization of public services in the United States and many other countries. While the
numerous participants in this very general consensus may differ sharply among
themselves on particulars, their overall agreement suggests that the distinctiveness of the public bureaucracy is obvious.

It is intriguing, however, that the authors reviewed above cannot by themselves overturn the opposing generic orientation in organizational theory. Whatever the degree of consensus among the analysts of public bureaucracy, their
work concentrates on the public bureaucracy, usually makes only implicit comparisons with private organizations, and usually provides no explicit evidence of
such comparisons. Hence the counterarguments of generic organizational theorists remain reasonably intact. Public and private bureaucracies do face similar
challenges and have similar general administrative functions—designing structures, motivating members, making decisions, etc. Critics of bureaucracy usually
chant the same litany of dysfunctions for private as well as public bureaucracies.
Political activities involving coalition formation, power relations, and persuasion
pervade all organizations, and relations with the external political environment
are likewise important to most organizations. Public and private bureaucracies
often do the same things, as in the cases of public and private schools, hospitals,
utilities, and universities. Public and private organizations also employ similar
professionals and specialists, such as lawyers, engineers, scientists, clerical and
custodial workers, and general managers.

Public and private bureaucracies also blur together through governmental
regulation of private firms, governmental contracts with private and nonprofit
organizations, lobbying and political activity by private and nonprofit organizations, and the involvement of private and nonprofit organizations in delivering
public services and finding solutions to social problems. In addition, such hybrid
organizations as governmental enterprises and authorities are designed to mix
public and private characteristics. As indicated by contingency theory perspectives and other developments in organizational theory, many variables other than
governmental or private auspices influence organizations—including their age
and life cycles; size, task, and technology; environmental uncertainty; and resource dependence. Public or private status often appears to exert less influence
than many of these other factors, and studies by organizational theorists over the

years have found many similarities between public and private organizations.[42] The public and the private sectors, and points of overlap and linkage in between, involve such a diverse array of organizational types that generalizations across those categories sometimes appear quite dubious.

Given all these complications, could we blame organizational theorists for arguing that the meaning of the very category of public bureaucracy remains unclear and that its distinctiveness is uncertain at best? But such an argument now must take into account some hard evidence to the contrary. Table 4.1 shows a steady accretion of empirical findings and other evidence on this issue. This body of research began to burgeon before the appearance of many of the references reviewed above, and its growth has accelerated in recent years. A full discussion of the contributions summarized in the table is impossible here, but those contributions and others in addition reflect a number of important developments in the analysis of the distinctiveness of public bureaucracies.[43]

**Definitions of Public, Private,
and Intermediate Organizational Forms**

Many of the entries in Table 4.1 show that researchers have hardly been intimidated by the problems in distinguishing the public and the private categories. Researchers have typically defined public organizations as those owned by government and private organizations as those not owned by government. Repeated findings that this simple dichotomy shows relations to important dependent variables have helped to keep this topic alive, and some researchers argue that this dichotomy is theoretically justified and parsimonious.[44]

Still, some researchers—I myself am included among them—emit scholarly grumbles about the oversimplifications inherent in the public–private dichotomy.[45] They argue that research employing more complex conceptions of the public-private continuum can produce better evidence about how and why public or private status influences bureaucracies. We have long been aware of the blurring and hybridization of the public and the private sectors described above. Dahl and Lindblom added to their observations about agencies and enterprises a depiction of the continuum of designs between the polar categories, including public corporations, heavily regulated utilities, and governmental contractors.[46] Wamsley and Zald later defined public and private organizations on the basis of their ownership and funding.[47] They defined public organizations as those both owned and funded by government and private organizations as those privately owned and receiving most of their funding from nongovernmental sources. Wamsley and Zald classified organizations owned by government but funded from private sources and those owned privately but primarily funded by government as hybrid or intermediate types. This classification helps to clarify the nature of the public and the private categories, but emphasizes the multidimensional nature of the distinctions between them. *(Text continues on p. 132)*

Table 4.1

Summary of Selected Research on the Uniqueness of Public Bureaucracies

Author(s)	Methodology	Findings and conclusions
A. *Positive and deductive theories of public bureaucracy and related social control processes*		
Banfield	Propositions about corruption in "typical" governmental agencies and "typical" business firms.	Governmental agencies have (a) greater fragmentation of authority and weaker requirements to avoid "selling" outputs below cost of production; (b) greater vagueness, multiplicity, and conflict among objectives and products; (c) stronger requirements to adhere to external laws and administrative procedures; and (d) less reliance on pecuniary incentives. Therefore, they spend more on reducing corruption than is gained in return and are less able to reduce corruption through strong central control.
Dahl and Lindblom	Theoretical analysis of societal decisions and allocation mechanisms.	"Agencies" under governmental control have more intangible goals, less incentive for cost reduction, more dysfunctions of bureaucracy (red tape, rigidity) than do "enterprises" controlled by markets.
Downs	Conceptual/theoretical model of bureaucracy.	Owing to the absence of the economic market, public bureaucracies tend toward more elaborate hierarchies. The political environment is more important and influences internal decisions. Agencies become rigid over time.
Wamsley and Zald	Conceptual/theoretical analysis of public organizations.	Public ownership and funding subject public organizations to unique political and economic environments and unique public expectations; for example, political sentiment toward the agency becomes more important.
B. *Organizational typologies and taxonomies that include a public–private distinction*		
Blau & Scott	Deductive typology.	Four-category typology of organizations: Commonweal, Business, Service, and Mutual Benefit. Commonweal organizations (public agencies) benefit the general public, and public accountability is the central organizational issue. Businesses benefit owners, and productivity is the central issue.

Table 4.1 *(continued)*

Author(s)	Methodology	Findings and conclusions
Haas, Hall, and Johnson	Empirically derived taxonomy.	Constructed nine taxonomic categories. Public and private organizations were mixed among categories, so the study did not support a public–private distinction.
Mintzberg	Typology of organizational structure based on review of research.	"Public-machine bureaucracies" are posited as one subcategory within "machine bureaucracies" because— owing to external constraints—public agencies tend toward highly bureaucratized form.
Pugh, Hickson, and Hinings	Empirical taxonomy of structural dimensions of fifty-two organizations in Great Britain, eight of which were governmental organizations.	Most of the public organizations were unexpectedly low on measures of internal structure, but high on concentration of authority at the top, with personnel procedures highly centralized or externally controlled. Noting that the governmental organizations were not typical governmental agencies but local "workflow" organizations, such as a water department, the researchers suggested that size and technological development determine internal structure, whereas concentration of authority is determined by government or other external auspices.

C. *Anecdotal observations by practitioners with experience in the public and the private sectors*

Blumenthal	Experienced practitioner's views on similarities and differences between public and business management.	Federal executives have less control over their organizations than executives. Federal organizations are more conglomerated and diverse. Congress and the press are more influential. The decision process is more cumbersome.

D. *Empirical research on public bureaucracy and public administrators*

Hood and Dunsire	Empirical taxonomy of British central governmental departments using archival data.	Arguing that public bureaucracies are a distinct set of organizations, the researchers developed a three-category empirical taxonomy of British central governmental departments.
Kaufman	Descriptive study of six federal bureau chiefs.	Much of bureau chiefs' work is generic management (motivating, communicating, decision making), but the political environment and congressional relations are highly significant.

Table 4.1 *(continued)*

Author(s)	Methodology	Findings and conclusions
Meyer	Empirical study of structural change using a national sample of state and local finance agencies.	Public bureaucracies are particularly open to external pressures for changes. Their hierarchies are stable, but there is frequent change in sub-unit composition. Their personnel systems are increasingly formalized over time due to federal emphasis on civil service rules. External pressures are mediated by political processes. Public bureaucracies have no alternative to Weberian hierarchy, and they are evaluated in terms of conformity with higher authority.
Warwick	Case study of U.S. Department of State.	Public organizations are heavily influenced by external political and institutional factors. They are prone to elaborate hierarchies and rules. Their internal structures are often imposed externally. They are resistant to change and to delegation of authority. Employees are security-conscious, especially in relation to potential political controversy.

E. *Empirical research comparing samples of public and private organizations and managers*

Author(s)	Methodology	Findings and conclusions
Boyatzis	Study of managerial competencies in four federal agencies and twelve Fortune 500 firms.	Private managers were higher on "goal-and-action" competencies. This is attributed to absence of such clear performance measures as profits and sales in the public sector. Private managers were also higher on leadership competencies of "conceptualization" and "use of oral presentations." This is attributed to more strategic decision making in the private sector and greater openness and standard procedures in the public sector.
Bretschneider	Survey of 1,005 computer and information-system managers in public and private organizations.	The public managers reported more interdependence from other organizations and more external accountability; more "red tape" (indicated by how long it takes for hiring, firing, creating positions, purchasing and contracting, and changing policy); less reliance on economic criteria in evaluating hardware and software; more formal planning processes that link the interdependent organizations and levels.

Table 4.1 *(continued)*

Author(s)	Methodology	Findings and conclusions
Buchanan	Compared questionnaire responses from managers in four "typical" federal agencies and four large business firms.	Public managers were lower on job satisfaction, job involvement, organizational commitment, and perceived organizational constraints and rules. Findings reflected weaker hierarchical authority, greater diversity of personnel, and weaker commitment expectations owing to civil service rules, political interventions, diffuse goals, and complex bureaucratic procedures.
Coursey and Bozeman	Survey of 210 upper managers in 39 public and private organizations concerning their perceptions of strategic decisions in their organizations	When asked to describe important strategic decisions, the managers identified types of decisions similar to those in the Hickson et al., study. Public managers were more likely to mention decisions about controls, services, and reorganization. Private managers more often identified decisions about technology, boundaries, and products. Managers in government-owned organizations reported higher levels of participation in decisions (number of persons involved, number of meetings); dimensions of publicness (degree of contact from governmental authorities) were even stronger predictors of participation. Public ownership and publicness did not, however, predict smoothness of decision processes.
Kilpatrick, Cummings, and Jennings	Survey of work-related values and attitudes at all levels in federal agencies and in business from 22 metropolitan sampling units. Include sample of 273 federal executives and 287 business executives.	Federal executives were comparable to business executives on job satisfaction, but federal scientists, engineers, and college graduates were lower than their private counterparts. Public sector respondents in all these groups were more favorably disposed to work in the other sector than were private respondents. There were conflicts between the public image of the federal service and the occupational values of highly educated, higher occupational status groups in the United States.
Lau, Pavett, and Newman	Compared U.S. Navy civilian executives to executives from a number of service and manufacturing firms.	Found general similarities in the work of the two types of managers, although the public managers devoted more time to "fire drills" and crisis management.

Table 4.1 *(continued)*

Author(s)	Methodology	Findings and conclusions
Mascarenhas	Analysis of financial data and characteristics of 187 state-owned, privately held, and publicly traded offshore oil drilling firms in many countries.	Form of ownership influenced the strategic domains of the firms. Publicly traded firms operated in more geographic markets and offered wider product lines. State-owned enterprises focused on domestic markets and had narrower product lines and a more stable customer base. Privately held firms also concentrated on domestic markets and had both narrow product lines and unstable customer bases.
Paine, Carroll, and Leete	Compared managers in one federal agency to managers in industry who were comparable in age and level.	Federal managers were lower on all thirteen items in Porter need satisfaction scale, with greatest difference on job security, autonomy, and self-actualization.
Rainey	Compared questionnaire responses from middle managers in four state agencies and a defense installation to those of middle managers in four private firms.	Public managers were lower on satisfaction with coworkers and promotion, relations of extrinsic rewards (pay, promotion, firing) to performance, perceived value of monetary incentives, and perceived organizational formalization (rules, channels). There were no differences on role conflict and ambiguity, task variability and analyzability, goal clarity, and self-reported motivation and job involvement.
Rhinehart, Barrel, Dewolfe, Griffin, and Spaner	Compared supervisory personnel in one federal agency to managers in a large sample from industry, with management level as a control variable.	Federal managers were lower on all thirteen items on Porter need satisfaction scale, especially on social and self-actualization need satisfaction. Among higher-level managers, federal managers were lower on autonomy and self-actualization. Results confirmed Paine et al.
Schwenk	Analysis of descriptions given by forty-two members of an executive MBA program of decision making in their organizations.	All the managers regarded conflict in decision making as unpleasant. Managers from for-profit organizations, however, perceived conflict as leading to confusion and low-quality decisions. Not-for-profit managers saw conflict as leading to more diagnosis and evaluation and higher-quality decisions; they reported more conflict during early stages of decision processes and more recycling from later stages back to earlier ones.

Table 4.1 *(continued)*

Author(s)	Methodology	Findings and conclusions
Smith and Nock	Comparison of results from 1976 General Social Survey of 1,499 adults by National Opinion Research Center and 1973 Quality-of-Employment Survey of 1,496 employed persons by Survey Research Center.	Blue-collar, public sector workers were more satisfied with most aspects of work than blue-collar, private sector workers. White-collar, public sector workers were much less satisfied with coworkers, supervision, and intrinsic aspects of work (interest, etc.).

F. *Empirical research comparing samples of public and private organizations in similar functional categories*

Chubb and Moe	Mail questionnaire survey of 11,000 principals and teachers in 450 public and private (Catholic, other private, and elite private) high schools.	Public school members perceived stronger influence by outside authorities, weaker parental involvement, more managerial and less professional orientations of principals, less emphasis on academic excellence, less clarity of goals and disciplinary policy, more formal constraints on personnel policy, weaker faculty influence on curriculum.
Savas	Review of numerous studies of private vs. public provision of services.	Reviews findings of greater cost-efficiency of private delivery systems for solid-waste collection, fire protection, transportation, health care, custodial services, landscaping, data processing, and legal aid. Comparisons of hospitals and utilities have been mixed and inconclusive.
Solomon	Compared 120 Israeli public sector top managers to 120 Israeli private sector top managers on questionnaire responses. Both samples were evenly divided between manufacturing and service organizations, and they represented a broad range of Israeli work organizations.	Private sector managers were much higher on perception that rewards were contingent on performance, that policies promoting efficiency were prevalent in their organizations, and on personal satisfaction with various dimensions of their work. On the latter two dimensions, differences between public and private service organizations were particularly strong.
Spann	Reviewed empirical studies of public vs. private provision of five types of services.	Private producers can provide airline, garbage collection, fire protection, and electric utility services at the same or lower costs than can public producers. Results for hospitals indicate little cost or quality difference.

Table 4.1 *(continued)*

Author(s)	Methodology	Findings and conclusions

G. *Organizational research in which the public–private distinction serves as a significant moderator*

Hickson, Butler, Cray, Mallory, and Wilson	Intensive longitudinal study of strategic decision processes in thirty public and private service and manufacturing organizations.	For both service and manufacturing organizations, public ownership increases tendency toward a "vortex-sporadic" mode of decision processes and the tendency toward higher levels of formal and informal interaction in strategic decisions. Both public/private ownership and purpose (service/manufacturing) showed important relations to decision processes.
Holdaway, Newberry, Hickson, and Heron	Analyzed structures of sixteen public and four private colleges in Canada, using procedures similar to Pugh et al.	Higher degrees of public control were related to higher levels of bureaucratic control (formalization, standardization of personnel procedures, centralization). The public colleges were higher than the private ones on degree of public control.
Kurke and Aldrich	Replication of Mintzberg study, observing four executives, including a school and a hospital executive, representing the public and the "quasi-public" sectors.	Mintzberg's findings were replicated and supported. Public managers spent much more time in contact with directors and outside groups. The school administrator spent much more time in formal activity (e.g., formal meetings).
Mintzberg	Observational study of five executives from a variety of organizations, including a hospital director and a superintendent of a large school system.	There were marked similarities in work roles of the five executives. The managers in public and "quasi-public" organizations—the school administrator and the hospital administrator, respectively—spent more time in contact with directors and external interest groups. The contacts were more structured and formalized (e.g., formal meetings), and the public administrators received more "status" requests.
Tolbert	Analysis of data on 167 public and 114 private colleges and universities from Higher Education General Information Survey.	For public colleges and universities, higher levels of private funding were related to existence of more administrative offices for private funding relations. For private colleges and universities, more public funding was related to more offices for public funding relations. The results support a combined institutionalization and resource dependence interpretation.

Source: Revised and expanded from James L. Perry and Hal G. Rainey, "The public–private Distinction in Organization Theory: A Critique and Research Strategy," *Academy of Management Review* 13 (April 1988): 182–201. Individual studies are cited in full in note 43.

Bozeman proposes that dimensions akin to ownership and funding be analyzed not as dichotomies but as continua.[48] He proposes that an organization can be classified according to its level of *publicness*, based on how much political and economic authority the organization has. Publicness, treated as a continuum, could then be related to properties of the organization. Bozeman and colleagues have reported research on governmental, business, and hybrid research-and-development laboratories showing that certain characteristics of the laboratories varied fairly consistently in relation to operationalizations of their publicness.[49] Somewhat similarly, Perry and Rainey propose that researchers employ a set of hybrid categories between the public and the private categories in designing research.[50]

Approaches to Analyzing the
Distinctiveness of Public Bureaucracies

Even pending the widespread use of such refinements in research designs, however, a substantial body of research pertaining to the distinctiveness of public bureaucracies now exists, as Table 4.1 illustrates. The table gives examples of a number of different forms of analysis and evidence on the topic. As described earlier, theoretical observations about public bureaucracies (section A of the table) have appeared for years, but these assertions about public bureaucracies have been countered by organizational theorists, such as those who work on organizational typologies and taxonomies. As the entries in section B of the table indicate, the organizational theorists did not find strong indications of all of the characteristics of public bureaucracies asserted by the economists and the political scientists. When the organizational theorists have mentioned public bureaucracies in their typologies, they have often treated them as a subcategory within broader categories.

On the other hand, other forms of evidence point to the distinctiveness of public bureaucracies. Section C contains the observations of a top executive who has served both in public and private bureaucracies about the distinctiveness of the public ones.[51] The testimony of such executives tends generally to corroborate the observations in the studies of public bureaucracies described earlier in this chapter and in section D of the table. Of course, executives' testimonials and general studies of public bureaucracies have some limitations as evidence. Other researchers have reported explicit comparisons of public and private organizations and sometimes of hybrid forms or additional categories. The table describes many examples and shows that researchers have adopted different approaches to the comparison.

As section E indicates, many researchers have compared samples of public and private organizations or managers.[52] So complex and varied are the public and the private categories that one has difficulty even conceiving of a fully representative sample of those categories. Some researchers have therefore employed samples of opportunity—including available sets of public and private organizations—or judgmental samples—including groups of public agencies and business firms asserted to be typical of those categories. Many early, exploratory studies of this type had limited samples and conducted fairly simplified public-versus-private comparisons without many persuasive controls for such important variables as organizational size and task. As the table shows, however, over time more and more studies report larger, more elaborate samples. Although the table does not show it, more recent studies have also employed better statistical designs and controls, providing more persuasive evidence of the distinctive aspects of public organizations.

Section F of the table provides examples of another alternative employed by researchers: the comparison of public and private forms of organization engaged in the same function or service. Some researchers conduct these comparisons to avoid confoundments caused by differences in organizational tasks and functions, arguing that the best way to assess public-versus-private differences is to compare similar organizations doing the same type of work in the two sectors. Other researchers perform these within-function comparisons out of interest in public policy questions about whether public and private organizations differ in their performance in service delivery. As indicated in section F, numerous studies now report public organizations to perform generally similar activities less efficiently than private organizations. Such differences do not always appear, however, especially in the cases of hospitals and utilities.

Direct comparisons of the overall effectiveness and innovativeness of public and private organizations are quite rare, probably owing to the difficulty of measuring many criteria of effectiveness other than efficiency. Critics of these studies who defend the public bureaucracy, including me, are quick to raise this point and to emphasize that even when public and private organizations perform the same general function, the public bureaucracies may face requirements to perform it differently, under more constraints, with more problematic clients.[53] Whatever the outcome of controversies such as this, the weight of the evidence supports the conclusion that many public organizations do face greater difficulty in performing as efficiently as comparable private ones. The research conducted thus far on this topic has created a strong base on which to develop additional research aimed at clarifying and resolving the points of controversy.

Areas of Accumulating Research and Evidence

In addition to the research on comparative efficiency, evidence on the distinctiveness of public bureaucracies has accumulated around certain of their dimensions. I shall briefly discuss below those concerning managerial roles, strategic decision processes, organizational structures, incentives, and work-related attitudes and values. Additional important streams of research cannot be covered here.[54] Sometimes—as the entries in Table 4.1 indicate—the evidence for the distinctiveness of public bureaucracies is slender, and many exceptions and contradictory findings exist.

Managerial Roles

In addition to the case studies described earlier and in section D of Table 4.1, and the testimonials of executives, a number of studies now show that, compared to their private sector counterparts, managers in governmental agencies experience more constraints, meetings, contacts, and interruptions from external political actors, groups, and oversight authorities. For example, see the entries in section E by Boyatzis, Bretschneider, Buchanan, and Lau et al. and those in sections F and G by Chubb and Moe, and Kurke and Aldrich, and Mintzberg.

Strategic Decision Processes

Similarly, researchers comparing major strategic decisions in public and private organizations find that the processes in public organizations focus on different types of decisions, employ different decision criteria, have different types of conflicts at different stages, and involve more interruptions and delays. For example, see the entries by Coursey and Bozeman and by Schwenk in section E, the Solomon entry in section F, and the Hickson et al. entry in section G.

Organizational Structure

In general, public organizations apparently do not show markedly higher levels on certain dimensions of organizational structuring, such as the pervasiveness of rules and procedures and the multiplicity of subunits, as suggested both by the cultural stereotype and the models of some positive theorists. Some studies find somewhat higher levels of rule orientation and formalization in public bureaucracies (see the Rainey entry in section E and the Holdaway et al. entry in section G), while others do not (see the Pugh et al. entry in section B). Other studies indicate particularly strong tendencies toward hierarchical structures in public bureaucracies (see the Meyer and the Warwick entries in section D).

Incentives and Incentive Structures

Public bureaucracies apparently do frequently differ from private ones on structural dimensions influenced by jurisdictionwide procedures and oversight bodies, such as civil service and procurement systems. A number of studies find that governmental bureaucracies tend to have more highly structured, externally imposed personnel procedures—apparently reflecting the effects of civil service systems—than private bureaucracies. See the Pugh et al. study in section B, the Meyer study in section D, the Chubb and Moe study in section F, and the

Holdaway et al. study in section G). In the United States and other countries, as compared to their private counterparts, public employees and managers consistently perceive greater structural constraints on the administration of such extrinsic incentives as pay, promotion, and disciplinary action. They also report that they perceive weaker relations between those types of incentives and individual performance. The Rainey study in section E and the Solomon study in section F are two among many studies on these matters.

Work-Related Values and Attitudes

Researchers also consistently find differences in the work-related values and attitudes of public and private managers and employees.[55] But the differences do not necessarily conform to the stereotypes and the potentially negative implications of the studies reported in the previous subsection. Many studies over the years have found that public employees tend to place a lower value on making a lot of money as an ultimate goal in work. They also tend to place a higher value on public and altruistic service. A variety of surveys have found that public employees report high levels of motivation and effort (see, for example, the Rainey study in section E).

Numerous surveys also report, however, that as compared to private employees and managers, public employees show somewhat more negative responses to questions about work-related attitudes. Public employees and managers report fairly high levels of general work satisfaction—at levels comparable to those of their private sector counterparts—but they have consistently reported somewhat lower levels of satisfaction with such specific facets of their work as autonomy and promotion policies. Some studies report somewhat less favorable responses from public employees on other measures of work-related attitudes, such as lower organizational commitment. See the entries in section E by Buchanan, Kilpatrick et al., Paine et al., Rainey, Rhinehart et al., and Smith and Nock, and the Solomon entry in section F.

Conclusion

Underlying all these streams of research are controversies and unresolved questions. In general, however, the body of research tends to support the arguments of the authors reviewed earlier concerning the general distinctiveness of public bureaucracies on many important dimensions. This research already provides useful evidence of some of the ways in which public ownership, political environments, and the absence of economic markets for the products and services of a bureaucracy can influence its organizational and managerial properties. Much additional work is needed to improve our understanding of these relations further, but the research reviewed here suggests the promising potential of such studies. The research suggests the potential for further developing a body of knowledge that relates important dimensions of political economy and institutional design, such as public or private ownership, to important properties and processes of organizations.

Notes

1. Charles Lindblom, *Politics and Markets* (New York: Basic Books, 1977).
2. Gibson Burrell and Gareth Morgan, *Sociological Paradigms and Organizational Analysis* (London: Heinemann, 1979), pp. 118–226.
3. Although contingency theory has become somewhat dated, it remains an important general perspective among organizational theorists. For an example of a recent text employing a contingency theory framework, as well as for additional description of the theory, see Richard Daft, *Organization Theory and Design*, 3d ed. (St. Paul, MN: West, 1989). One can also easily show that more recent streams of theoretical development in organizational theory—such as resource dependence, population ecology, transactions cost, and agency theory perspectives—tend to downplay the distinctiveness of public bureaucracies.
4. Peter Blau and Richard A. Schoenherr, *The Structure of Organizations* (New York: Basic Books, 1971).
5. For example, see Bill McKelvey, *Organizational Systematics* (Berkeley: University of California Press, 1982), p. 15.
6. This emphasis is one of the reasons why many political scientists refer to this body of work as the *bureaucratic politics* field. The emphasis is reflected in many books on the public bureaucracy, such as Kenneth J. Meier, *Politics and the Bureaucracy: Policymaking in the Fourth Branch of Government*, 2d ed. (Belmont, CA: Brooks/Cole, 1987); Francis E. Rourke, *Bureaucracy, Politics, and Public Policy*, 3d ed. (Boston: Little, Brown, 1984); Harold Seidman and Robert Gilmour, *Politics, Position, and Power*, 4th ed. (New York: Oxford University Press, 1986); and Peter Woll, *American Bureaucracy*, 2d ed. (New York: Norton, 1977).
7. The authors cited in footnote 6 devote some attention to internal structure and behavior, as do such books as Graham T. Allison, *Essence of Decision* (Boston: Little, Brown, 1971); Louis C. Gawthrop, *Bureaucratic Behavior in the Executive Branch: An Analysis of Organizational Change* (New York: Free Press, 1969); Michael Lipsky, *Street-Level Bureaucracy* (New York: Russell Sage, 1980); B. Guy Peters, *The Politics of Bureaucracy*, 3d ed. (New York: Longman, 1989); and Charles Goodsell, *The Case for Bureaucracy*, 2d ed. (Chatham, NJ: Chatham House, 1985). More recent books on public bureaucracy, such as James W. Fesler and Donald F. Kettl, *The Politics of the Administrative Process* (Chatham, NJ: Chatham House, 1991), and James Q. Wilson, *Bureaucracy: What Government Agencies Do and Why They Do It* (New York: Basic Books, 1989), often show more attention to internal management and organization; they were published, obviously, after the books summarized in this chapter and appear to reflect a continuation of the trend represented by those books.
8. Exceptions include the studies reported in Randall B. Ripley and Grace A. Franklin, eds., *Policy-Making in the Federal Executive Branch* (New York: Free Press, 1975), and a number of individual studies, such as John L. Foster and Judson H. Jones, "Rule Orientation and Bureaucratic Reform," *American Journal of Political Science* 22 (May 1978): 348–63. In spite of numerous exceptions, empirical studies are much less frequent in the bureaucratic-politics literature than in the organizational theory and organizational behavior literature.
9. Robert A. Dahl and Charles E. Lindblom, *Politics, Economics, and Welfare* (New York: Harper, 1953).

10. Ibid., 453–72.

11. Anthony Downs, *Inside Bureaucracy* (Boston: Little, Brown, 1967).

12. Ibid., p. 52.

13. Ibid., p. 59.

14. Ibid., pp. 145–46.

15. Ibid., ch. 9 and 12.

16. Ibid., pp. 4, 212.

17. Donald P. Warwick, *A Theory of Public Bureaucracy: Politics, Personality, and Organization in the State Department* (Cambridge, MA: Harvard University Press, 1975).

18. Ibid., pp. 8, 59, 188–91.

19. Since then, organizational theorists have paid more attention to external institutional contexts of organizations. See W. Richard Scott, "The Adolescence of Institutional Theory," *Administrative Science Quarterly* 32 (December 1987): 493–511.

20. Warwick, *Theory of Public Bureaucracy*, pp. 73–80, 162.

21. Ibid., pp. 69, 176.

22. Ibid., p. 79. Similar observations appear in Downs, *Inside Bureaucracy*, and in Gawthrop, *Bureaucratic Behavior*.

23. Warwick, *Theory of Public Bureaucracy*, p. 172.

24. Marshall W. Meyer, *Change in Public Bureaucracies* (London: Cambridge University Press, 1979).

25. Ibid., ch. 3–6.

26. Ibid., pp. 14, 21.

27. Ibid., p. 5.

28. Ibid., p. 192.

29. Ibid., p. 130.

30. Allen H. Barton, "A Diagnosis of Bureaucratic Maladies," in *Making Bureaucracies Work*, ed. Carol Weiss and Allen H. Barton (Beverly Hills, CA: Sage, 1980), pp. 27–36.

31. For example, see various entries in James L. Perry and Kenneth L. Kraemer, eds., *Public Management* (Palo Alto, CA: Mayfield, 1983), especially Graham T. Allison, "Public and Private Management: Are They Fundamentally Alike in All Unimportant Respects," pp. 72–93.

32. Laurence E. Lynn, *Managing the Public's Business* (New York: Basic Books, 1981).

33. Ibid., pp. 5, 12, 3.

34. Ibid., pp. 35, 72. The observation about inevitable bureaucracy resembles observations made by Warwick and by Meyer.

35. Herbert Kaufman, *The Administrative Behavior of Federal Bureau Chiefs* (Washington, DC: Brookings Institution, 1981).

36. D.C. Pitt and B.C. Smith, *Government Departments: An Organizational Perspective* (London: Routledge and Kegan Paul, 1981).

37. Ibid., pp. 9, 24, 79.

38. Christopher Hood and Andrew Dunsire, *Bureaumetrics: The Quantitative Comparison of British Central Government Agencies* (University: University of Alabama Press, 1981), pp. 5, 21.

39. Ibid., pp. 116, 21, 88, 109.

40. See, for example, Wilson, *Bureaucracy*.

41. See, for example, Seymour Martin Lipset and William Schneider, *The Confidence Gap: Business, Labor, and Government in the Public Mind*, 2d ed. (Baltimore: Johns Hopkins University Press, 1987), p. 288.

42. For example, see J.E. Haas, R.H. Hall, and N.J. Johnson, "Toward an Empirically

Derived Taxonomy of Organizations," in *Studies on Behavior in Organizations*, ed. R.V. Bowers (Athens: University of Georgia Press, 1957), pp. 157–80.
43. More comprehensive reviews of this research are provided in James L. Perry and Hal G. Rainey, "The Public–Private Distinction in Organization Theory: A Critique and Research Strategy," *Academy of Management Review* 13 (April 1988): 182–201; Hal G. Rainey, "Public Management: Recent Research on the Political Context and Managerial Roles, Structures, and Behaviors," *Journal of Management: Yearly Review of Management* 15 (June 1989): 229–50; and Hal G. Rainey, *Understanding and Managing Public Organizations* (San Francisco: Jossey-Bass, 1991). The references mentioned in Table 4.1 follow, arranged by section:

Section A. Edwin Banfield, "Corruption as a Feature of Governmental Organization," *Journal of Law and Economics* 18 (December 1975): 587–605; Dahl and Lindblom, *Politics, Economics, and Welfare*, pp. 453–42; Downs, *Inside Bureaucracy*, passim; Gary L. Wamsley and Mayer N. Zald, *The Political Economy of Public Organizations* (Lexington, MA: Lexington Books, 1973), passim.

Section B. Peter M. Blau and W. Richard Scott, *Formal Organizations* (San Francisco: Chandler, 1962); Haas, et al., "Toward an Empirically Derived Taxonomy of Organizations"; Henry Mintzberg, *The Structuring of Organizations* (Englewood Cliffs, NJ: Prentice-Hall, 1979); Derek S. Pugh, David J. Hickson, and C.J. Hinings, "An Empirical Taxonomy of Work Organizations," *Administrative Science Quarterly* 14 (March 1969): 115–26.

Section C. W. Michael Blumenthal, "Candid Reflections of A Businessman in Washington," in Perry and Kraemer, eds., *Public Management*, pp. 22–33.

Section D. Hood and Dunsire, *Bureaumetrics*; Kaufman, *Administrative Behavior*, passim; Meyer, *Change in Public Bureaucracies*, passim; Warwick, *Theory of Public Bureaucracy*, passim.

Section E. Richard E. Boyatzis, *The Competent Manager* (New York: Wiley, 1982); Stuart Bretschneider, "Management Information Systems in Public and Private Organizations: An Empirical Test," *Public Administration Review* 50 (September/October 1990): 536–45; Bruce Buchanan, "Government Managers, Business Executives, and Organizational Commitment," *Public Administration Review* 35 (July/August 1974): 339–47; and "Red Tape and the Service Ethic: Some Unexpected Differences Between Public and Private Managers," *Administration and Society* 6 (February 1975): 423–38; David Coursey and Barry Bozeman, "Decision Making in Public and Private Organizations: A Test of Alternative Conceptions of 'Publicness,' " *Public Administration Review* 50 (September/October 1990): 525–35; Franklin P. Kilpatrick, Milton C. Cummings, and M. Kent Jennings, *The Image of the Federal Service* (Washington, DC: Brookings Institution, 1964); Alan W. Lau, Cynthia M. Pavett, and Arthur R. Newman, "The Nature of Managerial Work: A Comparison of Public and Private Sector Jobs," *Academy of Management Proceedings* (1980): 339–43; Briance Mascarenhas, "Domains of State-owned, Privately Held, and Publicly Traded Firms in International Competition," *Administrative Science Quarterly* 34 (December 1989): 582–97; F.T. Paine, S.J. Carroll, and B.A. Leete, "Need Satisfaction of Managerial Level Personnel in a Governmental Agency," *Journal of Applied Psychology* 50 (June 1966): 247–49; Hal G. Rainey, "Perception of Incentives in Business and Government: Implications for Civil Service Reform," *Public Administration Review* 39 (September/October 1979): 440–48; and "Public Agencies and Private Firms: Incentive Structures, Goals, and Individual Roles," *Administration and Society* 15 (August 1983): 207–42; J.B. Rhinehart, R.P. Barrel, A.S. Dewolfe, J.E. Griffin, and F.E. Spaner, "Comparative Study of Need Satisfaction in Governmental and Business Hierarchies," *Journal of Applied Psychology* 53 (June 1969): 230–35; Charles R. Schwenk, "Conflict in Organizational Decision-Making: An Exploratory Study of Its Effects in

For-Profit and Not-for-Profit Organizations," *Management Science* 36 (April 1990): 436–48; M.P. Smith and S.L. Nock, "Social Class and the Quality of Life in Public and Private Organizations," *Journal of Social Issues* 36 (Spring 1980): 59–75.
    Section F. John E. Chubb and Terry M. Moe, "Politics, Markets, and the Organization of Schools," *American Political Science Review* 82 (December 1988): 1065–88; E.S. Savas, *Privatization* (Chatham, NJ: Chatham House, 1982); Esther E. Solomon, "Private and Public Sector Managers: An Empirical Investigation of Job Characteristics and Organizational Climate," *Journal of Applied Psychology* 71 (May 1986): 247–59; R.M. Spann, "Public versus Private Provision of Government Services," in *Budgets and Bureaucrats: The Sources of Government Growth*, ed. T.E. Borcherding (Durham, NC: Duke University Press, 1977), pp. 71–89.
    Section G. D.J. Hickson, R.J. Butler, D. Cray, G.R. Mallory, and D.C. Wilson, *Top Decisions: Strategic Decision-Making in Organizations* (San Francisco: Jossey-Bass, 1986); E. Holdaway, J.F. Newberry, D.J. Hickson, and R.P Heron, "Dimensions of Organizations in Complex Societies: The Educational Sector," *Administrative Science Quarterly* 20 (March 1975): 37–58; L.E. Kurke and H.E. Aldrich, "Mintzberg Was Right! A Replication and Extension of 'The Nature of Managerial Work,' " *Management Science* 29 (August 1983): 975–84; Henry Mintzberg, *The Nature of Managerial Work* (New York: Harper and Row, 1972); Pamela S. Tolbert, "Resource Dependence and Institutional Environments: Sources of Administrative Structure in Institutions of Higher Education," *Administrative Science Quarterly* 30 (March 1985): 1–13.
    44. Mascarenhas, "Domains of Firms."
    45. Barry Bozeman, *All Organizations Are Public* (San Francisco: Jossey-Bass, 1987), ch. 3; Perry and Rainey, "The Public-Private Distinction," p. 184.
    46. Dahl and Lindblom, *Politics, Economics, and Welfare.*
    47. Wamsley and Zald, *Political Economy of Public Organizations*, p. 10.
    48. Bozeman, *All Organizations Are Public*, ch. 4 and 5.
    49. Michael M. Crow and Barry Bozeman, "R&D Laboratory Classification and Public Policy: The Effects of Environmental Context on Laboratory Behavior," *Research Policy* 16 (October 1987): 229–58; Mark A. Emmert and Michael M. Crow, "Public, Private, and Hybrid Organizations: An Empirical Examination of Publicness," *Administration and Society* 20 (August 1988): 216–44.
    50. Perry and Rainey, "The Public–Private Distinction," p. 196. Researchers using more than two categories to represent the public–private continuum typically find that the additional categories show meaningful differences from the simple public and private ones. In addition to the studies in footnote 49, see F.R. Dobbin, L. Edelman, J.R. Meyer, W.R. Scott, and A. Swidler, "The Expansion of Due Process in Organizations," in *Institutional Patterns and Organizations*, ed. L.G. Zucker (Cambridge, MA: Ballinger, 1988); David Coursey and Hal G. Rainey, "Perceptions of Personnel System Constraints in Public, Private, and Hybrid Organizations," *Review of Public Personnel Administration* 10 (Spring 1990): 54–71; and Mascarenhas, "Domains of Firms," p. 591.
    51. See additional examples in Perry and Kraemer, eds., *Public Management.*
    52. Section G of Table 4.1 contains examples that illustrate approaches similar to those in sections E and F. Section G is separated from E and F to emphasize that some organizational researchers not pursuing direct public-versus-private comparisons have nevertheless found the distinction useful in analyzing important organizational dimensions.
    53. I elaborate these arguments in Rainey, *Understanding and Managing Public Organizations*. See also George W. Downs and Patrick Larkey, *The Search for Government Efficiency* (New York: Random House, 1986); and Steven Kelman, "The Grace Commission: How Much Waste in Government?" *The Public Interest* 78 (Winter 1985): 62–

82. After reviewing the limited evidence on innovativeness in the public and the private sectors, David Roessner concluded that there was no strong evidence that public sector organizations show less innovativeness than private organizations. See J. David Roessner, "Incentives to Innovate in Public and Private Organizations," in Perry and Kraemer, eds., *Public Management*, pp. 353–67.

54. Further discussion and references concerning these streams of research and additional ones are summarized in Rainey, "Public Management," and in Rainey, *Understanding and Managing Public Organizations*, where I also discuss research controversies and needs in more detail.

55. Rainey, *Understanding and Managing Public Organizations*, chapter 7, provides additional references supporting the points made in this subsection.

5

Bureaucracy, Power, Policy, and the State

Bert A. Rockman

The words "bureaucracy," "power," "policy," and the "state"—especially when used in combination—conjure up "big issues." These concepts are attractive entries in the lexicon of political science, since they encompass much that is important about political systems. Although each concept is attractive, controversy surrounds the definition of each. When the concepts are used in combination, the controversy is compounded. Perhaps a part of the attraction of the terms is a function of the "big" but vaguely articulated issues they address, that is, who really governs? In this chapter, I shall appraise these concepts from organizational, personnel, and systemic perspectives.

My initial step is to discuss briefly the first three of these concepts. I shall not provide an exhaustive analysis of each term, or provide a comprehensive survey of the literature on each, or even operationalize a specific definition. Instead, I shall discuss them from the perspective of their relationship with each other.

My second step is to treat the final concept in the list, the state. Through connecting the three aforementioned concepts, I shall set forth alternative perspectives about the relationship of the state bureaucracy to the state itself. This matter will be pursued from the standpoint of who controls, and is supposed to control, whom—as well as how, and whether, one can distinguish the state bureaucracy from the state.

Subsequent steps require distinguishing among units of analysis—between, for example, the level of the organization and that of personnel. What, on the one hand, is the relationship between bureaucratic structure and power? And what is the link between administrative officialdom and power?

A last, but most important, step is again to relate the administrative system to the state by sketching various images of the role of bureaucratic power within the state.

Bureaucracy, Power, and Policy

Bureaucracy

One basic complication in discussing the relationship between bureaucracy and power is that, both for the general public and for professional students of public administration, the word "bureaucracy" is a shorthand term for the executive organs of government. Yet, strictly speaking, bureaucracy encompasses more than that, and also less than that, since bureaucracy is but a subsector of the executive. According to shorthand usage, the term bureaucracy is frequently discussed from three main perspectives.

The first perspective views bureaucracy as a generic organizational form. Defined in the Weberian sense, bureaucracies are both public and private. To organizational sociologists, industrial psychologists, and other students of bureaucratic forms, the public/private distinction is to bureaucracy what the bear/raccoon distinction is to the animal kingdom. The bureaucratic nature of bureaucratic organization is its feature of defining relevance.[1] The organizational sociology, or micro perspective, tells us that it is organizational form, not legal proprietorship, that really matters. The "bureaucratic pathology" school, for instance, makes no distinction between public and private: according to this school, whether in the foreign office or the corporate office, bureaucracy stands as the enemy of revolutionary and egalitarian passions.

From the second perspective, bureaucracy is simply the public administrative agencies; we often use the word bureaucracy to refer to any part of the realm of the state administration. Yet this realm has become less clearly charted in recent times. Just as postindustrial economies produce an increased proportion of service jobs to production jobs, so postindustrial governments may be producing an increase in staff functions in proportion to line functions. These new forms of organization can be found in line departments, but they are especially likely to be located very close to political power. That is, they are often staff organs of central governmental institutions at the apex of government; in the United States they also may be agents of Congress. In traditional senses, they are not administrative. The staff shops that abound in the Executive Office of the President, for example, are there largely to circumvent or coordinate or monitor the line departments. As Heclo's analysis of the Office of Management and Budget indicates, some of these shops began as small organizations possessing professionalism and technical expertise, which are normally associated with bureaucracies in the Weberian mold.[2] Although the staffs of these agencies usually consist mainly of civil servants (especially outside the United States), they—as Campbell and

Szablowski note—are often different from the officials who staff the line departments; for example, in Canada, at least, the former are younger and more political than the latter. In addition, such agencies are said to lack a clear accountability to legislative authority.[3]

One can focus on *bureaucracy* defined as public (or state) administration in a number of ways, but the issues of coordination, control, and autonomy—which are at the heart of policy making and implementation—seem to be of special importance. From this vantage point, the bureaucracy (as a singular noun) seems often to be only a convenient fiction, for "the bureaucracy" dissolves rapidly into "bureaus" that interact with one another and with other actors.

From the third perspective, the bureaucracy is the personnel who are the permanent government—the servants of the state. This set of people may be looked at in a variety of ways. Deciding whether one should look only at executives or at all employees is important; here attention is given mostly to the former (the administrative elite), and only a brief glance is given to the legions of ordinary civil servants.

At the lower levels of officialdom, power frequently is exercised at the point where the state meets its citizens; certainly, the norms of the mass of officialdom are consequential for the legitimacy and the performance of the state.

Yet it is at the upper reaches of officialdom—the administrative elite—that the most important questions about who really runs things are raised. Among the concerns are issues of the administrative elite's social homogeneity or representativeness, of the elite's values and norms, of the elite's career paths, of the elite's ability to control the pathways to its own status and to other elite channels, and ultimately of the elite's ability to exert power over policy.

Power and Policy

The link between the administrative elite and policy deserves further consideration. Ezra Suleiman's brilliant first book-length analysis of the French *grands corps, Politics, Power, and Bureaucracy in France: The Administrative Elite,*[4] is divided into structural (sociological) and behavioral (political) components. According to a structural analysis, the administrative elite in France has strategic power over the passageways to key institutions and sufficient social and normative homogeneity to constitute a strategic elite in French society. Yet, according to a behavioral analysis, when Suleiman explores actual cases of policy making, the administrative elite's alleged homogeneity begins to dissolve; at an operational level, the elite is not imbued with a uniform definition of the public interest. This division is further elucidated in Suleiman's subsequent book, *Elites in French Society: The Politics of Survival,* wherein the "power" of the French administrative elite seems devoted less to some unified conception of proper policy than to a clear-eyed conception of group self-interest.[5] In other words, as a broad collective entity, bureaucrats rarely are united. Their differences of preference often are based upon the differences of mission represented by the organizations to which they belong.[6]

Viewed in the most microscopic form, decisions seem to be heavily influenced by a confluence of events, participants, and agendas—the so-called garbage can model.[7] Seen through these lenses, diversity is rampant and decision making is markedly fluid. Viewed through a lens with a wider angle, however, the issue is not what the decision is, but rather who gets to decide. To deal with this question, the structural (macroscopic) vantage point can be more useful to analyzing the power of bureaucracy in policy making.

To be sure, no modern state can function without a bureaucracy—which may well be the quintessence of the modern state. It is equally hard to imagine policy being made either in the implementation or the formulation phases without being influenced by bureaucrats and administrative agencies. Thus, the question arises, what is the relationship between the bureaucracy of the state and the authority of the state itself?

Bureaucracy and the State

Dependent upon its bureaucratic apparatus, a key issue for the modern state is whether those who putatively serve it (its functionaries, civil servants, bureaucrats) are in reality its masters. To some, the answer is apparent: public bureaucracies not only govern complex modern societies but have gained a predominant influence over the evolution of policy agendas.[8] According to this rationale, one studies bureaucracies and bureaucrats because they have a great deal of power over how public policy is shaped, a view that is shared in general, if not in all particulars, by elite theorists such as C. Wright Mills.[9]

By implication, of course, the question as to whether bureaucracies and their bureaucrats dominate or serve the state revolves around another question: Does the bureaucracy, in toto or in its parts, have an interest separate from the state itself? In real terms, does the bureaucracy define state interests and promote itself as the embodiment of these interests,[10] or does the bureaucracy faithfully follow directions provided by whatever authority is constituted to do so—whether that authority is the central committee of a ruling communist party, the cabinet of a parliamentary system, or the numerous claimants of authority in the American separation-of-powers system? The issue of bureaucratic autonomy and interest is especially poignant in systems that are organized as political democracies, but— as Trotsky and Mao feared—it is hardly confined to them.

One of the most central problems in analyzing the role of the bureaucracy in relation to the state lies in defining the state and determining who may legitimately speak for it. As slippery as this issue is, it is no doubt easier to define the legal authority of the state (who authoritatively acts in whose name?) than it is to locate responsibility for its behavior (who really ordered whom to do what?) or to arrive at satisfactory theories of the public interest. On the legal side, bureaucrats nowhere are constituted to exercise the authority of the state in the absence of the political direction contained in laws and rules, but they must frequently act without clear guidance. Broad constitutional theories of authority (e.g., party government) tend to be so all-encompassing as to be operationally irrelevant.[11] No matter who has ultimate constitutional authority, the inevitability of delegation necessarily gives some autonomy to the bureaucracy to exercise state power, which bureaucracy's permanence, specialization, and expertise allow it to cultivate further.

Providing a satisfactory empirical theory of the relation between the bureaucracy and the state is also problematic because the concept of the state is nebulous. Which of the following are included: the constituted political authorities, the permanent officials of the state and the bureaucratic apparatus, the dominant social classes or groups who shape the parameters of state action? Whereas constitutional theory specifies who is to act on whose account (that is, it specifies a hierarchical flow of authority), any analysis of the empirical relation between bureaucracy and the state must account for multiply directed flows of influence and segmented structures of authority. This complicates matters immeasurably, for we are used to employing such singular constructions in our parlance as "the state," "the bureaucracy," and even such connecting verbs as "serves" or "masters" or "is." These constructions produce sentences such as "The bureaucracy serves/masters/is the state."

These empirical-conceptual problems are partially the result of even deeper normative ones regarding the relationship between the bureaucracy and the state. Who is best positioned to define the state interest or the public interest? This immensely complicated question can be approached from several perspectives. Five perspectives are distinguished below: the Marxist; the idealist; the organic; the political; and the functional.

1. Strictly speaking, there is no *Marxist* perspective on state interest because the state is not conceived of as legitimately having autonomy. If bureaucrats serve the state, the state itself expresses principally the interest of its dominant social class. Although there is ample debate among Marxists themselves on the question of state autonomy, the conception of the state as an expression ultimately of class interest implies that only class interests, not a public or state interest, exist.[12]

2. The *idealist* perspective (a label given by Glendon Schubert) places great faith in the wisdom and internalized constraints of bureaucrats.[13] "The public interest" is assumed to be in their sights. Given sufficient discretion, it is assumed that their professionalism, trained judgment, expertise, and, especially, their role as "disinterested" servants of the state above the partisan interests and the interest-group struggles of the moment will lead to decisions that consider the long-run interests of the collectivity. The key assumption is that bureaucrats truly represent the interests of the state and are positioned literally and by their professional qualities to see and act on those interests. This perspective obvi-

ously assumes that the state does, in fact, represent the real and long-term interests of the society.

3. The latter assumption fits well with the *organic* perspective from which the notion is derived that the bureaucracy is the concrete manifestation of the state and the upholder of its legitimacy.[14] In nearly all important respects, by manifesting state authority the bureaucracy also manifests the interests of the state, and from this perspective, state interests advance the real interests of the society. To be sure, when "bureaucracy" is used in this context, what is really meant is not the bureaucracy in its particularized form—not bureaus or agencies or programs—but the bureaucracy as an institutional apparatus that provides for the coherent, centralized exercise of authority. In other words, the ability of the state to assert its own interests and not be a mere impartial regulator of the interests of others is emphasized. This view, intriguingly, is congruent with the growth and increased role of high-level central officials who coordinate and monitor the work of the ministries.[15] In Canada, Campbell and Szablowski call these officials "superbureaucrats." The principal role of the superagencies and the superbureaucrats is to ensure that the work of the departments, as well as their budgetary requests, is in accord with central priorities. To whom the superbureaucrats ultimately are responsible is not clear, however. Are they really agents of the state or merely of its present governors? If they are hybrids of a sort, is the dominant strain "political" or "civil servant"?[16] To the extent that their function is to oversee the fulfillment by the line departments of the priorities of central decision makers, strengthening the center also strengthens central political control, and thus the grip of politicians.[17]

4. According to the *political* perspective, the laws should be tightly written, their implementation should be scrutinized by the legislature, and the elected officials—their authority legitimated at the ballot box—should expect the bureaucracy to be responsive to the politicians' goals.[18] In other words, administrative discretion should be severely limited. In this model, precisely where political responsibility over administration should be located varies in accordance with both institutions and norms. The complexity of the channels of political responsibility in any system inhibits straight-out control, and the relative complexity or simplicity of these channels is evidenced by the communications patterns of the bureaucrats themselves.[19] Thus, even if it were possible to assume that more or less precise control over the bureaucracy could be accomplished by politicians, which politicians these would be—individual ministers, cabinet committees, prime ministers, or legislators—is an open question. Because the structure of political organization influences the structure of administrative organization (a matter that is explored below), there is no guarantee that political dominance strengthens the center against particalization.[20] Regardless of the mechanism of control, however, the political model stipulates that bureaucrats should be given only limited delegations of authority by elected officials and should be continuously supervised by them. Civil servants are to be smart and efficient "tools" of

the government of the day. Of course, owing obedience both to the government of the day and to tight laws limiting discretion may mean that civil servants are pulled in contradictory directions.[21]

5. Finally, the *functional* perspective develops the notion that the public interest results from an amalgam both of the effectiveness and knowledge of the administrative elite and of the representativeness and responsiveness of the political elite.[22] To the arts of government, bureaucrats and politicians are thought to bring distinctive skills and propensities—and equally distinctive blindspots. How to meld these diverse skills and propensities to achieve both an effective and a responsive state is at the core of this perspective. While no formulas for achieving this blissful state of affairs are immediately apparent, bureaucrats are perceived to be *one* (but not the only) important actor in the theater of government. The mechanisms through which they are linked to politicians and other important actors may be particularly relevant to how their skills are utilized in policy making.

Who should, and who does, have the power to make policy? The rise of the administrative state and of democratic polities makes these questions especially salient. The difficulty created by the rise of public bureaucracy as an agent in policy making often has been stated in terms of its mastery of, or servility to, the state. In the section above, three dimensions are suggested that help to define the nature of the problem: (1) the constitutional or legal definition (to whom is the bureaucracy formally accountable?); (2) the empirical definition (who influences whom, how, and in what ways?); and (3) the normative definition (does the bureaucracy guard or usurp the public interest?).

Normative theories are the most difficult to arrive at other than in an *ex cathedra* style because they rest ultimately on a satisfactory theory of the public interest, or at least on a theory of the responsibilities of the state as a corporate enterprise. A constitutional theory of the administrative role presumably derives from a normative theory of how the public interest is best arranged, the answer to the latter in democratic systems being universally through elected officials. Empirical theories of the role of bureaucracy and bureaucrats are dependent upon conceptual clarity. For example: what does bureaucratic autonomy mean? Precisely how is influence or dominance over agendas exercised? In what ways may the state be said to be separate from its bureaucracy, if at all? What, indeed, is policy? Most important, perhaps, to what extent is bureaucracy an "it," as distinct from a catch-all concept that houses a diverse and often internally conflictual set of entities, motives, and interests? If the answer to the last question is the complex one suggested by the second option, then—assuming that we wish to move beyond such concerns as salaries and pensions—using language that posits "the bureaucracy" as an undifferentiated interest seems overly simplistic.

In the next two sections, I treat the question of power first in terms of the level of the organization and then in terms of the level of individuals. Put in slightly different language, the first unit of analysis is that of bureaucratic form, the second that of bureaucrats. Following this, I shall present an appraisal of models of the state and the role of the administrative system in it.

Bureaucratic Organization and the Pathologies of Power

Bureaucratic organization, Max Weber argued, was the most technically efficient form of organization; this is an assertion that, to say the least, many find problematic. Indeed, for every characteristic that Weber identified as an element of the bureaucratic form, it is possible to identify an equal number of pathologies. Limited and fixed jurisdiction, for example, can mean tunnel vision and obsession with turf. Hierarchical authority can mean obsequious behavior, communications and information distortions, and a loss of imagination and innovation. Knowledge of the files also can mean routine and living by the book. Continuity may imply uncontrollability and a penchant for the comforts of the familiar. And, of course, full-time administrative officialdom, by virtue of its expertise, mastery of detail, and permanence, raises the spectre of its rulership.

Post-Weberian theories of complex organization tend to emphasize the downside of the Weberian characteristics ascribed to the bureaucratic form of complex organization. Victor Thompson summed up these negative aspects of the Weberian theory with the term "bureaupathology"—a condition resulting from the interplay of Weberian organizational attributes and "the need to control" that is inherently embodied in the hierarchy principle.[23] The implication of this kind of analysis, which is at the heart of organizational management theory, is that more effective organizations result in some measure from more felicitous organizational forms. Empirical research on the effects of variations in organizational form, however, tends to produce complicated, conditional, multivariate findings.[24]

Because it is microanalytic, the literature on organizational analysis was frequently ignored by political scientists until relatively recently. Many students of public administration, a field chiefly concerned with such issues as the political environment of public agencies and with personnel matters, also ignored this literature. Possibly, political scientists assumed that no broader issues emerged from looking at theories of organizational effectiveness. In addition, the complexity of the literature in this field is likely to discourage nearly all but the most focused students.

Yet organizational theories are also theories of human nature. Are we, for instance, attentive or inattentive creatures, perfecting or satisfying ones, programmable machines or social beings? Furthermore, these theories are laden with assumptions about power, and also with what it is that produces or motivates effective behavior. And what produces or motivates effective behavior certainly may have a bearing on policy—the uses of intelligence in decision making, for example.

Below I examine further the relationship between bureaucratic form, power, and policy, from two perspectives. The first, or internal, perspective looks at the impact of bureaucratic form on internal organizational processes—particularly on the wielding of organizational power—and then at the link to policy making via the effects of these processes on organizational decision making. The second, or external, perspective examines the impact of bureaucratic forms on clientele transactions, that is, how the bureaucracy deals with the public.

Internal Perspectives

Hierarchy and Decision Making

"If," writes Harold Wilensky, "an organization has many ranks and if in its administrative style and symbolism it emphasizes rank, the greatest distortion and blockage will attend the upward flow of communication."[25] Thus, Wilensky states a central difficulty of hierarchical organizations in processing information. Problem identification at the bottom rarely is able to be filtered to the top in an undistorted way. And while problems at the top command attention, they are frequently not formulated in a manner that accords with the task structures below.

The problem of obtaining adequate intelligence at the top is a function of numerous things: interest, sorting, problem definitions, and attention. Many of these are related to the characteristics of organizational leadership; some (such as the limits of attention) may be associated with ordinary human frailties. Among the causes of information distortion is the hierarchical chain of command associated with the bureaucratic form. Another type of distortion, discussed below, stems from a different feature of bureaucratic organization: segmented and competitive units.

Accurate intelligence, according to Richard Neustadt, is a presidential power lever. Because opaqueness is the essence of formal organization, to gain accurate intelligence presidents must dip directly into organizational intelligence sources.[26] This tactic, which is particularly identified with Franklin Roosevelt, was favored by Lyndon Johnson as well. Neustadt's prescription in its essence was to keep subordinates insecure. Yet insecurity below may well breed distortions in intelligence as information travels upward through an organization. Moreover, presidents can add to those distortions unless they are careful not to make their preferences known. Despite these prescriptive concerns, the assumption that presidents or other organizational leaders strive to maximize information is often unwarranted. For if they have a need to know, they may also have a need not to know—as exemplified by the Iran-Contra affair—in order to evade responsibility.

In crisis, small-group decisional processes have been employed to bring information immediately to the surface, and to debate it.[27] The famous EXCOM of the Cuban Missile Crisis stands out as such an informal organization—one that seemingly engaged in debate about the meaning of information and the implications of alternative choices, in large part because the preferences of the president were not clearly indicated. In noncrisis circumstances, Porter's analysis of the functioning of the Economic Policy Board under President Ford and Thayer's analysis of the National Security Council under Presidents Truman and Eisenhower stress the nonhierarchical and nonbureaucratic natures of these bodies and the presumably beneficial impacts of open discussion and cooperation.[28] On the other hand, Irving Janis detects across a number of cases of "committee" decision making a drive toward consensual thinking that is often risk-avoiding in decisional style, yet incautious and risk-bearing in result.[29]

A common denominator in information distortion that pertains both to small groups and bureaucratic processes is found whenever the strongly held preferences of those with responsibility for taking the decisions are known. If preferences are guarded, distortions in information seeking based on the known predispositions of top officials might be limited. If organizational leaders tend not to commit themselves, however, this may aggravate the tendency for subordinates to communicate only the face of the problem under consideration or only the information that bolsters their case. In other words, the exercise of hierarchical authority often causes information flowing upward to be distorted, whereas withholding information about leaders' preferences might alleviate such distortion. But the absence of strongly stated preferences also may encourage bureaucratic players to advocate their case even more strongly.

Unquestionably, information is a form of power, but, like electricity, it grows weaker the farther it travels. This is a problem for all forms of organization. The longer the distance, the more austerity there is to information and the more potential biases attach to it, whatever its direction. The most frequently examined aspect of informational biases in bureaucratic organization is that of communicating upward across sectors and statuses within the bureaucracy. In this sense, hierarchy distorts because communications traveling upward are liable to contain information consistent with what the subordinates believe the organizational elites want to hear; the more links in the chain, the more "delusions" may be passed on.

No doubt, good policy depends on accurate and nuanced information, and the assumptions about bureaucracy are that hierarchical authority shapes the information flow and distorts it at each link, thus producing decisions that fail to explore assumptions. Yet hierarchy, while an element of bureaucracy, is also not exclusive to bureaucratic forms of organization. Indeed, the distortions caused by knowledge of the aspirations of those at the top are probably greater in informal than in formal settings.

Clearly, the shape of knowledge varies throughout complex organizations, and actors at different levels of an organization pursue different informational strategies. At the top, transparency (getting to the bottom line) is what is desired;

at middle levels, opaqueness (avoiding definitions and criteria imposed at the top) is the strategy. The struggle for what information *is* and how it should be *displayed* is one that engages the attention and tactics of organizational actors. Formulas are workable and seemingly objective; nuances are seamless and often indigestible. This struggle to define what constitutes information is endemic in any complex organization.

Complex organizations typically are brimming with information, current and stored. The main problem in large organizations is moving information so as to coincide with any key decision maker's agenda. The frequently touted virtues of small groups—their informality and ability to explore the implications of alternative choices (which, as Irving Janis shows in his book *Groupthink*, are not inevitable outcomes)—concern their tendency to focus on a particular problem, often an especially compelling one that has reached a crisis. The difficulty for policy making in bureaucracy, however, is to push up information that is not necessarily immediately compelling. Therefore, in large organizations, the problematics of attention are important, since there seems usually to be a surplus of information available relative to attention.[30] Because important but noncompelling information is frequently unattended by decision makers in large-scale bureaucratic organizations, the strategies adopted by bureaucrats seeking to translate "important" into "compelling" information are crucial. The irony is that the power position imputed to bureaucrats with "information" assumes that they have someone's attention. In actuality, however, their so-called "power" rests upon the ability to find a niche in someone's agenda higher up who will make use of their valuable commodity. To translate what they know into action, bureaucrats have to behave politically rather than bureaucratically.

Hierarchy, Democracy, and Participation

The common complaint discussed above concerning the hierarchical chain of command in bureaucratic organizations is that hierarchy distorts communications and, thus, leads to inadequate decision processes. The alleged hierarchical impact discussed here, however, is that bureaucratic organization is undemocratic and alienating. The literature, empirical and theoretical, is voluminous. The reaction to the machine ideas of Taylorism and the classical and the neoclassical theories of bureaucracy in the industrial psychology/sociology literature is so vast that it comprises several schools of analysis. One fundamental assumption behind this literature is that when people participate in work decisions, alienation from their work is relieved; hence, they become more productive and their organizations more successful—a truly synergistic development!

Participation for "sociotechnical" reasons, Abrahamsson claims, is the most widely discussed value in the literature of organizational participation.[31] Such participation does not, however, satisfactorily accord with real democratic aspirations in the view of radical reformers such as Abrahamsson. According to this view, participation at lower organizational levels is only a palliative because it does not influence the organization's basic decisions. The mainstream sociotechnical-participation enthusiasts hope to lessen worker alienation so as to make workers more productive "citizens" of their organizations (a theme that is surfacing once again in light of the Japanese "managerial revolution"), but the scope of the prescribed participation remains limited. The basic logic of bureaucratic organization and hierarchical authority is not disturbed.

According to this critique, the democratization of organizations—especially workplace organizations—is thought to be essential because democracy in the larger political environment is imperfect and often meaningless.[32] If democracy and participation are to be meaningful, they must be acted upon in organizations that have meaning for people—the workplace being the most obvious of these. Victor Thompson comments in this regard that "the doctrines of democracy and liberalism which underlie our state have made almost no impact upon our bureaucratic organizations."[33] The hierarchical elements of bureaucracy, in short, are viewed as oppressive. Bureaucratic organization fundamentally is controlled by a few (the managerial elite) making the most vital decisions for the many (the workers), and that, according to the leveling theory, is about the most important social fact there is.

Hierarchy is a longer-running phenomenon, however, than is bureaucratic organization. Indeed, one of the leveling theorists suggests that Gulick's dictum regarding the unity of command has its roots in the movement from polytheistic religions to monotheistic ones.[34] I cannot here suggest a satisfactory theory that details how power should and can be allocated in a democracy, much less delve into the history of religion, but I will contend that bureaucratic organization is hardly the cradle of the hierarchy principle—only its efficient agent. Eliminating hierarchy and inequalities of power, to be sure, requires taking on bigger fish than bureaucratic theory. If such a brave (and, I suspect, short-lived) egalitarian world were to be achieved, however, bureaucratic organization certainly would have no place in it.

Local Rationality and Routine

The famous aphorism, "Where one stands depends upon where one sits," is especially relevant to bureaucratic organization. The specialization of task and the limited jurisdiction of bureaucratic units engender problems of organizational integration and are perhaps the characteristics of bureaucratic organizations that most frequently lead to breakdowns in their "efficiency." The simple fact that organizations have their own interests, imperatives, routines, and perspectives on problems accounts for much of the messiness invariably associated with policy making. Incoherence mostly means that the organizational participants are not neatly harnessed together pulling their weight, so to speak, on behalf of someone else's conception of "the public interest." A coherent policy process means an integrated policy process, and that often means the triumph of the command principle over the principles of differentiation of function and limited jurisdiction.

The problem of how systemwide organizational integration is to be accomplished in the face of existing suborganization or subsystem routines and interests is a very large one for any organization or government. It may even be said to lie at the heart of the problem of policy integration. Note that the critique of bureaucracy as conservative, wedded to routines, and self-serving is a critique almost always made by its would-be masters who hope to harness it to their ends. Because it tends to emphasize responsiveness to central authority, this critique contrasts with one that speaks of the oppressiveness of bureaucracy and calls for its democratization. The contrast in the logic of the critiques does not necessarily mean, however, that they are made in a mutually exclusive way. Those antipathetic to the very concept of bureaucracy often come at it with several cannons blazing, that is, bureaucracy is said to be both inefficient *and* oppressive.

Organizational tunnel vision—the predominance of subsystem or suborganizational interests—is often thought to result from the sole pursuit of organizational convenience, indicating a lack of commitment to a broader organizational or systemic unity. Although tunnel vision may result, it is doubtful that it is produced merely by convenient adherence to organizational routines. Ironically, it may well result from strong drives to fulfill programmatic missions. The more powerfully motivated bureaucrats are to achieve their mission (the more they may be said to have internalized the goals), the more troublesome they will be to those wishing to blend these goals, expressed as programs and budgets, with other priorities. Moreover, the more professionalized the bureaucracy is (that is, the more specialized the expertise it has), the more likely it will be to have ideas about what is correct policy. Guy Peters expresses this notion well: "Bureaucratic agencies frequently have well-developed ideas about what government should do. These ideas are not general statements, but rather are confined to the narrow area of the expertise of the agency."[35]

Yet the pulling together of organizational subunits or governmental subsystems need invoke neither the hierarchy principle nor aggressive efforts at organizational control.[36] Culture, according to analysts of Scandinavian systems in particular, is an exceedingly important consideration in determining how the diversity endemic to bureaucratic organization can be harnessed in the absence of powerful efforts to assert control from the center. Highly stylized rules of the game, for example, in which clear-cut winners and losers are avoided, in which building support is deemed more important than setting goals, and in which negotiation rather than leadership is stressed—all are thought to be successful in generating cooperation.[37]

Unfortunately, it is difficult to know how to build a widely accepted culture based on these values—assuming that we should wish to do so. Perhaps, as one analyst of the Norwegian system fears, the diminution in slack resources may bring forth more pronounced efforts at centralized control.[38] And in the views of still others, cultural diffusion (from the United States to Scandinavia) is more likely to favor a style of advocacy than of reserve, indicating that jeans may be only America's second-leading export.[39]

The main point is that the apparently disintegrative logic of bureaucratic organization can be influenced by exogenous factors, and systemic or more unified perspectives can be brought into play under the right conditions. But our knowledge of how to create those conditions is more like alchemy than modern science.

External Perspectives: The Problem of Universalism and Compassion

Bureaucracy as a means of evading the responsibilities of choice is a theme much played up in modern literature and armchair commentary. A related bureaucratic nightmare for those needing assistance or responsiveness from administrative agencies is perhaps the most negatively celebrated feature of bureaucratic form—going by the book. The boundary line between formality and employment of universalistic criteria on the one hand, and informality and particularistic behavior on the other is not clearly demarcated.

Strictly speaking, the logic of bureaucratic organization is universalistic. In practice, it is often something else. Where the line between the universalistic logic and the often particularistic practice should be drawn has a lot to do with questions of accessibility, influence, and responsibility. Whatever else, the logic of bureaucratic organization, when abetted by an appropriate cultural setting and a set of incentives, gives to the petty bureaucrat a power and status usually well beyond his meager compensation. In the circumstances of developing nations, for example, Fred Riggs noted that an ambiguous code of doubletalk often pervades bureaucratic-client relations—a code that promotes both overconformity to rules and evasion of them so that personalized choices can be made.[40] The prospects for corruption and also bureaucratic imperiousness are immense, but this has more to do with culturally defined incentives and prerogatives, corruptibility of top leadership, and a lack of professionalism than with bureaucratic administration, per se.

But even where culture and professionalism induce administrators to act in a way that balances universalistic with empathetic criteria, the equilibrium to be arrived at is always problematic. It boils down to the issue raised earlier of the permissible limits of bureaucratic discretion. A legalistic theory of accountability that, in the Wilsonian tradition, separates administration from politics will opt for clear and unmistakable legislative guidance and continuous legislative scrutiny. Theories such as those of Lowi, Hyneman, and Herman Finer, for instance, sharply circumscribe the judgment that administrators can exercise.[41] Presumably, according to this line of thinking, such limits ensure that bureaucracy serves the state and does not exercise independent power outside of strict statutory guidelines.

"Government by principle," asserts Victor Thompson, "means decision by problem category rather than by the individual case."[42] It is, in short, the triumph of impersonalism. Yet, unless other mechanisms are devised to gain access for those uneducated and without resources (those who are unskilled in dealing with a world of principle),[43] the class bias and the inequities of operating by pure principle will be great; possibly the result will be incompatible with a democratic society. Government purely by principle also may have the side-effect of delegitimizing institutions that appear to lose their capacity for responsiveness. Curiously, it is in the most bureaucratized systems that pure bureaucracy is most imperiled because distribution problems are apt to be partly a function of going exclusively by the book. The legendary trade-offs and pay-offs that were made in the former socialist-bloc bureaucracies to loosen up the system led to corruption and cynicism. But where should one draw the line? By definition, a theory that limits the application of principle cannot have much claim to be a theory. Not surprisingly, while theories of bureaucratic accountability abound, there are few of bureaucratic responsiveness. To achieve an adequate balance between the two values, accountability and responsiveness, some, like Carl Friedrich, would say that we must look to people rather than theory.[44] So, we turn now to people.

Guardians of the State: Officialdom

Most studies of bureaucrats are studies of the administrative elite. There are a variety of reasons for this, but the obvious one is that the top layers of officialdom are closest to the formulation of policy and most involved with politicians and interest groups. I therefore focus here mostly on administrative elites rather than on the minions below. I do so because the assumption that these officials are most closely linked to the triangulation of bureaucracy, policy, and power is obvious. Before setting forth to meet the elite, however, I want to pay some attention to the field officers beneath them, those who indeed do serve (or annoy) the public.

Where Public Administration Meets the Public

How do field officers deal with clients under conditions of strict legal limitations on their discretionary authority? Sociological theories suggest that officials at this level exhibit more concern about internal norms and structures than effectiveness with their clients. Goal displacement and self-interested behavior—the pathology of the petty bureaucrat—seem to be attractive focal points for examining the pathologies of bureaucratic systems.[45] This form of bureaucrat thrashing is regularly found in popularized form, for example, in the pages of the neoliberal *Washington Monthly*, not to mention in the collected speeches of recent past presidents.

Two studies suggest an alternative perspective, however. A survey of citizens who had direct dealings with federal agencies discovered that they were satisfied with how they were treated, even while they remained skeptical toward the bureaucracy in general.[46] Even when their situations were not always dealt with substantively to their satisfaction, the vast majority of citizens claimed to have been treated fairly.

A second study by Charles Goodsell examined field officials in a state welfare agency, finding a climate that he referred to as one of "compression."[47] Compression arises from the conflict between officials' desire to help their clients and the restraints on their legal authority to do so. Inasmuch as many of these officials are trained in what are euphemistically called "the helping professions," there is an obvious clash between professional norms and legal restrictions.

Even within tight discretionary limits and more or less classically bureaucratic settings, officials can be other than indifferent and surely something less than imperious. All of this suggests, furthermore, that cultural setting, agency leadership, and professionalism, rather than an abstract bureaucratic logic, are crucial determinants of variations in field officers' behavior. Universalistic rules, ironically, may impose stark psychological pressures on many of the most committed officials.

The Administrative Elite

Guardians of the State or of Their Own Status?

In what ways does the administrative elite hold power? Surely, they do not hold power as a unified force with a unified policy preference. Policy choices frequently do not place bureaucrats at odds with politicians, but in coalition with them—often against other bureaucrats. Moreover, the logic of bureaucratic and governmental organization ensures diversity of perspective based on where one sits or what one does. Nonetheless, administrative elites may possess some degree of group consciousness and seek to secure their role in society so as to exert a continuing influence over the terms in which policy options are considered and agendas defined. If this assumption is correct, the ability of the civil service elite to ensure its role depends greatly on its ability to generate beliefs about its indispensability.[48]

Such beliefs obviously will vary from one society to the next. By virtue of the relatively more limited view of the state in the United States as compared with Europe, the very low cohesion of the senior U.S. civil service, and the far less prestigious status U.S. civil servants enjoy relative to the European peers, American civil servants are widely believed to be quite dispensable. Furthermore, it would be difficult for United States civil servants to be considered an indispensable elite when the society holds to the belief that *all* elites are highly dispensable.

Institutional patterns in the formation and development of the state will affect the status and perceived indispensability of the administrative elite. In France, Sweden, and Japan, for example, the administrative state long preceded the development of parliamentary institutions, endowing the civil service in each case with great prestige. Bureaucratic prestige in both modern France and modern Japan is also closely linked to a few key educational institutions that regulate the flow of recruits into the upper levels of the administrative system and promote commonality of general outlook among them. The Ecole Nationale d'Administration in Paris and the Law Faculty of Tokyo University reflect somewhat different conceptions of appropriate training for the elite civil service, but they are carefully guarded points of entry endowed with the most exclusive of credentials. In all cases, of course, democratization of the polity has meant that bureaucratic elites have had to rub elbows with professional party politicians.[49]

Presumably, one indication of the ability of the administrative elite to guard its status under the aegis of its state guardianship is its ability to control recruitment by ensuring that entrants must pass through elite institutions. A more central indication is the ability of the administrative elite to control the pathways to other critical statuses in business (the French phenomenon of *pantouflage*) and in politics. Mattei Dogan notes, for example, the growing importance of an elite civil service background among France's cabinet members.[50]

One must still be cautious, though, about speaking in general terms of the civil service elite as a powerful corporate entity. Certainly, the bureaucratic elite does not commonly exercise cabalistic control over policy making to the exclusion of other actors, nor does it necessarily assert any particular policy position. Bureaucrats certainly hold attitudes that depend on factors other than their status as elite civil servants. But the procedures through which policy is debated and the influences that are brought to bear in shaping policy agendas may be closely related to the status and strategic role of the administrative elite.[51] These influences are facilitated by the elite's access to other strategic positions in society, especially politics and the management of nonpublic enterprises.

Thus, the position of the administrative elite in standing astride critical passageways and its ability to influence the framework of policy discussion invariably give it a certain kind of power. But the extent of the power of an administrative elite, *as a corporate entity*, varies greatly from one sociopolitical system to another.

Autonomy, Politics, and Politicization

To the extent that administration is deemed to be important or salient, it is inherently political. In that sense, a bureaucracy rarely expects autonomy; it can, however, hope for influence and accessibility to key decision makers at the center of government.[52] This necessarily involves politics—a more or less continuous interplay and effort at influence on the part of civil servants to have their perspectives taken into account and on the part of government politicians to have their preferences carried out.

Let me draw some unrefined distinctions between words here. First, autonomy in common parlance is a synonym for power—principally the power to run things as one wishes without external disturbances. Autonomy is sometimes used in the sense discussed in the previous section, which is to say in the tradition of elite theory, meaning an elite that controls critical passageways to strategic positions in society. From the standpoint of policy making, however, agencies and bureaucrats usually face a trade-off between autonomy and accessibility. The mystique of expertise is essential to creating an aura for an agency that would give it autonomy—that is, an aura that makes politicians feel the agency's business is too complicated for them to monitor closely. But most important policy questions travel not only upward to departmental ministers, but also outward to such bodies as interdepartmental committees. To influence key participants, bureaucrats need accessibility.

The need for accessibility also implies the need to practice politics, that is, the arts of influence. Such activity is normal in every bureaucratic setting, public or private. The need to practice politics, of necessity, means building political support. Some offices in a government are rarely touched by political controversy or are mainly self-contained. As a result, they may attract few officials of the "mover and shaker" variety. Any student of the Washington (or any other nation's) bureaucracy can readily point out the "green-eye-shade" offices within government. To continue to do what is being done in the absence of much policy change requires relatively little political initiative.

Trying to influence broader agendas or protect one's own in the face of threats, however, requires different behavioral forms. A steady effort at building bases of support and influencing political decision makers clearly is required.

In this regard, politics is a continuous activity in the executive arm of governments as well as in the executive suites of enterprises. Its form varies according to the channels available for wielding influence.

Administrative elites, like any other, vary in temperament. Some civil servants see themselves as part of a political process and display an impressive drive to gain influence and push their perspectives; others are much less active. How close one is to decision makers counts impressively, of course. But so do motivations, as Aberbach, Putnam, and Rockman show.[53] Since policy making is inherently a political process, whether in the executive suite or the executive branch, it is not surprising that political skills are an important ingredient. In this sense, and also in the sense that higher-level officialdom connects policy in concrete terms to specific interests and thus mediates between formal political decision makers and society,[54] one can say that the pristine Wilsonian duality of administration and politics is operationally meaningless.

The system in which administrative elites are embedded determines, of course, their routes of access to influence. Very broadly speaking, the European and the Japanese routes involve going to the top; having access to the minister is the key to influence. In the United States, however, the phenomenon of layering-in numerous political appointees between department secretaries and senior civil servants clogs the access route. In addition, since U.S. cabinets are that in name only and exercise no collective decision-making powers, the departmental secretary is not necessarily an influential figure. In this uncertain situation, one needs to go elsewhere as well. An independent legislature, with its numerous subcommittees and large staffs, is a rich vein of influence to mine. Enterprising and aggrieved officials of the administration (but not of *The* Administration) often accept the legislature's tacit invitation.

European bureaucrats, therefore, are involved in the subtleties of small-group and interpersonal influence; that is, they play a relatively sedate form of bureaucratic and even court politics. They play the game knowing they will continue to be game players. On the other hand, the Americans begin at a point of relative strategic or locational disadvantage (farther down and ignored), and they must therefore be more politically adventurous and inevitably more assertive. In contrast to their European counterparts, they also have more outlets to ply.[55] Furthermore, it may well be that in the American case, as apparently in Canada, the "movers and shakers" are to be found at the executive center, recruited through irregular channels, and better-positioned to influence policy making on a positive (what should be done?) rather than a defensive (what can be saved?) note.[56]

If politics is an intrinsic part of administrative activity at its higher reaches,[57] regardless of its form and style, then what does it mean to talk about politicization of the bureaucracy? Ronge uses the term politicization to talk about the growing role of political mediation played by top bureaucrats in the advanced industrial democracies.[58] This use of politicization, though, implies a sharp separation between administration and politics that is drawn from the classical tradition. I use the term politicization in quite a different way.

By politicization, I mean the effort of a government (in the United States, a presidential administration) to manipulate the bureaucracy by organization and/or personnel so as to ensure the loyalty of the bureaucracy to the government's (president's) preferences and political interests. The ways this may be tried are numerous. I will hardly exhaust the list.

The most obvious possibility is to imprint a strong partisan mold or tendency onto the bureaucracy; this is most easily achieved when a party or dominant and exclusionary coalition has been in power for some time. La Palombara's analysis of the "parentelistic" behavior of the Italian bureaucracy prior to the opening-to-the-Left in Italian politics in the early 1960s is an obvious case in point.[59] The exclusion of the Left from access to the administration was its hallmark. Similar, if less stark, phenomena appear to have been operative during the pre-socialist years of the French Fifth Republic and also, to some extent, in Japan where the bureaucracy and the Liberal Democratic party seem to be at least tacit allies. On the American side—especially from the period of Nixon to Reagan—there was a deepened concern about presidential administrations trying to get the bureaucracy to work exclusively on behalf of their sometimes very controversial goals and to do so with an enthusiasm bred of conviction. A leading student of the Washington executive establishment suggests that the Washington bureaucracy, largely created in its present form in the 1930s, came into being to serve the goals of the political leadership of the day, which thus had an extensive opportunity to mold it. As the goals have changed, presidential administrations, especially Republican ones, have been trying to remold the structures and the personnel of the bureaucracy in order to serve different goals.[60] From the perspective of the displaced and their proponents, the process is seen as politicization, whereas its advocates no doubt see the process as one of developing political responsiveness.

The process of permeating political change into the executive may mean centering more of the action at the top or building up coordinative and monitoring powers.[61] On the other hand, such political change may mean centering more and more political control within the departments themselves. Layering-in numerous loyalists, as in the American case, is a way in which this possibility is promoted.[62] This tactic may politicize the bureaucracy by ignoring its civil servants. Another tactic lies in personnel flexibilities (newly built into the American system) that enable political personnel to ship out recalcitrant bureaucrats to less politically sensitive positions. Still another tactic is a change in the nature of civil service personnel systems (really a variant of the layering-in phenomenon) that creates a distinctively "political" class of civil servants who can expect, as American appointees now can, to move on when a new government moves in.[63]

No doubt the politicization of bureaucracy is testimony to the growing importance that the governors attach to the administrative aspects of policy making and the need to ensure that its direction is in safe hands. Yet culture is again important. For the tendencies that are afoot in developing bureaucratic responsiveness to the regime are much less notable in Scandinavia. Social Democratic rule did not produce a party bureaucracy during the lengthy period in which the Swedish Social Democrats held power up to the 1970s. Nor is there evidence that the mode of politicization—especially evident in the United States and, to a lesser degree, in the brave new (but now, past) world of British government under Mrs. Thatcher—has yet reached the shores of Scandinavia. Culture counts, in other words. And a consensual culture is one that is favorable to bureaucratization rather than politicization.

Images of the State and of Bureaucracy

One's conception of the power and the role of the state bureaucracy is firmly wedded to one's conception of the state or, in less grandiose terms, to one's notion of what it is that governments can and should do. My conceptual list is brief and neither exhaustive nor mutually exclusive. The idea is simply to see how the issue of bureaucratic power might be related to some central images of the state. In this limited foray, I explore four images of the state: the state as interest, the state within itself, the state as expert navigator, and the state as object.

The State as Interest

The idea that the state is an autonomous force apart from the society it governs is one that is fundamental to the organic model of bureaucracy discussed earlier. Although the tradition of statism is much stronger in some European systems than it is in the United States, some recent literature has emphasized the idea that even "weak" states such as the United States have definitions of self-interest that they will pursue even in the presence of strong interest-group pressures to do otherwise. Stephen Krasner's study of foreign investment, *Defending the National Interest*, and Eric Nordlinger's theoretical work, *On the Autonomy of the Democratic State*, have emphasized the role of state interest and autonomy.[64]

Decrying the limitations of the interest group—or liberal perspective — of the state, Krasner claims forthrightly that his "is a study of the aims of central decision makers and their relationship with private corporations. Its basic analytic assumption is that there is a distinction between the state and the society."[65] Krasner's use of the term "central decision makers" is explained only in passing, but the term is said to comprise "the Presidency and some cabinet offices, particularly the Secretary of State."[66] Although these certainly are central, they hardly exhaust the list of such actors. One wonders, for example, who the central actors might be in a field such as health policy?

From the present perspective, the most fascinating element of Krasner's and Nordlinger's books is that their discussions of the statist approach do not consider the bureaucracy to be powerful or autonomous. What energizes the bureaucracy is leadership from the central actors, presumably the president and other executive leaders. Krasner rejects the supposition that these central actors are mere agents of bureaucratic outcomes and bargains. In this perspective, bureaucrats truly are the servants of the state, not *the* state.

While I have no quarrel with Krasner's central thesis, namely that in a particular domain the executive leadership can be successful in asserting its policy definitions over and above powerful societal or bureaucratic interests, I have more trouble with the terms in which his argument is couched. Normally, executive leaders who have their own, frequently partisan, conception of the policy universe come and go. Alternatively, the bureaucracy often is viewed as the real locus of longer-term and more stable definitions of policy. Couching the argument in terms of "the state" should lead one to conclude that it is the bureaucracy that has a vested interest in stable policy (state interests?), whereas the ephemeral central actors merely assert partisan or momentary perspectives. Of course, Krasner finds a fairly stable definition of state interests over time by the central executive actors, and that leads him to conclude that an ideologically defined "national interest" was asserted across various presidential administrations. Accordingly, stable policy preferences at the top seem necessary to assert the proposition of a state able to define its interests and act autonomously on them. By this proposition, neither the Congress nor the bureaucracy is central to the state.

The equation may be written thus: stable preferences at the center + central leadership = state autonomy. Thus, the ultimate irony is that the image of the state as interest more or less excludes the bureaucracy as a central agent of the state and considers it as but another societal interest to be overcome.[67]

The State within Itself

The portrait of the state within itself is a familiar one to students of political science. The modern state is said to be sectoralized, segmented, colonized by interests, replete with subgovernments, and essentially subsystem-dominant. This portrayal renders the state as a corporate entity weak, but its parts strong. The bureaucracy, like the state itself, is stronger in its parts than as a whole. It is a bureaucracy of bureaus, a government of subgovernments, a state absorbed with interests but without an interest. In the view of many, the modern state is in essence big but also weak at its center.[68]

This condition, paradoxically, produces a significant degree of autonomy for the bureaucracy at the level of the bureau (or other appropriate unit) but not at the level of the system. In France, for instance, the coalitions of the parties in the governments of the Fourth Republic gave opportunities to bureaucrats to deal with politicians in the Assembly. These opportunities were cut off when authority was centralized (i.e., the state strengthened) and the Assembly weakened.[69] As Ripley and Franklin indicate, when policies are salient and highly centralized, bureaucracies become less relevant to their outcomes, even though some organizational elites (cabinet members) may be central actors.[70]

One of the major struggles taking place in modern governments (especially now in the United States and Great Britain) is that between central decision makers and the subgovernmental parts. This struggle is especially problematic in the United States But it is doubtful either in the United States or the United Kingdom (or other systems, for that matter) that the issues can be boiled down simply to a struggle of executive politicians against bureaucrats. Some bureaucrats, after all, will be positioned at the center of things seeking to impose a system-defined rationality on the parts. If they succeed, which they can do only with strong political leadership, they will enhance the role of central decision makers and probably weaken the operational powers of line bureaus.

The State as Expert Navigator

The central mythology propagated by the French administrative elite is its indispensable role as the navigator of the state. Birnbaum describes the objectives of the navigator state and the mindset of navigators thus:

to create a state capable of arbitrating conflicts by reducing social tensions, integrating society from above. In their view, the rationality that guides their action guarantees neutrality: the more state intervention is guided solely by scientific knowledge and expertise, they argue, the more legitimate that action will be.[71]

The navigator state is a state guided by technical-rational suppositions. It may be either interventionist and directly involved in economic planning (a strategic conception of the state), or it may provide guidance in a form that minimizes intrusive interventionism but emphasizes rational outcomes (an expert conception of the state). Whether one adopts a big- or a small-state (étatist or market-oriented) approach, the conception of the state as navigator rests upon an assumption of rational (coherent) policy and rational (unified) policy-making processes. In such a state, exceptionally well trained bureaucrats will be important figures placed at the apex of power, but bureaucratic interventionism and sectoral particularism will be eroded.

The reign of the technocratic state in a conflictless society implies that the demand (political) side of governing can or should be regulated or ignored. The technocratic state is not so much a bureaucratic state as it is one influenced by experts who are bureaucrats. It rests in large part on the unity of politicians and experts and increases the importance of the former being descended from the latter.

Technocratic guidance assumes that rational decisions, unlike political ones, are calculable and that feasibilities are defined by economics and engineering— not by politics. Thus, the expert state probably will calculate the public interest for good or ill outside of the framework of politics. In this regard, an outstanding study of alternative forms in the regulation of public utilities across American states noted that expert and resource-rich regulatory commissions tended to do such things as adopt rate structures that gave utilities a large return—a highly unpopular action.[72]

The ability of the technocratic state to resist popular political pressures undoubtedly rests on the relative unity of the political elite (which, of course, might be imposed artificially via authoritarian rule) and on the elite's success in persuading others that the language of technocracy should be used as a guide to public policy. But it is unlikely that even the technocratic state can resist the most severe political pressures—except in the short run. In the longer run, the cumulative effects of resistance are apt to delegitimize the apparatus of the state, especially when effectiveness also is called into question.

The State as Object

Behind the image of the state as object is the basic assumption that governmental latitude is shaped by the results of past activity. Yesterday's solutions become today's problems. The idea of the state as object suggests limits to the growth of state programs as the state attempts to meet those future commitments that are the product of past choices. Under these conditions, the climate for policy entrepreneurship (new programs) by bureaucrats within government will become more restricted.[73]

In short, to view the state as object is to view it as reacting and adapting to the consequences of past acts. Thus, the prospects of policy promotion and the market for policy initiatives shrink. The shift in "company" work accordingly moves from the policy-production line to the finance office. This probably means a shift from the operating bureaus to the central financial institutions of government or from one set of bureaucrats with one set of key constituencies (external interests) to another set of bureaucrats with a different set of key constituencies (central leadership).

Conclusion

How bureaucracy links to power and to policy has been, however obliquely approached, the topic of this chapter. The subject is as complex analytically as it is exciting topically. I have looked at it from three angles: that of the organization of bureaucracy itself, that of administrative personnel (especially the administrative elite), and that of the state. The issues that lie at the heart of the relationship between bureaucracy, power, and policy at whatever level—whether of the individuals to the subunits, the subunits to the departments, the departments to the government, or the bureaucracy (in toto) to the state—are those of coordination, control, and autonomy. The basic issues of government and the political order are contained within the topic we have examined. Included among these issues are the following: What constitutes proper authority? Who are the proper authorities? How can integration and coherence be achieved? How can the instruments of the state serve it? Is there a public or a state interest aside from the interests made manifest in the policy process?

When used in relation to the term "power," the term "bureaucracy" succumbs readily to holistic, monolithic, and systemic modes of thinking.[74] As a sociological phenomenon, bureaucracy is seen as an "it"; bureaucrats, especially the administrative elite, are seen as a quite distinctive "them." "It" is accordingly a principal repository of power in the society, whereas "them" are the elites who stand at or near the top of these great institutional sources of power. Seen in this light, the state administration—like the steel industry—is linked to many other factors of production (corporate enterprise and the political elite, for instance). Accordingly, the bureaucracy *is* a powerful institution. It follows that those who are at or near its apex are powerful people.

Studies of the policy making process, however, yield pictures that rarely are highly congruent with the monoliths of "it" and "them." In decision making, "it" and "them" are shown typically to be compartmentalized and frequently possessed of divergent interests. From the "one" of the sociological perspective, there is the "many" of the policy-making perspective. Moreover, from this perspective, policy itself rarely has well-defined boundaries and may be better viewed as a continuous rather than a discrete process. This makes the issue of power particularly problematic.

How are these conflicting perspectives to be reconciled? Indeed, can or ought they to be reconciled? While I doubt that these distinctive perspectives are easily reconcilable, each perspective has a legitimate niche in the ecology of social and political analysis. As distinctive approaches to political analysis, they each yield important insights.[75]

To theorists of social forces, the emergence of bureaucratic institutions has been one of the most compelling aspects of modern life. The organizational continuities of bureaucracy across diverse environments are impressive. Bureaucracies' capacity to swallow up the half-baked thoughts and impulses of less than persistent leaders is equally impressive. The role of bureaucracy in mediating between "high policy" and "real policy" is without doubt a critical power and one that, ipso facto, makes bureaucracy into a policy making apparatus, not a mere piece of machinery.

If we accept this supposition, then it follows that the administrative elite sits atop important and continuously powerful instruments of policy. Consequently, this elite *must be* powerful. The administrative elite, therefore, is worthy of study not because we can demonstrate that it acts as a unified force but because we can learn much about its political psychology and its sociology. From the psychological perspective, *how* bureaucrats think is as important as *what* they think because the perspective tells us how they are apt to define problems, solutions, and processes—the assumption being that they are key participants in determining these definitions for the polity. From the sociological perspective, the ability of the administrative elite to populate other centers of power and to reproduce the bases of its own standing is a classic concern in theories of the elite. Thus, if the administrative elite is a powerful elite, it is so not because of its unity on decisions but because of its unity over how decisions should be made, and because of its accessibility to other significant institutional centers.

To the student of "What's going on on Planet Earth?" much of the above may sound detached from the real world of decision making, a world in which interests are clashing and coalitions are being constructed and dissolving. In this more clamorous world, bureaucratic politics and diversity are everywhere, and singular nouns are strictly *verboten*. Here, the question is not, "Does the bureaucracy (or bureaucrats) have power?" but rather "What coalition of forces was constructed to take advantage of an opportunity?"

How can we mediate between these two worlds—the one (of unifying abstraction) and the many (of concrete diversities) as William James put it? We live, as James wrote, like fishes swimming in the sea of sense and of facts, needing to be redirected from time to time by the abstract determinants in the air above, yet unable to draw life directly from it.[76] We need to be aware of our dependence on each of these elements—the direct and the indirect, the proximate and the distant. We need to pose unifying questions but be satisfied with plural and contingent answers. And we need to pose pluralizing and operational questions without ending our quest with the answers they produce.

In a direct institutional sense, the major impact of bureaucracy on policy making lies in its persistence and ability to stabilize its immediate environment—in other words, to develop tacit (but not immutable) alliances and agreements with other interdependent actors. In decision making, the power of the bureaucracy is never uniformly exerted because it is virtually never an "it." Ultimately, the independence of operating agencies lies in their inherent connection to the institutional power of central leadership. To the extent that central mechanisms of political leadership are powerful, to the extent that central leaders are persistent in policy direction, and to the extent that they provide clear and operational guides, to that extent is the bureaucracy their servant.

Notes

1. For example, see Bengt Abrahamsson, *Bureaucracy or Participation: The Logic of Organization* (Beverly Hills, CA: Sage, 1977); Victor A. Thompson, *Modern Organization: A General Theory* (New York: Alfred A. Knopf, 1964); and Frederick C. Thayer, *An End to Hierarchy and Competition: Administration in the Post-Affluent World*, 2d ed. (New York: New Viewpoints, 1981).

2. Hugh Heclo, "OMB and the Presidency—The Problem of 'Neutral Competence,' " *The Public Interest* 38 (Winter 1975): 80–98.

3. Colin Campbell and George J. Szablowski, *The Superbureaucrats: Structure and Behavior in Central Agencies* (Toronto: MacMillan, 1979).

4. Ezra N. Suleiman, *Politics, Power, and Bureaucracy in France: The Administrative Elite* (Princeton, NJ: Princeton University Press, 1974).

5. Ezra N. Suleiman, *Elites in French Society: The Politics of Survival* (Princeton, NJ: Princeton University Press, 1978).

6. See, for instance, Graham T. Allison, "Conceptual Models and the Cuban Missile Crisis," in *Essence of Decision: Explaining the Cuban Missile Crisis* (Boston: Little, Brown, 1971); Morton Halperin, *Bureaucratic Politics and Foreign Policy* (Washington, DC: Brookings Institution, 1974), esp. part one; and Robert Axelrod, "Bureaucratic Decisionmaking in the Military Assistance Program: Some Empirical Findings," in *Readings in American Foreign Policy: A Bureaucratic Perspective*, ed. Morton H. Halperin and Arnold Kanter (Boston: Little, Brown, 1973), pp. 154–71.

7. See James G. March and Johan P. Olsen, *Ambiguity and Choice in Organizations* (Bergen: Universitetsforlaget, 1976); Michael D. Cohen, James G. March, and Johan P. Olsen, "A Garbage Can Model of Organizational Choice," *Administrative Science Quarterly* 17 (March 1972): 1–25; James G. March and Johan P. Olsen, "What Administrative Reorganization Tells Us About Governing," *American Political Science Review* 77 (June 1983): 281–96; John W. Kingdon, *Agendas, Alternatives, and Public Policies* (Boston: Little, Brown, 1984), esp. ch. 8; and Johan P. Olsen and James G. March, "The New Institutionalism: Organizational Factors in Political Life," *American Political Science Review* 78 (September, 1984): 734–49.

8. See, for example, Robert D. Putnam, "The Political Attitudes of Senior Civil Servants in Western Europe: A Preliminary Report," *British Journal of Political Science* 3

(July 1973): 257–90; and Hugh Heclo, *Modern Social Politics in Britain and Sweden* (New Haven, CT: Yale University Press, 1974). Putnam puts the matter audaciously; he asks: "Can there really be much doubt about who governs our complex modern societies?" (p. 257). The question is rhetorical.

9. The classic work of Mills in this regard is his *The Power Elite* (New York: Oxford University Press, 1956). Mills's argument, while exceedingly vague in its particulars, pinpoints the bureaucracy (but apparently the high-level appointees rather than its permanent officers) and the military (which must include permanent officers) as two of the leading actors, along with business elites, in the triangulation of power within the American system.

10. See, for instance, Kenneth Dyson, *The State Tradition in Western Europe* (New York: Oxford University Press, 1980), and Pierre Birnbaum, *The Heights of Power: An Essay on the Power Elite in France* (Chicago: University of Chicago Press, 1982). See especially in this regard, Suleiman, *Elites in French Society*.

11. On this, see, for example, Glendon Schubert's critique of theories encompassing broad normative principles of administrative behavior. See *The Public Interest: A Critique of the Theory of a Political Concept* (Glencoe, IL: Free Press, 1960).

12. See, for instance, Nicos Poulantzas, "The Problem of the Capitalist State," *New Left Review* 82 (November/December 1969): 67–78; Ralph Miliband, "The Capitalist State—Reply to Nicos Poulantzas," *New Left Review* 59 (January/February 1970): 53–60; and Ralph Miliband, "Poulantzas and the Capitalist State," *New Left Review* 82 (November/December 1973): 83–93.

13. This is the view that Schubert labels "Idealism." "The Idealists," Schubert ways, "would maximize (or, at the very least, expand) the scope of official autonomy and discretion, thus placing all public servants in the heart of the policy making process" (*The Public Interest*, p. 80). For a clear expression of this view, see Carl J. Friedrich, "Public Policy and the Nature of Administrative Responsibility," in *Bureaucratic Power in National Politics*, 3d ed., ed. Francis E. Rourke (Boston: Little, Brown, 1978), pp. 399–409.

14. See, for example, Dyson, *The State Tradition*; for a more tepid American version of the same line of argument, see James L. Sundquist, "The Crisis of Competence in Our National Government," *Political Science Quarterly* 95 (Summer 1980): 183–208.

15. Campbell and Szablowski, *The Superbureaucrats*. See also Colin Campbell, *Governments under Stress: Political Executives and Key Bureaucrats in Washington, London, and Ottawa* (Toronto: University of Toronto Press, 1983).

16. For a discussion of this image, see Joel D. Aberbach, Robert D. Putnam, and Bert A. Rockman, *Bureaucrats and Politicians in Western Democracies* (Cambridge, MA: Harvard University Press, 1981), p. 16, passim.

17. See Richard P. Nathan, *The Administrative Presidency* (New York: John Wiley, 1983).

18. There are various versions of this view that Schubert calls the "rationalist" theory. In this body of theory, "The model of authority . . . is hierarchical, with the public on top and bureaucrats on the bottom." Thus, "Human discretion is minimized or eliminated by defining it out of the decision making situation" (*The Public Interest*, pp. 30–31). Among the various versions of this view are Theodore Lowi, *The End of Liberalism: The Second Republic of the United States*, 2d ed. (New York: Norton, 1979); Charles S. Hyneman, *Bureaucracy in a Democracy* (New York: Harper, 1950); Herman Finer, "Administrative Responsibility in Democratic Government," in Rourke, ed., *Bureaucratic Power*, pp. 410–21; Nathan, *Administrative Presidency*.

19. For empirical evidence on this, see Aberbach, Putnam, and Rockman, *Bureaucrats and Politicians*. And for a more extended discussion of the implications of these patterns for political responsibility and administration, see Joel D. Aberbach and Bert A. Rock-

man, "The Administrative State in Industrialized Democracies," National Public Radio Module on Bureaucracies, Global Understanding Project, 1984; and also Bert A. Rockman, "Executive–Legislative Relations and Legislative Oversight," *Legislative Studies Quarterly* 9 (August 1984), esp. pp. 406–14.

20. See especially James Q. Wilson, "The Rise of the Bureaucratic State," in *The American Commonwealth—1976*, ed. Nathan Glazer and Irving Kristol (New York: Basic Books, 1976), pp. 77–103.

21. This point was made salient during the Nixon administration's abuse of the executive power.

22. For further explorations of these mixed needs or functional models of bureaucratic contributions to "the public interest," see Aberbach, Putnam, and Rockman, *Bureaucrats and Politicians*, ch. 8; S.E. Finer, "Princes, Parliaments, and the Public Service," *Parliamentary Affairs* 33 (Autumn 1980): 353–72; and Sir Douglas Wass, "The Public Service in Modern Society," *Public Administration* 61 (Spring 1983): 7–20.

23. Thompson, *Modern Organization*, ch. 8.

24. For example, see Paul R. Lawrence and Jay W. Lorsch, *Organization and Environment* (Homewood, IL: Richard Irwin, 1969); Paul E. Mott, *The Characteristics of Effective Organizations* (New York: Harper and Row, 1972); Christopher C. Hood and Andrew Dunsire, *Bureaumetrics: The Quantitative Comparison of British Central Agencies* (University: University of Alabama Press, 1981).

25. Harold L. Wilensky, *Organizational Intelligence: Knowledge and Policy in Government and Industry* (New York: Basic Books, 1967), p. 44.

26. Richard E. Neustadt, *Presidential Power: The Politics of Leadership from FDR to Carter* (New York: John Wiley, 1980).

27. Allison, "Conceptual Models and the Cuban Missile Crisis."

28. Roger B. Porter, *Presidential Decision Making: The Economic Policy Board* (Cambridge: Cambridge University Press, 1980), esp. ch. 7; and Thayer, *An End to Hierarchy*, esp. ch. 5.

29. See Irving L. Janis, *Groupthink*, 2d ed. (Boston: Houghton Mifflin, 1982).

30. For example, Martha S. Feldman and James G. March, "Information in Organizations as Signal and Symbol," *Administrative Science Quarterly* 26 (June 1981): 171–86.

31. Abrahamsson, *Bureaucracy or Participation*, p. 193.

32. See here Carole Pateman, *Participation and Democratic Theory* (Cambridge: Cambridge University Press, 1970); Paul Blumberg, *Industrial Democracy: The Sociology of Participation* (New York: Schocken, 1973); Thayer, *An End to Hierarchy*; and Abrahamsson, *Bureaucracy or Participation*.

33. Thompson, *Modern Organizations*, p. 65.

34. See Thayer, *An End to Hierarchy*, pp. A–11–A–22.

35. B. Guy Peters, "The Problem of Bureaucratic Government," *Journal of Politics* 43 (February 1981): 65–66.

36. For an indication of the penchant to achieve a uniform hierarchical objective defined through OMB, see Richard Rose, *Managing Presidential Objectives* (New York: Free Press, 1976).

37. Thomas J. Anton, *Administered Politics: Elite Political Culture in Sweden* (Boston: Martinus Nijhoff, 1980), 184–85.

38. See Johan P. Olsen, *Organized Democracy: Political Institutions in a Welfare State* (Bergen: Universitetsforlaget, 1982), pp. 145–46.

39. For arguments suggesting that the American political style of advocacy is penetrating Scandinavian political culture, see Steven Kelman, *Regulating America, Regulating Sweden: A Comparative Study of Occupational Safety and Health Policy* (Cambridge, MA: MIT Press, 1981), esp. pp. 228–37; and Anton, *Administered Politics*, pp. 186–87.

40. Fred W. Riggs, *Administration in Developing Countries: The Theory of Prismatic Society* (Boston: Houghton Mifflin, 1964), p. 201.

41. Lowi, *The End of Liberalism*; Hyneman, *Bureaucracy in a Democracy*; and Herman Finer, "Administrative Responsibility."

42. Victor A. Thompson, *Without Sympathy or Enthusiasm: The Problem of Administrative Compassion* (University: University of Alabama Press, 1975), p. 68.

43. For example, see Gideon Sjoberg, Richard A. Brymer, and Buford Farris, "Bureaucracy and the Lower Class," in Rourke, ed., *Bureaucratic Power in National Politics*, pp. 40–53.

44. Friedrich, "Public Policy and the Nature of Administrative Responsibility."

45. Mohr distinguishes between transitive goals and reflexive goals, the former being outer-directed toward the organization's mission and the latter being inner-directed toward the needs of organizational members. See Lawrence B. Mohr, "The Concept of Organizational Goal," *American Political Science Review* 67 (June 1973): 470–81.

46. Daniel Katz, Barbara A. Gutek, Robert L. Kahn, and Eugenia Barton, *Bureaucratic Encounters: A Pilot Study in the Evaluation of Government Services* (Ann Arbor, MI: Institute for Social Research, 1975).

47. Charles T. Goodsell, "Looking Once Again at Human Service Bureaucracy," *Journal of Politics* 43 (August 1981): 763–78.

48. See Suleiman, *Elites in French Society*.

49. In the case of Japan, where this tendency is a recent one, see Michio Muramatsu and Ellis S. Krauss, "Bureaucrats and Politicians in Policy Making: The Case of Japan," *American Political Science Review* 78 (March 1984): 126–46.

50. Mattei Dogan, "How to Become a Cabinet Minister in France," *Comparative Politics* 12 (January 1979): 1–25.

51. Freeman illustrates, for example, the central role of the bureaucracy in France in defining the terms and language of debate regarding the issues of immigrant labor in contrast to the salience of the parliamentary role in Britain in phrasing the terms of debate over the same issue. In France, the issues became technical ones; in Britain, the issues became part of a very deep and intense political debate. See Gary P. Freeman, *Immigrant Labor and Racial Conflict in Industrial Societies* (Princeton, NJ: Princeton University Press, 1979).

52. The point here is that to gain power over policy formulation that leads beyond the jurisdiction of a single unit or requires interaction among units, access to appellate political authority is essential.

53. Aberbach, Putnam, and Rockman, *Bureaucrats and Politicians*, pp. 224–26.

54. See Volker Ronge, "The Politicization of Administration in Advanced Capitalist Societies," *Political Studies* 22 (March 1974): 86–93.

55. Aberbach and Rockman, "The Administrative State in Advanced Industrial Societies."

56. Campbell and Szablowski, *The Superbureaucrats*. Also see Bert A. Rockman, "America's *Departments* of State: Regular and Irregular Syndromes of policy making," *American Political Science Review* 75 (December 1981): 911–27.

57. Yet administrative politics in this sense is not necessarily a day-to-day occurrence. Management is. But politics in the sense of strategic maneuver (and thus in any sensible definition of management) is omnipresent, even though outright challenges or clashes are infrequent. In normal routines, of course, politics over high policy flashes only rarely. Note in this regard, Herbert Kaufman, *The Administrative Behavior of the Federal Bureau Chiefs* (Washington, DC: Brookings Institution, 1981).

58. Ronge, "The Politicization of Administration."

59. Joseph LaPalombara, *Interest Groups in Italian Politics* (Princeton, NJ: Princeton University Press, 1964).

60. Personal communication from Professor Joel D. Aberbach.

61. A plea that began in the United States with the Brownlow Commission Report. In the spirit of Brownlow, see Richard E. Neustadt, "Presidency and Legislation: The Growth of Central Clearance," *American Political Science Review* 48 (September 1954): 641–71.

62. This phenomenon has been spotted both by Hugh Heclo, *A Government of Strangers: Executive Politics in Washington* (Washington, DC: Brookings Institution, 1977); and Nathan, *Administrative Presidency.*

63. For evidence of this in the British and other European systems, see F.F. Ridley, "Career Service: A Comparative Perspective on Civil Service Promotion," *Public Administration* 61 (Summer 1983): 179–96; and Hans-Ulrich Derlien, "Zur einstweiligen Quieszierung politischer Beamter des Bundes, 1949–1983," Universität Bamberg, Verwaltungswissenschaftliche Beitrage, No. 16, 1984. Derlien's analysis suggests that this "political" class of civil servants is no recent phenomenon in German postwar history. Ridley contends similarly that the continental tradition (comparable with, but more decorously fashioned than the United States tradition) has been to ensure regime loyalists at the top. His fear was that the U.K. personnel system under Margaret Thatcher was being continentalized.

64. See Stephen D. Krasner, *Defending the National Interest: Raw Materials Investments and U.S. Foreign Policy* (Princeton, NJ: Princeton University Press, 1978); and Eric A. Nordlinger, *On the Autonomy of the Democratic State* (Cambridge, MA: Harvard University Press, 1981).

65. Krasner, *Defending the National Interest*, p. 5.

66. Ibid., p. 33.

67. Ibid., p. 75.

68. See, for example, Lowi, *The End of Liberalism*; Hugh Heclo, "Introduction: The Presidential Illusion," in *The Illusion of Presidential Government*, ed. Hugh Heclo and Lester M. Salamon (Boulder, CO: Westview Press, 1981), pp. 1–17; and Hugh Heclo, "The Changing Presidential Office," in *Politics and the Oval Office*, ed. Arnold J. Meltsner (San Francisco: Institute for Contemporary Studies, 1981), pp. 161–84.

69. Vincent Wright, "Politics and Administration under the French Fifth Republic," *Political Studies* 22 (March 1974): 44–65.

70. Randall B. Ripley and Grace A. Franklin, *Congress, the Bureaucracy, and Public Policy*, 3d ed. (Homewood, IL: Dorsey Press, 1984), esp. ch. 8.

71. Birnbaum, *The Heights of Power*, p. 85.

72. William T. Gormley, Jr., *The Politics of Public Utility Regulation* (Pittsburgh: University of Pittsburgh Press, 1983), pp. 215–16.

73. Richard Rose notes in this regard that "The past constrains the present size of government. The bigger government is the greater the constraints, for there is less scope for new initiatives and fewer unmobilized resources" (*Understanding Big Government: The Programme Approach* [London: Sage, 1984], p. 29).

74. See Bill Jenkins and Andrew Gray, "Bureaucratic Politics and Power: Developments in the Study of Bureaucracy," *Political Studies* 31 (June 1983): 177–93.

75. For a more extended discussion of these lines of analysis, see my "Conclusion: Elites and Social Inquiry," in *Elite Studies and Communist Politics: Essays in Memory of Carl Beck*, ed. Ronald H. Linden and Bert A. Rockman (Pittsburgh: University Center for International Studies and University of Pittsburgh Press, 1984), pp. 325–348.

76. William James, *Pragmatism* (New York: Meridian Books, 1960), p. 90.

6

Explorations in
Bureaucratic Responsiveness

Grace Hall Saltzstein

Organizational theorists from at least the time of Marx have worried about the controllability of bureaucracy in any governmental system.[1] Few theorists, or citizens, would dispute the need for bureaucratic responsiveness in a representative democracy. If bureaucrats are not subject to direct popular control, can bureaucratic policy making be considered "democratic" in any meaningful sense? How can responsiveness to public interests and wishes be assured in organizations that are not subject to direct popular control? These questions and their implications have long been the subject of scholarly concern.

Despite the attention devoted to these questions, an examination of the theoretical, conceptual, and empirical analyses of bureaucratic responsiveness reveals considerable confusion and ambiguity. Assessments of the extent and the nature of bureaucratic responsiveness vary tremendously, conflicting definitions of the central concept are commonly utilized, and competing—perhaps equally valid—conceptualizations are often ignored. Drawing upon relevant literature, this chapter examines the concept of bureaucratic responsiveness and attempts to delineate the major parameters of the concept, the principal theoretical and methodological limitations of various approaches, and the main questions that have been thus far overlooked or inadequately addressed.

The early interest in bureaucratic responsiveness grew out of an awareness that administration could not be divorced from politics, but rather represented a "continuation of the legislative process."[2] During this period, concern focused on the implications of a policy-making bureaucracy for democratic control, and debates raged over the extent of the problem and the proper mechanisms to ameliorate it.[3] At this stage, responsiveness came to be equated with accountability, and, as Hill notes, this "traditional accountability literature tends to be pitched at a high theoretical level."[4] Scholars eventually began to focus on the effects of accountability mechanisms, however, examining the impact of such traditional reforms as overhead controls as well as newer reforms, adopted in the 1960s and the 1970s, that involved direct control by the public.[5] Other scholars, influenced by research on legislative responsiveness,[6] turned their attention to general analyses of bureaucratic representation and responsiveness.[7] These latter enterprises began to develop measurable indicators of responsiveness; this activity refocused scholars' attention on basic theoretical and conceptual issues about the meaning of bureaucratic responsiveness.

Differentiating Two Perspectives on Responsiveness

Unfortunately for theoretical development, analyses of specific mechanisms to enhance responsiveness have tended to adopt a narrow view of the subject, while general analyses have tended to borrow ideas from studies of legislative responsiveness. Although bureaucratic responsiveness is more complex than legislative responsiveness, little effort has been devoted to exploring the former as a potentially unique concept. At least two principal perspectives toward bureaucratic responsiveness—distinguished mainly by their respective definitions of bureaucracy's representational role—are evident in the public administration literature.

Bureaucratic Responsiveness as Responding to the Public's Wishes

The first perspective, which is the one adopted by most of the recent literature on bureaucratic responsiveness, sees the bureaucracy as a representative of the public, and defines bureaucratic responsiveness in much the same fashion as legislative responsiveness. Thus, bureaucratic responsiveness is assumed to require responsiveness to the wishes of the public. Few authors who take this perspective indicate any awareness of the existence of two competing views about the mechanism by which public wishes are entered into bureaucratic deliberations. Both the theory and the practice of public administration reflect pronounced disagreement as to the proper channels of interaction between citizens and bureaucracy.

The traditional view assigns responsibility for interest representation to elected officials, who then grant authority to the bureaucracy. Elected officials are defined as the legitimate representatives of the public, and the bureaucracy serves as a neutral instrument that elected officials are to use in meeting public demands. According to this view, the bureaucracy provides no independent assessment of public wishes; responsiveness to the public is provided solely through the bureaucracy's faithful adherence to elected officials' interpretation of public wishes.

Obviously compatible with Woodrow Wilson's 1887 treatise on administration, which stimulated the acceptance of the politics–administration dichotomy, this view retained strong support among administrators and analysts even after support for the politics–administration dichotomy waned. Thus, in their analysis of school administration, Ziegler, Jennings, and Peak examine the conflict between the public's and the professionals' attempts to influence policy, and conclude: "At the risk of oversimplification, the thrust of standard political theory is that, even though a balance between efficiency and responsiveness must be maintained, the ultimate policy initiative should rest with the elected representatives."[8] Accepting this position while expressing alarm over the difficulties of maintaining such legislative dominance has been a staple of social criticism over the past four decades.[9] Furthermore, studies indicate that many practicing administrators continue to believe that elected officials can and should be dominant over them.[10]

A competing view, which holds that the bureaucracy legitimately exercises independent representational functions that are equivalent to the functions performed by elected officials, also finds considerable support in democratic theory and administrative practice. It is argued that "the people" delegate their authority to three *equal* branches of government, that elections are simply one of several means of selecting authorized agents of the people, and that elected and nonelected officers alike may "represent" the public in direct fashion.[11] Pluralist theorists reach similar conclusions about bureaucratic representation, assuming that the representational functions performed by the bureaucracy are equivalent to those performed by elected officials.[12] Support for this view has waxed and waned in the practice of administration, with high points evident during the New Deal period and during the heyday of the "new public administration" in the 1970s. Even now, adherents contend that the bureaucracy has a right and an obligation to respond to public interests in a direct fashion, without the mediation of elected officials.[13]

Thus, one main perspective on bureaucratic responsiveness sees the bureaucracy as a representative of the public. The two competing versions of this perspective see responsiveness as occurring either—according to the traditional view—as the bureaucracy *indirectly* carries out the public's mandate by following explicitly the directions set by elected officials, or—according to a more recent view—as the bureaucracy *directly* and independently responds to the public.

Bureaucratic Responsiveness as Responding to the Interests of the State

The major alternative perspective toward bureaucratic representation emphasizes the responsibility of the bureaucracy to "represent" the state in interactions with the public.[14] Indeed, Rosenbloom argues:

The history of the United States bureaucracy and some of the most fundamental features of the personnel system support this view more than they support any other. Political neutrality regulations, loyalty-security provisions, procedures regarding the removal of federal servants, and the traditional judicial doctrine concerning the constitutional rights of public employees have all been premised largely on a conception of federal servants as being representatives of the government or state, rather than of any outside group or as their own agents.[15]

Looking at the representative function of bureaucracy from this perspective focuses attention on the instrumental nature of bureaucratic existence and the objective, substantive functions performed by bureaucracy. Thus, it is emphasized that administrative agencies were created for specific purposes and that their primary responsibility is to provide "good administration," defined as "the apolitical application of technical competence to politically defined ends."[16] Responsiveness, then, is assessed according to the extent to which bureaucracy meets various standards of good administration, however those may be defined.

While the standards applied to bureaucracy have varied over time, a list of commonly used standards includes efficiency, fiscal integrity, accountability, and equity, as well as neutral competence, expertise, and professionalism.[17] From this perspective, as Schumaker and Loomis note:

> . . . responsiveness is conceptualized in terms of the actions that policymakers take to reduce specific problems. According to this conceptualization, police departments are responsive when they react quickly and effectively to crime. . . . In short, [the studies reviewed] suggest that policymakers are supposed to respond to an "objective measure of need," even when these responses are independent of, and perhaps contrary to, public preferences.[18]

Thus, bureaucracies are assigned responsibility by the public and its representatives for certain policy problems, and responsiveness is measured according to what the bureaucracies do about those problems. In recent years, such assessments have looked both at the procedural aspects of that response (i.e., were the allocated funds actually spent as intended? were programs developed based on the best available information?) and at the substantive outputs and impacts (what effect did the program have on the problem?). Requirements for program and performance evaluation are obviously designed to encourage responsiveness in this form.[19]

The Bureaucratic Consequences
of Choosing a Responsiveness Perspective

Although the different perspectives inevitably lead to contradictory conclusions as to what responsiveness requires in any given situation, no single perspective on bureaucratic responsiveness has gained dominance in either the practice or the study of public administration. Of course, the selection by bureaucrats of a perspective on responsiveness is crucial. The chosen perspective becomes an important component of the bureaucrats' generalized role conceptions, which—presumably—affect their behavior.

Those bureaucrats who adopt one or the other version of the first perspective—the one that emphasizes direct or indirect responsiveness to the public's wishes—are likely to behave in characteristic ways. For example, those whose theoretical conception of the bureaucratic role has been influenced by notions of administrative pluralism are likely to employ such "political" decision-making techniques as bargaining, coalition building, and compromising among competing groups. Others may be guided by conceptions of bureaucrats as administrative statesmen responding to their interpretations of the public interest or as change agents with primary responsibilities to achieve social equity.[20] On the other hand, those bureaucrats who adopt the second perspective—the one that emphasizes responsiveness to the interests of the state—are likely to behave in other characteristic ways. For example, those influenced by the vestiges of a politics–administration dichotomy and by norms of neutral competence are likely to approach substantive responsiveness in terms of expertise or professionalism. Administrators adopting this perspective, referred to by Dotson as the corporate objectivity approach to administrative responsibility, assume that scientific standards and expertise should provide the basis of administrative response, especially when policies cannot easily be judged by the public.[21] In those cases, rationality will determine bureaucratic responses to substantive policy needs.

Defining Responsiveness

In addition to the complexities that are associated with multiple perspectives on bureaucratic responsiveness, administrators and researchers must confront difficult questions in defining the general concept of responsiveness.

All operationalizations of the concept of responsiveness make certain assumptions about the appropriate targets of governmental responsiveness, the wishes or interests to which government should respond, and the form that governmental responses should take. Hence the boundaries of the concept are established by answering the questions of responsiveness to whom, to what, and in what form? Yet answering these questions is anything but simple. Because notions of responsiveness inevitably assert a relationship between "the people" and public officials and institutions, some attempt must be made to define the relevant public. An initial problem of "appropriate inclusion" arises in defining the population to be considered as the community for decision-making purposes.[22] How are we to determine where the boundaries of the community should be drawn? Should the relevant community be defined at the level of neighborhoods, cities, states, regions, or at the level of the nation as a whole? Since we can easily demonstrate that a bare majority within a particular community can become a minority in a slightly larger community, we can see that "however impeccable democratic decision making may be within a given community, the outcomes are in some sense determined by the previous and inescapably undemocratic decisions that defined them in the first place."[23]

Thus, a decision by bureaucrats to be responsive to a particular population, such as residents of a suburb, may preclude responsiveness to an alternately defined population, such as residents of the central city bordering the suburb. Yet, despite the fact that bureaucrats often are afforded discretion in designating a target population,[24] analysts of bureaucratic responsiveness usually examine a single population as the appropriate target of responsiveness and ignore the effect of bureaucratic decisions on other potential populations. As will be demonstrated later, shifting the definition of the target populations may lead analysts to differing conclusions about the extent of bureaucratic responsiveness.

Even if we agree on the geographic scope of the community, related questions arise in regard to whose interests within that community should engender a response. Should institutions be responsive to the interests of the mass public, voters, attentive elites, organized groups, or individuals? Potential targets are numerous in the bureaucratic setting; administrators may face demands from all of the above, as well as from at least the following additional actors: individual legislators, legislative committees, legislative chambers, chief executives, agency superiors, agency constituents, individuals affected by a policy, immediate clientele, or some other specific group, such as the socially disadvantaged.

It would be a rare situation, indeed, if all of these potential populations desired mutually compatible outcomes. In the absence of such agreement, which combatants should be heard? Various persuasive theories enjoy widespread support, but produce contradictory conclusions. Proponents of legislative dominance would defer to the legislature, pluralists would defer to group interest, whereas public choice proponents would maximize individual utility in market-exchange terms; of course, the conclusions of any approach could be challenged by questioning the premises of the argument. Yet if we cannot definitively decide to whom bureaucracies should respond, can we assess the extent of responsiveness in bureaucracy?

Because much research on bureaucratic responsiveness has focused on the impact of a particular reform mechanism on a single group, the possibility of inaccurately assessing responsiveness is a serious problem. For example, public health services frequently find that policies designed to meet the needs of low-income clients displease the local medical establishment that is at the core of the health services' constituencies.[25] Responsiveness to actual users of a public service is often enhanced by bureaucratic actions to "screen out" or discourage difficult or hard-to-please potential applicants.[26] Furthermore, deference to elected officials may come at the expense of responsiveness to public demands.

Researchers looking at different target groups could thus reach radically different conclusions about the responsiveness of the bureaucracy.

Similar problems confront the researcher in determining which aspects of a target population's wishes or interests require a response. In general, it has been assumed that responsiveness is owed either to the demands and preferences of the designated population or to the interests or needs of the population or to some combination of the two.[27] Those who assume that responsiveness means "reflecting and giving expression to the will of the people" must still determine how to measure the people's will.[28] Should we measure articulated demands, general public opinion, or some combination of the two?[29] Furthermore, which demands must be met—all of them, even if they are contradictory, or only the most intensely felt?[30] Analogously, if general public opinion is the basis of action, which opinions are relevant? How much support must an opinion have before action is taken? What about uninformed opinions, strongly felt minority opinions, or situations in which opinion is simply divided? Is responsiveness a winner-take-all proposition, or does it require some attempt to balance competing claims and provide something for everyone? Does the concept have any meaning when the public is apathetic or has no opinion?

The difficulties are even more pronounced if we accept the notion that responsiveness may entail responding to community "needs," as well as, or even opposing, community wishes.[31] This potential for conflict is acknowledged as the "mandate/independence" problem in representation theory: should the representatives blindly respond to the wishes of their constituencies or do they have a right or obligation to act independently in terms of what they think is best for the constituents?[32] The likelihood of administrators taking the latter position is enhanced by the increasing professionalism of public bureaucracies and the emphasis on expertise and neutral competence. More and more, administrators are selected, evaluated, and rewarded according to their technical expertise in areas outside the common knowledge of either elected officials or the public. In fulfilling their "functional" responsibilities by applying this expertise, administrators are apt to think they have a better understanding of public needs than the public has.

Tension arises when officials who have been trained to apply substantive expertise to policy problems are confronted with citizen demands that are at odds with the expert's solution. How much and under what circumstances should professionals or other experts defer to public opinion in policy making? An analyst who looks only at responsiveness to citizens' preferences might conclude that a lack of deference to public opinion represents a lack of responsiveness. Is this necessarily the case if the administrator was acting upon clear, unambiguous expertise that was at odds with citizen preferences?[33] As Sharp raises the question in regard to one type of responsiveness, "perhaps agenda responsiveness does not consist of a correspondence between policymaker priorities and those of the public, but rather a willingness to strike some balance between professional standards and values and community priorities."[34] On the other hand, critics of professionalism have long noted the tendency of professionals to inflate the value of their training and to redefine value-laden issues as narrow, technical issues to be decided by experts.[35] Thus, the excuse of responding on the basis of neutral competence can provide administrators with a convenient rationalization for ignoring outside opinion.[36] How is the researcher to differentiate the genuine response from the rationalization?

The final definitional issue to be considered is the different forms that responsiveness can take. Responsiveness has been variously operationalized by researchers as opinion concurrence between representatives and the designated public, as procedural openness, as agenda setting, as advocacy of or support for specific policies during the decision-making stage, as policy enactments, as policy implementation, and as policy impacts.[37] Schumaker categorizes the basic forms of responsiveness as (1) access responsiveness; (2) agenda responsiveness; (3) policy responsiveness; (4) output responsiveness; and (5) impact responsiveness.[38]

Many of the problems that arise in operationalizing each of these types of responsiveness have been discussed elsewhere.[39] The difficulties are more pronounced as the researcher's attention moves from opinion concurrence to policy impacts. In addition, problems of operationalizing each type of responsiveness are more complex in the bureaucratic setting than in the legislative setting. Thus, if the test of responsiveness is concurrence on policy agendas, the researcher must decide whether administrators' agenda preferences should match those of citizens or of elected officials. Is the administrator's opinion regarding the matter salient to operationalization of the concept? What if the administrator's expertise dictates an agenda different from that of the public or of elected officials? Should impact responsiveness be assessed in terms of substantive policy impacts (i.e., improved health care) or in terms of citizen satisfaction (i.e., approval of the health delivery system)? As Mann has illustrated, professional judgments of what is needed in dealing with a particular policy problem may conflict with citizen preferences, so how the concept is operationalized may affect evaluations of administrative responsiveness.[40]

Analyzing the Studies of Responsiveness

Although research that deals explicitly with bureaucratic responsiveness is relatively limited, a considerable amount of empirical research that touches on or has implications for responsiveness does exist. The following discussion delineates the models used in conducting much of that research, with examples taken from various studies to illustrate the important problems associated with this field of research.

Research Models and Foci

Empirical analyses of bureaucratic responsiveness have tended not to utilize the full range of definitions of the concept. With some notable exceptions to be mentioned later, virtually all recent research dealing with bureaucratic responsiveness has defined the concept in terms of response to the wishes or demands of the public in general or some particular segments of the public.[41] This dominant research orientation ignores both the traditional public administration orientation to bureaucratic responsibility, which requires responsiveness to elected representatives of the public, and the perspective that requires responsiveness to the interests of the state in favor of an exclusive focus on the direct link between administrative agencies and citizens. Ostrom's approach to responsiveness is representative: "Let us define responsiveness as the capacity to satisfy the preferences of citizens. . . . The responsiveness of any particular institutional arrangement is the capacity of those who act within the constraints of a set of decision-making rules to satisfy the preferences of others who are dependent upon the institution."[42]

As Sharp argues so persuasively, this approach represents a "consumer model" of responsiveness:

> By a consumer model of responsiveness, I mean the approach that treats responsiveness in the public policy realm in a manner similar to responsiveness in the marketing realm. Citizens are viewed as consumers of policy outputs, and public officials are expected to base their actions on citizen evaluation of those outputs, in much the same way that the marketplace supposedly provides signals to producers of any product. Citizen demand is therefore a keystone of the consumer model of responsiveness, in much the same way that consumer demand is central to any marketing approach. Under the consumer model, responsiveness has to do with the satisfaction of citizen preferences or demands, or at least with the relationship between citizen preferences/demands and policy maker priorities, beliefs, or actions.[43]

While this consumer model is consistent with standard approaches to legislative responsiveness, its focus on direct interactions between citizens and bureaucrats is not the only valid perspective on bureaucratic responsiveness. Indeed, as the earlier discussion of perspectives on bureaucratic responsiveness indicates, the responsiveness-to-public-wishes perspective is not even the dominant orientation in public administration theory. Yet, as Mladenka notes in regard to studies using a consumer model, "these efforts have ignored competing perspectives on the appropriate role of public organizations in a democratic society even though no compelling reasons are offered as to why we ought to favor the public preference position and reject the others."[44]

Sharp argues that the consumer model "strips the responsiveness concept of an important dimension and diverts attention from significant responsiveness issues."[45] She posits an alternative, "professional responsibility" model that equates responsiveness with "action based on professional judgments of need." This model would also assume a direct relationship between bureaucracy and citizens, but would allow the bureaucrat to respond at the independence end of the mandate–independence continuum. This alternative is consistent in many ways with the view of bureaucrats as representatives of the state who have an overriding obligation to respond to objective needs.

The previous discussion of public administration theory and practice suggests yet a third model that might be termed the "neutral executor" model. Under this final model, responsiveness would be measured in terms of bureaucratic response to elected officials. While analyses of administrative receptivity to political control are evident in such areas as regulation, iron triangles, oversight mechanisms, and legislative/executive interactions, the findings and implications of those strands of literature have yet to be incorporated into studies of bureaucratic responsiveness.[46] Adopting such an approach would incorporate in research what is probably the most widely accepted theoretical perspective on bureaucratic responsibility.

The research thus far conducted on bureaucratic responsiveness has adopted a variety of substantive foci. As noted previously, a small body of empirical research has focused on general issues of bureaucratic responsiveness, while a wide variety of more specific topics has been examined. For example, research on decentralization and citizen participation focuses on the extent to which such mechanisms increase the responsiveness of the bureaucracy to its immediate constituencies.[47] Research on urban service distribution and alternative service delivery systems addresses the link between services provided and neighborhood or group needs or wishes.[48] A subset of research on representative bureaucracy focuses on the links between "passive" representation of groups in bureaucracy and "active" representation, or responsiveness to the group interest, in policy making.[49] Research relating to the "public encounter" with bureaucracy has delved into questions about bureaucracy's responsiveness to individuals or classes of individuals.[50] Numerous other research strands might be seen as touching on questions of bureaucratic responsiveness, but the above-listed studies illustrate the general dimensions of empirical research in the area. Hence, the following discussion relies on examples from those studies to illustrate different kinds of problems caused by the general lack of conceptual clarity regarding the topic and by the lack of reliance on alternative models of responsiveness.

Conceptual and Operational Problems

As noted above, any number of problems are evident in research on bureaucratic responsiveness. Even where responsiveness is conceptualized at the relatively undemanding level of opinion concurrence, disagreements inevitably arise in deciding *which* administrators' views should match those of *which* citizens or officials, which values are to be considered, how variations in knowledge or intensity are to be handled, and how much value congruence is required to suggest that responsiveness has occurred. As a consequence, some scholars have been interested only in top-level administrators, while others have looked at street-level bureaucrats.[51] Some scholars have looked at specific segments of the community, such as citizen activists; others have looked at general public opinion, and yet others have looked at the opinions of elected officials.[52]

While most analysts now agree that access and agenda responsiveness alone are insufficient as indicators of responsiveness, policy and impact models continue to raise severe problems of operationalization. First, researchers encounter problems in identifying a policy that can be linked unambiguously to a group's or a population's interests or wishes. This may not be a problem where survey data indicate clear public support for a specific policy, but few researchers are fortunate enough to obtain such data. Frequently, researchers are faced with the hazardous undertaking of inferring a group interest as well as a policy designed to satisfy it.[53]

In addition, the output, or impact, selected by the researcher must be something over which the bureaucracy reasonably might be expected to have some control. The difficulty of meeting this condition has plagued research on service distribution from the start, when the inclination was to use expenditures and/or deployment of capital facilities as indicators of bureaucratic policy. Only recently has that procedure been criticized on the grounds that such measures may more accurately reflect legal and economic constraints imposed by extrabureaucratic actors and developed over a considerable period of time than current policies and decisions willfully adopted by bureaucrats.[54] Use of surveys of citizen satisfaction with governmental services as an indicator of service responsiveness has been criticized in similar fashion because of the lack of evidence of linkage between agency actions and survey results.[55] Furthermore— and perhaps most important—many bureaucratic outputs are determined by elected officials working with bureaucrats and are not subject to the exclusive control of the bureaucracy. Consequently, considerable disagreement may exist among researchers as to whether a given situation is or is not evidence of bureaucratic responsiveness.[56]

In addition to the extensive operationalization problems that lead to contradictory conclusions, analysts of bureaucratic responsiveness also disagree about the appropriate level of analysis. Most researchers in the areas mentioned above simply accept some particular level of "appropriate inclusion." Those interested in opinion concurrence in school administration examine citizen opinion within the school district, analysts of service distribution look primarily at intracity distribution, and students of public encounters may examine the individual agency's responses to client requests.[57] Critical analysts in virtually every case contend that the level of analysis selected may mask more pervasive system or societal unresponsiveness.[58] Thus, critics of public choice service delivery strategies argue that increasing intrajurisdictional homogenity may indeed enhance responsiveness within that jurisdiction, but only at the cost of decreased responsiveness across jurisdictions.[59] Similarly, Hill argues that the problem of metropolitan areas is not the lack of governmental responsiveness within communities but rather the resource inequities that exist among jurisdictions.[60]

Within a given community, the extent of bureaucratic responsiveness may be overestimated, critics charge, by focusing only on the part played by the bureaucracy. If responsiveness is a function both of bureaucratic and political forces, is it valid to assess bureaucratic responsiveness according to the actions of the bureaucracy only, or should that assessment address the contributions of the bureaucracy to overall levels of responsiveness? Should we conclude that an agency that provides prompt, thorough investigation of citizen complaints is responsive even if administrators know that no money is available to correct the problems and make no effort to obtain additional funds?[61] Or, as Sharp asks in regard to access responsiveness, "does access responsiveness mean that all elements of the local governmental system are working together to find out about citizen concerns?"[62]

This set of questions takes us back once again to a major problem with existing research on responsiveness: the lack of integration of alternative models of responsiveness. Even the research that specifically addresses the subject of bureaucratic responsiveness has minimized or ignored at least one of the possible approaches to responsiveness. Thus, Mann, Tucker, and Ziegler; and Gormley, Hoadley, and Williams—all downplay the role of responsiveness to elected officials, apparently because overhead controls through elected officials are relatively weak in the administrative settings they examine.[63] Similar problems plague the urban service distribution literature as well, with political influences usually explored according to a simple consumer model examining the links between electoral votes and bureaucratic outputs, in a narrow range of policy arenas, despite other research demonstrating links between minority and female representation in elective office and bureaucratic outcomes or the influence of overhead controls in other policy areas.[64]

Yet the possibility of responsiveness to elected officials or to professional standards instead of or in addition to citizen wishes makes the adaptation of legislative models of representation to administration difficult. For example, the standard trustee/delegate distinction so frequently applied to legislators becomes more ambiguous when applied to administrators. Mann, for example, would include as delegates those administrators who take direction from either elected officials or the public. But his own data suggest some significant differences between those who feel they owe responsiveness to the board and those who feel they owe such responsiveness to the public directly. Some additional distinctions need to be made between the two groups in studying bureaucratic responsiveness.

Similar problems arise with the trustee category in such research. Most analysts classify as a trustee anyone "whose decisions are based on his own values, even though the represented might disagree."[65] But, according to classical standards of organization, bureaucrats are to be selected, advanced, and rewarded on the basis of expertise. Under the influence of good-government norms, communities and their elected officials frequently *select* administrators on the basis of expertise and expect those administrators to act on their professional values to do what is "best" for the community. Over 80 percent of the administrators in Mann's suburban school districts were classified as trustees in his study, despite his corollary finding that the bulk of the community and the school boards in those districts were allegiant and satisfied with having such administrators. Does the trustee model convey an accurate image in such a situation, or is some revision warranted under the professional responsibility model? Such questions become more pressing as bureaucratic responsiveness is examined using additional models.

Charting Future Research Directions

What does the preceding discussion suggest about directions for future research? First, the key questions, as Salamon and Wamsley note, "may not be whether the bureaucracy is responsive, but to whom, and under what circumstances."[66] Hence, empirical analyses that address those questions are needed. At the same time, it is clear that responses to questions about whether the bureaucracy is responsive are crucially dependent upon researchers' decisions as to the appropriate level of inclusion, the level of analysis, standards of assessment, and so on. If comparisons are ever to be made across strands of research, and if general conclusions are to be drawn from varied research, some heightened awareness of the impact of such decisions must be obtained.

Continued research is needed on the relationships among various types of responsiveness. Such research should address a variety of questions, such as those regarding the links among access, agenda, policy, output, and impact responsiveness, both over time and across different types of agencies. In addition, more needs to be known about the relationships among responsiveness to different target populations. For example, what trade-offs, if any, are required among responsiveness to individual clients, to agency constituencies, to other groups, and to the community? How is responsiveness to particularistic interests related to responsiveness to societal needs or to the general interest?

Another important question that has yet to be adequately addressed refers to the second part of Salamon and Wamsley's concern: under what circumstances is bureaucracy responsive? Numerous studies have suggested a wide variety of potential correlates of bureaucratic responsiveness. Empirical studies have only recently begun to examine in systematic fashion, however, the relative influences of different correlates or the interactions among correlates.[67]

One potentially significant correlate is the representational role adopted by administrators. Analysts must look beyond the delegate/trustee conceptions of role to tap the range of roles currently adopted by administrators. As noted earlier, widely divergent conceptions of bureaucratic representation are evident in the training given to public administrators. We need to know who adopts which role and why. Do administrators alter their conceptions of representational role over time or in response to their environment? How accurate are their perceptions of the public's or elected officials' wishes? How are the representational roles adopted by individual administrators related to administrative responsiveness?

Similarly, we need to know more about how agency characteristics and agency/legislature/clientele characteristics are related to responsiveness. Does the nature of the policy involved make a difference? How do the size, age, or organizational structure of the agency matter? What differences do agency rules and regulations or professionalism make? Among these groups demanding responsiveness, do those that obtain bureaucratic attention share certain characteristics? What effects do different community norms and values cause? How do economic and social constraints impinge upon administrative responsiveness?

In any event, more needs to be known about the relative importance of various factors in influencing responsiveness and how these factors interact. Certain kinds of agencies clearly seem to attract individuals with distinctive views of responsiveness, and certain types of communities demand particular styles of administration and select administrators to fit those styles.[68] Such interactions have important implications for the types of bureaucratic responsiveness that will be possible as well as for the scope of responsiveness.

Finally, more research should focus on the *impact* of bureaucratic responsiveness. Studies that define responsiveness in terms of impact already focus on the tangible benefits and gains that accrue from responsiveness. In addition, strong arguments can be made for the absolute virtue of bureaucratic responsiveness in a democracy, and most analyses assume implicitly that responsiveness must be demonstrated if we expect the public to accept and defer to administrative discretion. Mann, for example, argues that "Responsiveness is the price schools pay for community support."[69] Yet the link between bureaucratic responsiveness and system support—either in the very narrow sense of satisfaction with particular services or the broader sense of regime support, trust, and allegiance—has not been carefully explored. Further research might begin to focus on the impact of bureaucratic responsiveness or unresponsiveness on how citizens perceive of their government and on their willingness to support it.

Notes

1. Nicos Mouzelis, *Organisation and Bureaucracy: An Analysis of Modern Theories* (Chicago: Aldine, 1968).

2. E. Pendleton Herring, *Public Administration and the Public Interest* (New York: Russell and Russell, 1936), p. 218.

3. For a classic discussion of the need for control of the bureaucracy, see Paul Appleby, "Public Administration and Democracy," in *Public Administration and Democracy*, ed. Roscoe Martin (Syracuse, NY: Syracuse University Press, 1965), pp. 333–47. For the classic dispute over control mechanisms, see Herman Finer, "Administrative Responsibility in Democratic Government," *Public Administration Review* 1 (Summer 1941): 335–50; and Carl J. Friedrich, "Public Policy and the Nature of Administrative Responsibility," *Public Policy* 1 (1940): 3–24. For a recent analysis of the problem of accountability, see John P. Burke, *Bureaucratic Responsibility* (Baltimore: Johns Hopkins University Press, 1986).

4. Larry B. Hill, "Bureaucratic Monitoring Mechanisms" in *The Public Encounter*, ed. Charles T. Goodsell (Bloomington: Indiana University Press, 1981), p.162.

5. For example, see Judith E. Gruber, *Controlling Bureaucracies* (Berkeley: University of California Press, 1987); William T. Gormley, Jr., *Taming the Bureaucracy* (Princeton, NJ: Princeton University Press, 1989).

6. For example, Helen Ingram, Nancy Laney, and John McCain, *A Policy Approach to Political Representation* (Baltimore: Johns Hopkins University Press, 1980); Heinz Eulau and Kenneth Prewitt, *Labyrinths of Democracy* (Indianapolis: Bobbs-Merrill, 1973).

7. For example, William Gormley, John Hoadley, and Charles Williams, "Potential Responsiveness in the Bureaucracy: Views of Public Utility Regulation," *American Political Science Review* 77 (September 1983): 704–17; Dale Mann, *The Politics of Administrative Representation* (Lexington, MA: Lexington Books, 1976); Harvey Tucker and L. Harmon Ziegler, *Professionals versus the Public* (New York: Longman, 1980).

8. L. Harmon Ziegler, M.K. Jennings, and J. Wayne Peak, *Governing American Schools* (North Scituate, MA: Duxbury Press, 1974), p. 6.

9. See, for example, Herman Finer, "Administrative Responsibility in Democratic Government"; John K. Galbraith, *The New Industrial State* (Boston: Houghton Mifflin, 1967); Charles Hyneman, *Bureaucracy in a Democracy* (New York: Harper, 1950); and Theodore Lowi, *The End of Liberalism* (New York: W. W. Norton, 1969).

10. Kenneth R. Greene, "Municipal Administrators' Receptivity to Citizens' and Elected Officials' Contacts," *Public Administration Review* 42 (July/August 1982): 346–53.

11. Herbert Storing, "The 'Other' Federalist Papers: A Preliminary Sketch," *Political Science Reviewer* (1976): 214–47.

12. See Robert Dahl's discussion of the "American Hybrid" in *A Preface to Democratic Theory* (Chicago: University of Chicago Press, 1956), ch. 5; see especially his discussions of the role of bureaucracy, pp. 136–37, 147–48; see also David Truman, *The Governmental Process* (New York: Alfred A. Knopf, 1955), ch. 8–9.

13. See John Rohr, *To Run a Constitution* (Lawrence: University of Kansas Press, 1986), pp. 171–94. Burke, *Bureaucratic Responsibility*, p. 35, argues that utilitarian concepts of bureaucratic responsibility inevitably lead to such conclusions. Furthermore, even where the bureaucracy is seen as owing primary responsiveness to elected officials, legislative mandates may require bureaucratic responsiveness to the public as well.

14. Hannah Pitkin, *The Concept of Representation* (Berkeley: University of California Press, 1967), p. 41.

15. David Rosenbloom, "Forms of Bureaucratic Representation in the Federal Service," *Midwest Review of Public Administration* 8 (July 1974): 163.

16. Annemarie Walsh, *The Public's Business* (Cambridge, MA: MIT Press, 1978), p. 38.

17. James Fesler, *Public Administration Theory and Practice* (Englewood Cliffs, NJ: Prentice-Hall, 1980), pp. 302–09; Herbert Kaufman, "Emerging Conflicts in the Doctrines of Public Administration," *Public Administration Review* 29 (January/February 1969):

3–12; James Q. Wilson, "The Bureaucracy Problem," *The Public Interest* 6 (1967): 3–9.

18. Paul Schumaker and B. Loomis, "Responsiveness to Citizen Preferences and Societal Problems in American Communities," in *South Atlantic Urban Studies*, ed. S. Hines and G. Hopkins (Columbia: University of South Carolina Press, 1979), p. 46.

19. Bruce Rocheleau, "Evaluation, Accountability, and Responsiveness in Administration," *Midwest Review of Public Administration* 9 (October 1975): 163–72.

20. For arguments favoring the administrative statesman position, see Appleby, "Public Administration and Democracy"; Herbert Storing "American Statesmanship: Old and New," in *Bureaucrats, Policy Analysts, Statesmen: Who Leads?*, ed. Robert A. Goldwin (Washington, DC: American Enterprise Institute, 1980), pp. 88–113; and Dwight Waldo, *The Administrative State* (New York: Ronald Press, 1948). For advocacy of administrators as change agents, see Frank Marini, ed., *Toward a New Public Administration* (Scranton, PA: Chandler, 1971).

21. Arch Dotson, "Fundamental Approaches to Administrative Responsibility," *Western Political Quarterly* 10 (September 1957): 701–27. Obviously, difficulties arise because professionals and the public disagree as to when the public is incapable of judging public policies.

22. Robert Dahl and Charles Lindblom, *Politics, Economics, and Welfare* (New York: Harper and Row, 1953), pp. 51–54.

23. Frederick Whelan, "Prologue: Democratic Theory and the Boundary Problem," in *Liberal Democracy: Nomos XXV*, ed. J. Roland Pennock and J. Chapman (New York: New York University Press, 1983), pp. 13–47.

24. For example, see Lester Salamon and Gary Wamsley, "The Federal Bureaucracy: Responsive to Whom?" in *People vs. Government*, ed. Leroy Rieselbach (Bloomington: Indiana University Press, 1975), pp. 165, 178–79.

25. Joseph Viteritti, "Organizational Environments: The Significance of the Constituent–Client Distinction." Paper presented at the 1983 annual meetings of the American Political Science Association.

26. Daniel Katz, Barbara Gutek, Robert L. Kahn, and Eugenia Barton, *Bureaucratic Encounters: A Pilot Study in the Evaluation of Governmental Services* (Ann Arbor: Institute for Social Research, University of Michigan, 1975), pp. 190, 195–96; Barbara Nelson, "Help-seeking from Public Authorities: Who Arrives at the Agency Door?" *Policy Sciences* 12 (1980): 175–92.

27. The basis of this disagreement centers on the question as to whether responsiveness is simply "reaction" to demands or if it can occur in the absence of public opinion or demands.

28. J. Roland Pennock, "Responsiveness, Responsibility, and Majority Rule," *American Political Science Review* 66 (1952): 790–807.

29. Albert Karnig, "'Private-Regarding' Policy, Civil Rights Groups, and the Mediating Impact of Municipal Reforms," *American Journal of Political Science* 19 (1975): 91–106, and Ziegler, Jennings, and Peak, *Governing American Schools*, look at articulated demands. Susan B. Hansen, "Participation, Political Structure, and Concurrence," *American Political Science Review* 69 (1975): 1181–99; and Sidney Verba and Norman Nie, *Participation in America* (New York: Harper and Row, 1972), look at general public opinion, while Russell Getter and Paul Schumaker, "Contextual Bases of Responsiveness to Citizen Preferences and Group Demands," *Policy and Politics* 6 (1978): 249–78, argue for looking at both.

30. Pennock, "Responsiveness, Responsibility, and Majority Rule," discusses the problem of contradictory demands, while Willmore Kendall and George Carey, "The Intensity Problem and Democratic Theory," *American Political Science Review* 62 (1968): 5–24, raise the intensity issue.

31. See Schumaker and Loomis, "Responsiveness to Citizen Preferences."

32. Pitkin, *Concept of Representation*, p. 164.

33. Mann, *Politics of Administrative Representation*, pp. 21–24, considers these problems, but tends to downplay their significance for representational theories.

34. Elaine B. Sharp, "Responsiveness in Urban Service Delivery," *Administration and Society* 13 (May 1981): 44.

35. Clarence Stone, "The Implementation of Social Issues," *Journal of Social Issues* 36 (1980): 15–34.

36. Greene, "Municipal Administrators' Receptivity."

37. Representative examples of each approach follow: see Verba and Nie, *Participation in America*, and Gormley, Hoadley, and Williams, "Potential Responsiveness in the Bureaucracy," for opinion concurrence; Tucker and Ziegler, *Professionals versus the Public*, for procedural openness and agenda setting; Roger Davidson, "Congress and the Executive: The Race for Representation," in *Congress: The First Branch of Government*, ed. A. DeGrazia, (New York: Anchor, 1967), pp. 365–402, for policy and advocacy; Karnig, " 'Private-Regarding' Policy" and Rufus P. Browning, Dale Rogers Marshall, and David Tabb, *Protest is not Enough* (Berkeley: University of California Press, 1984), for policy enactments; Schumaker and Loomis, "Responsiveness to Citizen Preferences," for policy implementation; and Dennis Dresang, "Ethnic Politics, Representative Bureaucracy, and Development Administration: The Zambian Case," *American Political Science Review* 68 (1974): 1605–17; and Frank Thompson, "Minority Groups in Public Bureaucracy: Are Passive and Active Representation Linked?" *Administration and Society* 8 (1976): 201–26, for policy impacts.

38. Paul Schumaker, "Policy Responsiveness to Protest-Group Demands," *Journal of Politics* 37 (February/May 1975): 488–521.

39. See ibid.; Sharp, "Responsiveness in Urban Service Delivery"; Kenneth Mladenka, "Responsive Performance by Public Officials," in Goodsell, ed., *The Public Encounter*, pp. 143–59; Kenneth J. Meier and Robert England, "Black Representation and Educational Policy: Are They Related?" *American Political Science Review* 78 (June 1984): 392–403; and Gormley, Hoadley, and Williams, "Potential Responsiveness in the Bureaucracy."

40. Mann, *Politics of Administrative Representation*, pp. 16–17.

41. Mladenka, "Responsive Performance by Public Officials."

42. Elinor Ostrom, "The Design of Institutional Arrangements and the Responsiveness of the Police," in *People vs. Government*, ed. Leroy Rieselbach (Bloomington: Indiana University Press, 1975), p. 275.

43. Sharp, "Responsiveness in Urban Service Delivery," pp. 34–35.

44. Kenneth Mladenka, "Citizen Demands and Urban Services: The Distribution of Bureaucratic Response in Chicago and Houston," *American Journal of Political Science* 25 (November 1981): 145.

45. Sharp, "Responsiveness in Urban Service Delivery," p. 34.

46. See Marver Bernstein, *Regulating Business by Independent Commission* (Princeton, NJ: Princeton University Press, 1955); William Gormley, *The Politics of Public Utility Regulation* (Pittsburgh: University of Pittsburgh Press, 1983), on regulation; Lee Fritschler, *Smoking and Politics: Policy Making and the Federal Bureaucracy* (Englewood Cliffs, NJ: Prentice-Hall, 1975), on iron triangles; Bruce Smith and D.C. Hague, eds., *The Dilemma of Accountability in Modern Government* (New York: St. Martin's, 1971); Bernard Rosen, *Holding Government Bureaucracies Accountable* (New York: Praeger, 1982), on oversight mechanisms; Lawrence C. Dodd and Richard Schott, *Congress and the Administrative State* (New York: John Wiley, 1979); H. Douglas Arnold, *Congress and the Bureaucracy: A Theory of Influence* (New Haven, CT: Yale University Press, 1979), on legislative–executive interactions.

47. For example, see Robert Yin and Douglas Yates, *Street-Level Governments* (Lexington, MA: Lexington Books, 1975); R.L. Cole, *Citizen Participation and the Urban Policy Process* (Lexington, MA: Lexington Books, 1974).

48. Mladenka, "Responsive Performance by Public Officials," George Antunes and John Plumlee, "The Distribution of an Urban Public Service: Ethnicity, Socioeconomic Status, and Bureaucracy as Determinants of the Quality of Neighborhood Streets," *Urban Affairs Quarterly* 12 (March 1977): 313–32; John Boyle and David Jacobs, "The Intra-City Distribution of Services: A Multivariate Analysis," *American Political Science Review* 76 (June 1982): 371–79.

49. Thompson, "Minority Groups in Public Bureaucracy"; Dresang, "Ethnic Politics, Representative Bureaucracy, and Development Administration"; Kenneth J. Meier and Lloyd Nigro, "Representative Bureaucracy and Policy Preferences: A Study in the Attitudes of Federal Executives," *Public Administration Review* 36 (July/August 1976): 458–69; and Kenneth J. Meier, "Representative Bureaucracy: An Empirical Analysis," *American Political Science Review* 69 (June 1975): 526–43.

50. Katz et al., *Bureaucratic Encounters*; Goodsell, ed. *The Public Encounter*; and Elihu Katz and Brenda Danet, eds. *Bureaucracy and the Public*, (New York: Basic Books, 1973).

51. For example, Meier, "Representative Bureaucracy"; and Gormley, Hoadley, and Williams, "Potential Responsiveness in the Bureaucracy," look at top-level administrators, while Michael Brown, *Working the Street* (New York: Russell Sage, 1981), and William K. Muir, *Police: Street Corner Politicians* (Chicago: University of Chicago Press, 1977), examine street-level bureaucrats.

52. Representative examples include Gormley, Hoadley, and Williams, "Potential Responsiveness in the Bureaucracy," on citizen activists; Meier and Nigro, "Representative Bureaucracy and Policy Preferences," on general public opinion; and Mann, *Politics of Administrative Representation*, on opinions of elected officials.

53. Grace Saltzstein, "Representative Bureaucracy and Bureaucratic Responsibility," *Administration and Society* 10 (1979): 465–75.

54. See Boyle and Jacobs, "Intra-City Distribution of Services," p. 373; David Koehler and Margaret Wrightson, "Inequality in the Delivery of Urban Services: A Reconsideration of the Chicago Parks," *Journal of Politics* 49 (1987): 80–99.

55. Brian Stipak, "Citizen Satisfaction with Urban Services," *Public Administration Review* 39 (January/February 1979): 46–52.

56. See, for example, Koehler and Wrightson, "Inequality in the Delivery of Urban Services," pp. 93–95, regarding the findings of Mladenka, "Citizen Demands and Urban Services."

57. See Ziegler, Jennings, and Peak, *Governing American Schools*; Bryan Jones, *Governing Urban America* (Boston: Little, Brown, 1983); and Yeheskel Hasenfeld and Daniel Steinmetz, "Client–Official Encounters in Social Service Agencies" in Goodsell, ed., *The Public Encounter*, pp. 83–101.

58. See Kenneth J. Meier, Joe Stewart, Jr., and Robert England, "The Politics of Bureaucratic Discretion: Educational Access as an Urban Service," *American Journal of Political Science* 35 (February 1991): 155–77.

59. Gary Miller, *Cities by Contract* (Cambridge, MA: MIT Press, 1981), pp. 196–202.

60. Richard Hill, "Separate and Unequal: Governmental Inequality in the Metropolis," *American Political Science Review* 68 (1974): 1557–68.

61. See Mladenka, "Citizen Demands and Urban Services"; Lynn Bachelor, "Service Equity and Citizen Complaints," paper presented at the 1983 annual meetings of the American Political Science Association.

62. Sharp, "Responsiveness in Urban Service Delivery," p. 39.

63. See Mann, *Politics of Administrative Representation*; Tucker and Ziegler, *Professionals versus the Public*; and Gormley, Hoadley, and Williams, "Potential Responsiveness in the Bureaucracy."

64. See Peter Eisinger, "Black Employment in Municipal Jobs: The Impact of Black Political Power," *American Political Science Review* 76 (1982): 380–92; Saltzstein, "Representative Bureaucracy and Bureaucratic Responsibility"; Browning, Marshall, and Tabb, *Protest Is Not Enough*; Meier and England, "Black Representation and Educational Policy."

65. Mann, *Politics of Administrative Representation*, p. 11.

66. Salamon and Wamsley, "Responsive to Whom?", p. 152.

67. See David L. Cingranelli, "Race, Politics and Elites: Testing Alternative Models of Municipal Service Distribution," *American Journal of Political Science* 25 (1981): 664–92; Meier, Stewart, and England, "Politics of Bureaucratic Discretion"; Browning, Marshall, and Tabb, *Protest Is Not Enough*.

68. See James Q. Wilson, *Varieties of Police Behavior* (Cambridge, MA: Harvard University Press, 1969); Barbara Romzek and J. Stephen Hendricks, "Organizational Involvement and Representative Bureaucracy: Can We Have it Both Ways?" *American Political Science Review* 76 (March 1982): 75–82; Thomas Henderson, "The Relative Effects of Community Complexity and of Sheriffs upon the Professionalism of Sheriffs' Departments," *American Journal of Political Science* 19 (February 1975): 107–32.

69. Mann, *Politics of Administrative Representation*, p. 69.

Part Two

The Future State of Public Bureaucracy

7

The Problem of Predicting Bureaucracy's Future

Larry B. Hill

How will we be governed in the future? Will the large-scale organizations, which we call "bureaucracies," that have developed in modern society to implement public policies continue to exist in recognizable form? Will they expand in scale and scope? If these organizations undergo significant change, what will be the nature (evolutionary or abrupt) and direction (democratic or totalitarian) of this change? If bureaucracies are replaced, what will postbureaucratic organizations look like, and how will they affect citizens?

These are the kinds of questions that those who would forecast the future of government must address. Of the myriad positions that might be taken on these issues, most prophecies about bureaucracy seem to fit more or less comfortably into one or the other of two general views. One view predicts increased bureaucratization; the other predicts some form of debureaucratization. Of course, further bureaucratization may not necessarily be deplored, just as debureaucratization may not necessarily be applauded. Like Cassandra, prophets of bureaucracy may not be sanguine about their prophecies, which may not be heeded. Unfortunately, we cannot be sure which bureaucratic prophets have Cassandra's gift, or curse, of prophesying correctly.

The Coming Bureaucratization of American Government

Among those who predict an increase in bureaucratization, important differences arise in the nature of the organizations forecasted and in the explanations given for their development. The following is a brief summary of several views rather than an exhaustive treatment. A caveat is in order: the discrete views identified below on the causes of bureaucratization often have been separated artificially; in the course of prophesying, authors frequently blend several views together. And some explanations cannot readily be classified. In the assembly of those who hate bureaucracy, implicating an ill-defined, general conspiracy is not at all rare.

Why Bureaucracy Grows

Many of those who foresee greater bureaucratization would agree with Max Weber's contention that bureaucracy's growth is concomitant with the development of rational-legal society. The following passages from *Economy and Society* indicate the basis for Weber's assessment:

—Experience tends universally to show that the purely bureaucratic type of administrative organization—that is, the monocratic variety of bureaucracy—is, from a purely technical point of view, capable of attaining the highest degree of efficiency and is in this sense formally the most rational known means of exercising authority over human beings.

—The development of modern forms of organization in all fields is nothing less than identical with the development and continual spread of bureaucratic administration. This is true of church and state, of armies, political parties, economic enterprises, interest groups, endowments, clubs, and many others. Its development is . . . at the root of the modern Western state.

—The choice is only that between bureaucracy and dilettantism in the field of administration.[1]

According to Weber's analysis, if bureaucracy is the appropriate organizational form for rational-legal society—assuming that the trends toward increased rationalism in society are not reversed—then greater bureaucratization can be safely predicted.

Other analysts who agree that bureaucracy's growth is inexorable believe the explanation lies elsewhere than in the evolution of rational-legal society. One popular alternative explanation for bureaucracy's growth—which seldom is fully articulated—finds the cause within bureaucratic agencies themselves. According to this view, the organizational structures of bureaucracies provide a powerful framework within which bureaucrats—who seek self- and organizational aggrandizement—acquire resources and nurture political alliances; these advantages then are pursued so that the organizations at least perpetuate themselves and probably expand.[2]

According to a second alternative explanation, which really subsumes at least three separable explanations, bureaucratic growth is caused by the activities of external, nonbureaucratic political actors:

1. Some theorists believe that bureaucracy expands because politicians compete for votes by promising more services and bigger grants (particularly entitlement grants), which must be dispensed by an ever-larger bureaucracy.[3]

2. Others believe that bureaucracy expands because political groups press their claims within a rudderless policy process that gives legitimacy and access to virtually all organized groups; the public interest is defined merely as the outcome of the various pressures, and government's main role is simply "ratifying the agreements and adjustments worked out among the competing leaders."[4] Since policy follows no theoretical or ideological pattern, government (and bureaucracy) tends to grow as the system's chief participants attempt to satisfy as many competing claimants as possible.

3. Yet others believe that welfare bureaucracies are not designed as benevolent service providers but as institutions of social control: determined to protect itself, our capitalist-dominated political system created welfare bureaucracies as a response to actual or potential pressure from the poor; the preeminent goal of these institutions is to pacify and control the poor—including the permanent "underclass" that has been created by economic policies designed to favor the rich.[5] Because capitalist economies are subject to recurrent crises, the price of pacification tends to increase, and government grows.

Evaluations of Bureaucratic Growth

Just as authors who predict increased bureaucratization do so for different reasons, so also they may present a variety of normative evaluations of the prospect. Those who take an instrumental approach to bureaucracy may view this form of organization simply as an efficient tool that ought to be used to accomplish whatever public purposes are identified through the political process. According to this view, bureaucracy's advantages over other organizational forms—including speed, reliability, impartiality, universality, continuity, precision, and economy—are obvious. Since these advantages outweigh any associated costs, choosing to use a nonbureaucratic form of administration would be irrational, and political legitimacy should be accorded to our bureaucratic institutions. Bureaucracy's public defenders have been both few and subdued, at least, until recently.[6]

But those who take a demonic approach to bureaucracy long have been numerous and vociferous. Some of bureaucracy's critics worry about its seeming propensity to promote a form of government that could end in totalitarianism.[7] Of course, this view is taken by many popular writers; the world that we describe as "Orwellian" is quintessentially bureaucratic. Other critics point to bureaucracy's alleged "dysfunctions": these organizations are rigid and rule-bound, secretive, unaccountable, slow, inefficient, et cetera. In this view, if bureaucratic agencies of the future are not totalitarian, they are likely to be dehumanized.[8]

Perhaps ironically, the pessimistic view of bureaucratic growth came to be shared by the man who developed the ideal-typical view of bureaucracy. Writing before either the rise of fascism in Europe or the development of computers, Max Weber expressed his fears in a passage, which has become well known, at the end of *The Protestant Ethic and the Spirit of Capitalism.* Speaking of the "iron cage" of the future, he cited the possibility of it being inhabited by those having

> a mechanized petrification decked out with a sort of obsessive self-importance. Then indeed could it be said of the "ultimate" men of that stage of cultural development: "Technicians without souls, sensualists without hearts—this nothingness imagines it has climbed to a level of humanity never reached."[9]

The authors of the next two chapters present different visions of the ways in which they believe American government will become increasingly bureaucratic in the decades to come. In "The Political Marriage of Information Technology and Bureaucracy," Theodore J. Lowi, who takes a generally jaundiced approach to bureaucracy, charts the recent growth of expenditures for information technology within public bureaucracies and predicts that the already high level of such spending will continue to increase. Because the implementation of information technology facilitates management's control of bureaucracies and their environments, he says, the leaders of bureaucracies have every incentive to use the available technology. But Lowi identifies a number of serious political costs that may be incurred in uniting public bureaucracy and information technology. This marriage, he concludes, may promote a rational, well-managed, but boring society.

The discussion thus far has treated the notion of bureaucratization as a straightforward, unidimensional concept. But, in "On Predicting the Bureaucratization of American Government," James Q. Wilson points out that the concept actually is multidimensional. In constructing his forecast of the future, he uses the public choice perspective, the social control perspective, and the interest-group liberalism perspective in analyzing three different meanings of bureaucratic growth: (1) all three perspectives predict that the *size* of government and its bureaucracies will grow; (2) the perspectives vary about whether the *discretionary authority* of bureaucracies will grow; (3) the perspectives have little to say about the likelihood of the bureaucracies becoming more *structurally complex*, but Wilson argues that the proliferation of interest groups will stimulate bureaucratic complexity. Wilson is not daunted by his analysis; from a comparative viewpoint, he claims, the bureaucracy of the United States is perhaps the least Orwellian of those belonging to the major industrial democracies.

The Coming Debureaucratization of American Government

Whereas most of those who foresee an increasingly bureaucratized future do so with at least some trepidation, those who foresee debureaucratization frequently are filled with utopian zeal. Two main views about the nature of debureaucratization and its causes may be identified. Some futurists hold that—owing mainly to changes in society—bureaucracy will be superseded by more advanced organizational forms. Other futurists hold that—through shrinking the role of government—bureaucracy will be engineered out of existence. Of course, these views may overlap, and many of their adherents would not endorse the extreme form in which the views have just been stated.

Beyond Bureaucracy

During the mid-1960s and the early 1970s, a number of theorists began to say that what Warren Bennis called Weber's "machine model" of bureaucracy was outmoded and unable to cope with the rapid changes occurring in its environment. Advances in science and technology, greater interdependence between government and all other social and economic actors, declines in environmental stability and increases in turbulence—all posed important challenges for bureaucracy, Bennis said, "It is the requirement of adaptability to the environment which leads to the predicted demise of bureaucracy and to the collapse of management as we know it now."[10]

Because bureaucracies cannot successfully cope with these challenges—nor can they cope with others concerning the difficulties in motivating workers and providing leadership in a hierarchical structure—new kinds of organizations, which Bennis called "organic-adaptive" structures, were evolving. Important features of these new organizations included their temporary nature, their organization around particular problems to be solved, their conceptualization upon organic rather than mechanical models, and their differentiation on the basis of flexible criteria related to skill and professional training rather than hierarchy and role.

According to Bennis, change would be endemic in these new types of organizations. Many changes would occur as a result of the kinds of work being done; if activity is organized around a problem, the "project team," or "task force," will be designed to disband when it is no longer needed.[11] Other changes will occur as a matter of policy; managers will frequently redesign the organization, breaking down calcified and obsolete structures as a means toward the goal of creating a "self-renewing organization."[12]

Some aspects of Bennis's evolving organic-adaptive structures (which were popularized by Alvin Toffler in Future Shock as "Ad-hocracies"), especially their temporary and rapidly changing character, would place strains on workers' psychological coping mechanisms. But Bennis believed that compensations could be found in the increased scope the new structures would allow for creativity and for freedom from the evils of hierarchy.[13]

In the intervening years since Bennis first sketched his highly influential ideas about the future of organizations, a number of other writers belonging to the same genre have contributed to the discussion. Among the predictions frequently made are the following: organizations of the future will adopt a networking style of management that features horizontal rather than vertical (hierarchical) linkages; organizations of the future will be characterized by bottom-up and decentralized authority relationships rather than top-down and centralized relationships; organizations of the future will be products of an "information society" in which computers play a vital and liberating role; organizations of the future will pay a great deal of attention to the "human side of management," emphasizing noneconomic motivators, worker participation, quality circles, and Type Z managerial styles borrowed from Japan.[14] If this vision of the post-bureaucratic future is not idyllic, it is generally optimistic.

Shrinking Government and Bureaucracy

Quite a different strand of thought agrees with the Jeffersonian dictum, "that government is best which governs least." The growth during the past half-century in government's scope and in its administrative reach has profoundly alarmed many conservative futurists who have a vision of a minimalist state.[15]

Perhaps the most important program advocated for shrinking bureaucracy is the practice of "load shedding" in which government would simply rid itself of the obligation, which advocates point out was recently assumed in many cases, to provide expensive and intrusive social services—particularly in various aspects of education, health care, housing, and income maintenance—that previously were considered private. Precisely how far load shedding should be taken is a matter of debate among these theorists; some argue that national defense is the only function that is legitimately governmental, but recognize as a political reality that government will continue to provide many other services.

For the remaining services that cannot be shed, a variety of antibureaucratic strategies and institutional arrangements has been foreseen:

1. Governments could introduce *user charges* that reflect actual costs for many municipal services (refuse pickup, swimming pools, libraries), for bridges, for rescues by the Coast Guard.

2. Governments could adopt *voucher systems* that promote competition among suppliers—possibly including both public and private suppliers (education at all levels)—or that otherwise provide a less bureaucratic delivery system for services (food stamps and Medicaid enrollment cards rather than commodity food distribution and comprehensive governmental health care delivery programs).

3. Governments could promote *intergovernmental agreements*, the already widespread practice in which one governmental unit decides not to duplicate a service established by another unit—frequently at a different governmental level—but to sign a contract with that unit to provide the service (counties providing water supply, sewage treatment, jails for municipalities).

4. Governments could implement *contracting out* with private suppliers to provide a service (street sweeping and maintenance, refuse collection, ambulance service) or to provide components of a service (data processing, secretarial and clerical services, training, food service, janitorial service).

5. Governments could conclude *franchise arrangements*, which usually grant a monopoly to a private firm for providing a service and which feature regulation by the government and payment for the services by the consumer (cable television, bus transportation, stadium and airport concessions).

6. Governments could introduce *grant programs* to award governmental subsidies for services—either in the form of money or tax-exempt status—to the producers (subsidized mass transit, universities, hospitals, cultural institutions).

7. Governments could promote *mandatory recourse to the market*, which occurs in many small cities that require citizens to have their trash picked up regularly but allow them to select any company to provide the service.

8. Governments could encourage *voluntary mutual-aid associations* that provide a variety of services under more or less direct governmental auspices (recreation facilities, neighborhood patrols, volunteer fire departments—the latter account for more than 90 percent of the fire departments in this country).

Those who foresee a minimalist state believe that creative combinations of these sorts of strategies and structures can shrink bureaucracy—perhaps drastically. For example, adopting the negative income tax, which really is a type of voucher scheme, could have a dramatic impact on the size and scope of the federal bureaucracy—assuming that the plan finally adopted stays true to the original intent. Milton Friedman, the proposal's intellectual father, has emphasized the importance of the latter point: "The negative income tax would be a satisfactory reform of our present welfare system only if it *replaces* the host of other specific programs that we now have. It would do more harm than good if it simply became another rag in the ragbag of welfare programs."[16]

Although the negative income tax scheme has just been discussed as a prototypical example of the thinking of those who foresee a minimalist state, it also may be viewed as an example of the kinds of programs that might be characteristic of more advanced postbureaucratic organizations. Thus, the scheme illustrates how the two views that have been presented on debureaucratization may overlap.

In his sketch of the coming "cybernetic state," Allen Schick mentions the negative income tax—along with such other programs as family allowances—as an example of the more-or-less self-executing programs favored by this form of the state in which "government functions as a servomechanism, conjoining the polity and the economy to achieve public objectives."[17] In Schick's cybernetic state, "bureaucracy presumably will shrink in size and importance," but—through self-regulative means—the government will continue to play an important role in the economy and in society.[18] Schick's vision of the debureaucratized future is probably closer to Bennis than to Friedman, but contains elements of both.

After gazing into their crystal balls, the authors of this part's final two chapters foresee different types of less bureaucratized futures for American government. Among the writers who predict debureaucratization, both essayists are atypical because their visions can hardly be labeled utopian.

In "Catastrophic Errors and the Changing Shape of Bureaucracy," Martin Landau argues that the potential for bureaucracies to make errors of truly catastrophic proportions—allowing nuclear reactors to undergo core meltdowns or unleashing dangerous genetically engineered viruses upon the environment—requires that significant changes be made in the structure of bureaucracy. Because governmental agencies will be forced to take action in newly developing policy areas in which knowledge is very uncertain and experimentation is not possible, Landau says that new organizational forms promoting the goal of reliability will develop. Since a broad empirical base for ensuring reliable organizational performance does not exist, he concludes, we shall have to employ our theoretical knowledge; perhaps computer simulations could be used as a strategy for conducting quasi-experiments. Landau predicts that postbureaucratic organizations will be flatter (hierarchy will be undermined by the wide dispersion of knowledge), more pragmatic, and more competitive than our present bureaucracies.

Quite a different view of the future is taken by Francis E. Rourke in "American Exceptionalism: Government without Bureaucracy." Rourke describes "American exceptionalism" as the tendency in this country to pursue strategies for dealing with social and economic problems that will minimize the role of bureaucracy. While most other Western democracies have reconciled themselves to the inevitability of bureaucracy in the modern state, Americans have resented and resisted this development. Rourke says that this rejection has been visible across the entire spectrum of American politics. The criticism comes even from reformers, who cannot achieve their most cherished objectives without relying on bureaucratic organizations. As a result, one of the most striking characteristics of modern American politics is the extraordinary range of ways in which the system has sought to find alternatives to bureaucracy in both the design and the implementation of public policy. Rourke takes a nonutopian attitude toward the variety of debureaucratization he sees developing.

Notes

1. Max Weber, *Economy and Society: An Outline of Interpretive Sociology*, vol. 1, ed. Guenther Roth and Claus Wittich (Berkeley: University of California Press, 1978), p. 223.

2. See William A. Niskanen, *Bureaucracy and Representative Government* (Chicago: Aldine-Atherton, 1971).

3. See Morris P. Fiorina, *Congress: Keystone of the Washington Establishment* (New Haven, CT: Yale University Press, 1977), p. 49.

4. For a discussion of "interest-group liberalism," see Theodore J. Lowi, *The End of Liberalism: The Second Republic of the United States*, 2d ed. (New York: Norton, 1979), p. 51.

5. See Francis Fox Piven and Richard A. Cloward, *Regulating the Poor: The Functions of Public Welfare* (New York: Pantheon, 1971); Walter I. Trattner, ed., *Social Welfare or Social Control? Some Historical Reflections on "Regulating the Poor"* (Knoxville: University of Tennessee Press, 1983).

6. Prominent examples of texts that defend bureaucracy include Francis E. Rourke, *Bureaucracy, Politics, and Public Policy,* 3d ed. (Boston: Little, Brown, 1984); Charles T. Goodsell, *The Case for Bureaucracy: A Public Administration Polemic,* 2d ed. (Chatham, NJ: Chatham House, 1985); Kenneth J. Meier, *Politics and the Bureaucracy: Policymaking in the Fourth Branch of Government,* 2d ed. (Monterey, CA: Brooks/Cole, 1987); James W. Fesler and Donald F. Kettl, The Politics of the Administrative Process (Chatham, NJ: Chatham House, 1991).

7. See Hannah Arendt, *The Origins of Totalitarianism,* new ed. (New York: Harcourt Brace Jovanovich, 1973).

8. The literature assuming this viewpoint is voluminous. As examples, see Ralph P. Hummel, *The Bureaucratic Experience,* 3d ed. (New York: St. Martin's, 1987); Henry Jacoby, *The Bureaucratization of the World,* trans. Eveline L. Kanes (Berkeley: University of California Press, 1973).

9. Max Weber, *The Sociology of Religion,* vol. 1 (Boston: Beacon Press, 1964), p. 204.

10. Warren G. Bennis, *Changing Organizations: Essays on the Development and Evolution of Human Organization* (New York: McGraw-Hill, 1966), p. 10; see also the essays in Warren G. Bennis and Philip E. Slater, *The Temporary Society* (New York: Harper and Row, 1968).

11. For an overview of what has come to be called "matrix" management, see David I. Cleland, *Matrix Management Systems Handbook* (New York: Van Nostrand Reinhold, 1984).

12. See John W. Gardner, *Self-renewal: The Individual and the Innovative Society* (New York: Harper and Row, 1964).

13. Alvin Toffler, *Future Shock* (New York: Random House, 1970), ch. 7. See also Frederick C. Thayer, *An End to Hierarchy and Competition: Administration in the Post-Affluent World,* 2d ed. (New York: New Viewpoints, 1981).

14. For a popular compendium of these ideas, see John Naisbitt, *Megatrends: Ten New Directions Transforming Our Lives* (New York: Warner Books, 1984); for a perspective from public administration, see Harlan Cleveland, "The Twilight of Hierarchy: Speculations on the Global Information Society," *Public Administration Review* 45 (January/February 1985): 185–95.

15. A concise statement of these ideas, upon which I relied heavily in the following synopsis, may be found in E.S. Savas, *Privatizing the Public Sector: How to Shrink Government* (Chatham, NJ: Chatham House, 1982).

16. Milton Friedman and Rose Freidman, *Free to Choose: A Personal Statement* (New York: Avon Books, 1980), p. 113; emphasis in original.

17. Allen Schick, "Toward the Cybernetic State," in *Public Administration in a Time of Turbulence,* ed. Dwight Waldo (Scranton, PA: Chandler, 1971), p. 222; emphasis deleted.

18. Ibid., p. 225.

8

The Political Marriage
of Information Technology
and Bureaucracy

Theodore J. Lowi

In *Nineteen Eighty-Four,* George Orwell presaged the information revolution in public bureaucracies by inventing such office machines as the "speakwrite," the "versificator," and the interactive "telescreen." Very recently, information technology has progressed by leaps and bounds, and the influence of this technology on public organizations—which has thus far been largely neglected by political scientists—is the aspect of bureaucracy's future that I shall explore.

The Growth of Information Technology
within Public Bureaucracies

I start a brief overview of this particular technological revolution with an examination of only the public sector developments. This leaves aside the vast industry of information technology in the private sector. A survey conducted by the National Bureau of Standards in 1981, which examined the situation in the late 1970s, estimated that in the federal government alone total indirect investment in information technology amounted to $6 billion. That did not count expenditures for contracting out for such information services from the private sector. In a 1984 survey the bureau found that during the fiscal year 1983, the federal government expended more than $10 billion for information technology. The bureau estimated that the federal government spent nearly $14 billion during 1985.

There are at least two reasons why federal expenditures on information technology rose substantially in the 1980s. First, since the federal government was a leader in the adoption and integration of information technology, a lot of its machinery was obsolete and had to be replaced. Second, since so much investment in information technology has always been in the Defense Department and related agencies, and since the Reagan administration placed its budgetary emphasis on these agencies, there was every reason to expect that expenditures for these matters would rise. But the value of information technology is not lost on agencies outside the Defense establishment.

What are the uses to which this technology has been applied? In many areas, information technology has become commonplace. For instance, information retrieval is very important to the personnel function; somebody has estimated that there are fourteen computerized dossiers on every man, woman, and child in this country. Computerized information retrieval also is used on data other than personnel data, for example, scientific information of various types and the Library of Congress card catalog. Another important use of computers is in fiscal and budgetary management. Of course, word processing is now ubiquitous. Well before the end of the 1980s, more than half a million personal computers were in the hands—or at the fingertips—of federal bureaucrats. More important, information technology is increasingly used in decision making itself, not only through simulating various scenarios but through creating situations in which indicators become trigger or threshold variables to decisions. These developments in information technology have resulted in a significant expansion of the role of the management component of public bureaucracies.

Information Technology and
the Managerial Control of Bureaucracies

Management may be defined as the use of information to manipulate the fact and value premises of workers. Thus, management is virtually information processing. This interpretation would be supported by an examination of the curricula of the major business schools offering the MBA degree. Furthermore, the graduates of these schools hope to become managers; some 90 percent of the graduates of the Harvard and the Wharton Business Schools, according to the *Wall Street Journal*, prefer to go into the management aspects rather than the hands-on manufacturing aspects of the businesses they join. Hence, management has become an important, distinguishable professional component, interchangeable between the private and the public sectors.

The government investment in information technology is almost entirely devoted to facilitating management's control of the bureaucracies and their external environments. In other words, this technology has been adopted for purposes of social control. One can generally predict that a new technology will be experimented with as an additional instrument of social control; this one certainly is working out that way.

To give a sense of the extent of this commitment to social control within and without the agencies themselves, let us consider the Communications Act of 1934—the only comprehensive effort by the national government to deal with information in any form. In that act, Congress gave AT&T a monopoly in the area in return for an agreement that they would make the new information technology universally available; everyone could possess the telephone. Although comparable new technology is now at hand, we certainly have no governmental policy that has a comprehensive vision of the importance of access and that values the ability of citizens to use information technology for spontaneous communication among themselves, as opposed to sponsored communications between individuals and large organizations, including government. In contrast, everything about information technology that I can see, at the risk of slight overstatement, is an investment in social control—in the controlling of the processes of large administrative agencies and in facilitating their direct control of their immediate environment.

Why Information Technology Will Continue to Expand within Bureaucracies

To predict that we will make a much higher investment in information technology in the future does not depend solely upon making extrapolations from the studies and situations alluded to above. This prediction also can be made simply by coming to an understanding of the nature of public organizations. That is, when we understand exactly what bureaucracies are, then we can generate predictions about the kinds of investments they will choose to make. Thus, let me spell out four dimensions of bureaucracy, which are certainly applicable to public bureaucracy, that show how inherently compatible this form of organization is with information technology and formally defined information processing. On the basis of this analysis, I shall suggest that we can predict the direction of public bureaucracy's future growth.

The first dimension concerns routine. In his early days as a student of public administration, Arnold Brecht once defined bureaucracy as "voluminous routine business." I can think of no better definition of the direct function of computer technology than that. IBM stands for International *Business* Machines; the company has been successful precisely because its machines efficiently handle the voluminous routine tasks of large business establishments, that is, private bureaucracies.

The second dimension of this very intimate compatibility between information technology and bureaucracy is that information, not knowledge, is the life of both. Information is formally defined knowledge. According to the definition that technologists themselves use, information is artificial knowledge. It is knowledge transformed into power, into means of greater power. It is an enhancement, but nevertheless it is artificial. That is why one can measure information, but one cannot measure knowledge. Information comes in bits, knowledge does not. I am not saying this as a Luddite; it is a fact by definition.

The third dimension of compatibility concerns costs. Bureaucratic organizations can easily handle the costs of being informed. Information is a resource, but it is unique in relation to other resources in that it is not used up in the process of being used. When additions are made to an agency's information technology bank, the addition is a marginal cost because any information already used does not need replenishing. Information needs only to be added as a marginal adjustment.

The fourth dimension of compatibility between information technology and bureaucracy relates to interdependence. In one sense, information is comparable to other resources, such as energy, in that any resource provides additional power in dealing with the environment. Here, however, information parts company with other resources. While information adds power, it does so through creating interdependence, not independence. Information is a process whose value as a resource must be understood in terms of that interdependence. This analysis suggests the compatibility between information technology and bureaucracy because even traditional conceptions of bureaucracy stress the importance of its highly interdependent parts, which specialize in certain tasks.

The Political Costs of Unifying Bureaucracy and Information Technology

Bureaucracies certainly have used information technology to their advantage in developing a separate management component, in controlling their environments, and in creating rational operating procedures that increase their power. But what are the likely political costs of this marriage between bureaucracy and modern information processing? I suggest that the costs will be considerable. Perhaps identifying them will help promote reform and invalidate my forecast.

The first of these political costs of uniting bureaucracy and information technology is the magnification of error. When an organization increases by a large factor the ability to coordinate and to take the total universe of the operation into account, it also magnifies the consequences of errors that occur, for example, brownouts of the whole East Coast.

A second political cost of an information-based bureaucracy is stalemate. Information-processing capabilities allow bureaucracies to interact with the environment to an increased degree, but they also produce differences of opinion so that bureaucracies are cross-pressured and may have difficulty in getting their jobs done. No public works megaprojects have been accomplished in recent years, for example. I am very critical of governments, but when they have a job to do and cannot act, stalemate must be counted as a cost.

A third political cost of combining bureaucracy with information technology is the loss of sensory experience between bureaucracies and the outside world, between law makers and the citizens, between people and people. The act of formalizing knowledge moves one or more steps away from sensory experience, which causes problems in policy making. My favorite example is the Bill Mauldin cartoon that shows a general standing on an alpine peak poring over a map spread out on a rock; his aide has a finger on the map and says, "General, Sir, according to our calculations, we are on that hill right over there." This is the kind of error that comes from removal from sensory experience.

A fourth political cost of the adoption of information technology by bureaucracies is the decline of the rule of law. The rule of law had been abandoned in *Nineteen Eighty-Four*. Orwell wrote: "This was not illegal (nothing was illegal, since there were no longer any laws)."[1] The rise of cost-benefit analysis is associated with the decline of legal substance. Economics has replaced law as the language of the state.

A fifth political cost of an information-based bureaucracy is the denigration of amateurs in favor of professionals, who know how to manipulate the new technology. This process is already happening, but certainly it will be accelerated at the very time when broad-ranging capacities for analyzing complex problems—capacities that many amateurs are likely to possess but that many narrowly trained professionals are not likely to possess—are most needed.

The last political cost I shall mention of combining bureaucracy and information technology is the decline of spontaneous politics and the rise of sponsored politics. Because agencies have increased their ability to interact with their environments through adopting information technology, they then may sponsor communications from "approved" groups that become inputs to the policy process. Whether this procedure produces stalemate or produces a more legitimate action, it is, nevertheless, sponsored politics in which you translate your complaints into the language that bureaucracy can deal with, just as we have to have a lawyer in court to translate our language into judicial language. This further denigrates spontaneity in politics.

Conclusion

In taking a final overview of the bureaucratic future I foresee, I want to invoke a Lasswell-type developmental construct, which I draw from his friend and colleague, Karl Mannheim. The developmental construct is what Mannheim called "bureaucratic conservatism." This is the society I envision. Mannheim predicted a rationalized society where the unpredictable (read "political") is irrational. Therefore, politics is viewed as bad and as something to be controlled.[2]

Now, the outcome from that developmental construct is not necessarily a tyranny of the Orwellian or any other violent type. Totalitarianism is a possibility, but I do not see it as a high probability. To me, the higher probability is one that I began to conceptualize fifteen years ago but did not fully understand then. Also, I did not appreciate how likely it was to come into being. That is the hell of administrative boredom—a society so rationalized that the citizen's freedom has become translated and prismatic. In this future society *managers* are the epitome of civic virtue. That, I fear, is what we shall mean just a few years from now when we speak of the modern state.

Notes

1. George Orwell, *Nineteen Eighty-Four* [1949] (Oxford: Clarendon Press, 1984), Vol. p. 161.
2. Karl Mannheim, *Ideology and Utopia: An Introduction to the Sociology of Knowledge* [1929] (New York: Harcourt, Brace, and World, 1968), pp. 104–106.

9

On Predicting the Bureaucratization of American Government

James Q. Wilson

Will American government become significantly more bureaucratic in the next several decades? To answer that question, we first have to explain what we mean by more bureaucratic. Although there are at least three possible meanings of that term, the meanings are often not distinguished one from the other—and this leads to global and perhaps mistaken conclusions.

First, we can say that the government is becoming more bureaucratic if it grows in size measured by employees, outlays, or proportion of the gross national product it consumes. This is the customary way in which bureaucratization is measured; the great bulk of the literature attempting to explain the rates of growth of the American government—as well as that of other industrial states— uses this method of measurement. Second, we can mean that the government becomes more bureaucratic in that its agencies exercise more discretionary authority. By discretionary authority, I mean the opposite of the rule of law in A.V. Dicey's terms or "juridical democracy" in Theodore Lowi's phrase.[1] Discretion allows agencies to constrain the behavior of others while remaining free of clear legislative standards. Finally, the government may become more bureaucratic because its agencies become internally more complex. According to this definition of bureaucratization, authority within each agency becomes more widely divided among various appointed officials.

Governments may become more bureaucratic in one or the other, but not necessarily in all three of these senses. If we compare governments across states within the United States or across the world, we may decide that they are highly bureaucratic with respect to one measure, but not with respect to another.

In an effort to answer the question, "Is the American government in the decades to come likely to become significantly more bureaucratic in any one of these three senses?," we can turn to a political science literature that contains at least three dominant ways of thinking about the question. First, we can examine the "public choice" perspective, which treats political actors as individuals and groups who maximize in a rational manner their self-interest, usually narrowly conceived. Second, we can repair to the view sometimes called the "social control" perspective, sometimes called (albeit more loosely) the "neo-Marxist" perspective, namely, that the government exists in order to reproduce or retain control of the processes of capital accumulation so as to protect and reproduce the dominant social class, variously defined as business, bourgeois, or capitalists. Finally, we can consider our old friend, "interest-group liberalism," in Theodore Lowi's terms,[2] or putting a better face on it, the perspective of "well-intentioned pluralism." The question is, what predictions might each of these three schools of thought offer about the likely changes in the nature of the bureaucratic state?

Bureaucratization and Governmental Size

Dealing first with the question of size, I believe all three views would predict that there will be a continued growth in the size of the government as measured by total expenditures, percentage of gross national product consumed, number of employees, or whatever. In this regard, the United States will become more like Sweden, which has nowhere left to go in terms of bureaucratization. Sweden is at the asymptote of the curve, at least among the democratic industrial states. The United States, from this perspective, has only up to go. According to the public choice perspective, because of the competitive struggle for votes, politicians promise more and more in order to win office. In this view, Ronald Reagan will be a brief and perhaps not very lasting exception. Indeed, advocates of the public choice perspective claim that he did not reduce government at all, but that he, in fact, increased it. Reagan's critics agree; they only disagree about which aspect of government he increased the most. The social control theory suggests that the government will grow in order to appropriate more resources to buy off political dissent and thereby maintain legitimacy, or in order to subsidize industries that are running out of markets. The interest-group liberalism view will, I think, claim that the government will grow because there are "unmet needs" out there. And as long as there is an unmet need, there will be a group pressing government to take some new step.

Each of these perspectives offers a different rationale for the prediction that the size of government size will grow. In my view, the difficulties in these perspectives tend to cancel each other out. My net assessment is that—however it is measured—the government will grow; Ronald Reagan was, indeed, an aberration. The public choice perspective vastly overstates self-interest maximization as a motive of politics, and cannot explain why until the 1960s the United States government so rarely relied on deficit financing, except in war time, and why until the 1930s (or, even better, the 1960s) this competitive struggle for votes did not lead early on to the creation of the national welfare state, which clearly it did not. I find the social control perspective to be an interesting one, but it has not yet established empirically the proposition that the key function of welfare is to buy off potential dissent in order to establish the legitimacy of the state. With respect to interest-group liberalism, one always wants to know what is an unmet need, but we can be assured that that question will always be answered. Although criticisms can be brought against each of the paradigmatic ways of thinking of the problem about the size of the government, a surprising degree of unanimity exists among the perspectives that the *size* of the government will grow.

Bureaucratization and Discretionary Authority

A much more complicated issue arises when we ask the more interesting question: will the discretionary authority of government agencies grow? Will the rule of law, as Dicey saw it, retreat even further into the background? To me, this is the most important question to be asked about bureaucratization. After all, depending on which definition of bureaucratization we prefer, we could have a government that consumes a very large fraction of the gross national product, but if it uses the resources only to issue checks so as to transfer income among individuals or localities with the aid of a well-programmed computer located in the basement of the Treasury Department, we might not have a bureaucratic state at all—provided, of course, we could keep Congressmen from going into the basement of the Treasury Department and reprogramming the computer at night in order to benefit their constituents (a heroic assumption, I grant you). The rise in discretionary authority, I think, is what George Orwell was talking about: nothing was illegal in *Nineteen Eighty-Four* because there was no law. That overstates the matter, but overstatement was Orwell's point.

If we assess what these three schools of thought have to say about the likelihood of increased discretion, some problems arise with all three. The net assessment I offer on this issue, therefore, is more complicated.

The public choice theorists would have us believe that bureaus grow rapidly in authority in order to maximize the wealth and power of the members of the bureaus. But that assessment, which has not been empirically demonstrated, runs up against the fact that bureaus are not autonomous. Bureaus and their important subdivisions grow only as the legislature permits; therefore, the theory of a bureau must be linked with the theory of a legislature. Furthermore, the wealth of individual bureaucrats is not, in fact, dependent upon the size of their bureau. It is, instead, dependent on systemwide civil service and financial compensation laws.

The social control perspective argues that the growth of discretionary authority has been inevitable as the dominant social class has used government instrumentalities at the local and the federal levels in order to control the workers. In this view, the history of the public schools, the asylums, the prisons, the jails, the mental institutions, the police, and the judiciary is a history of creating and energizing institutions whose social function, if not their stated purpose, has been to control dissident activity. The difficulty with that view, it seems to me, is twofold. First, it has not to my satisfaction been established by the historical evidence. Second, the agencies of social control about which social control theorists write the most have been precisely those agencies of government that have suffered a net *reduction* in their discretionary authority in the last two or three decades. We can all think of government agencies that have acquired more discretionary authority. I will mention some in a moment. What is striking is that the schools, the prisons, the jails, the mental hospitals, and the police have suffered a net reduction in discretionary authority. The reduction has not occurred in their total size or in the magnitude of their impact on society. Measured in these ways, their authority is probably larger. But their capacity to alter the fate of human beings in a way that is unconstrained by the rule of law has decreased. We have decriminalized a larger and larger number of offenses, and we have deinstitutionalized a larger and larger number both of persons who formerly were put in prison for relatively minor offenses and of persons who were once in asylums but are now on the streets. The schools have seen the rise of the students' rights movement, prisons have seen the rise of prisoners' rights movements, and the courts have sharply reduced the power of the police to arrest and interrogate.

The rights movement has had the effect of reducing the discretionary authority of social control agencies at the very time when the discretionary authority of other agencies—notably those engaged in environmental regulation or the delivery of health care—have grown. Although the evidence is not complete, I think there has been a net decline in the discretionary authority of most of the "street-level" bureaucracies, to use Michael Lipsky's term—the police, the asylums, the schools, the prisons, and the jails.[3] Although their size and net impact remain as large or larger than ever, their discretionary authority has been reduced.

At the same time, the discretionary authority of welfare agencies that deal with certain kinds of relatively powerless clients has increased. I am thinking of those agencies that deal with such matters as Aid to Families with Dependent Children and those agencies that engage in quality-of-life issues, or what is sometimes called social regulation, as opposed to rate setting or entry regulation. We see an enormous expansion in the number of rules governing the behavior of welfare recipients and an enormous expansion in the number of rules governing the behavior of industrial entities. Why welfare mothers and DuPont should find themselves in the same fix is not altogether clear. I predict that DuPont will get out of the fix faster than will the welfare mothers, but this does suggest that some important distinctions have to be made when we analyze changes in discretionary authority.

Finally, my sense is that there has been relatively little change in the discretionary authority of agencies that transfer funds by means of entitlement programs or intergovernmental transfers. The largest entitlement program, Social Security retirement insurance, has been relatively free of significant changes in eligibility rules or in procedures that empower bureaucrats to make unconstrained choices among potential recipients. The rise of disability insurance, by contrast, has greatly increased bureaucratic discretion. Intergovernmental transfers became for a while more clearly standardized with the rise of block grants and general revenue sharing; the latter has, of course, ended. But as anyone who has looked at the federal budget over the last few years is all too aware, intergovernmental transfers through block grants and general revenue sharing has been the slowest-growing component of intergovernmental transfers. In fact, in the aggregate, it is not growing at all. Those transfer payments among units of government that are earmarked and that are specific grant proposals tend to be constrained by as many rules as once was the case. Of course, there is a reason for this. No one in that particular system has an interest in deregulating it because these intergovernmental transfers represent, to some degree, the shared objectives of federal administrators and state and local administrators, each of whom uses the rules and constraints of the others in order to justify resistance to legislative intervention.

Bureaucratization and Agency Complexity

Finally, there is the question of the complexity of government agencies. Are agencies becoming more complex such that the citizen experiences more red tape, more delays, more paperwork, more problems? Most of the theories that I have alluded to—certainly the public choice theory, and to some degree the social control and interest-group theories—have relatively little to say about the internal life of agencies.

My sense is that the internal life of agencies has become more complex and will continue to become more complex. Hugh Heclo has a graphic illustration of this in his famous essay on issue networks in which he shows the organization chart of the higher command of the Department of Labor in 1933, 1960, and 1976. During those four decades, that organization experienced a proliferation of assistant secretaries and special-assistant-deputy-undersecretaries.[4] Such a proliferation also is happening in other kinds of organizations; I see it in universities, for example. The Kennedy School of Government at Harvard is training people for administrative service, and the hierarchy of that school has become as complex as the hierarchy of the Department of State. Perhaps a process of emulation is at work: in order to train people for being deputy assistant secretaries, the school has created deputy assistant deans.

This process of complexity occurs not because people like to proliferate offices or because the supply of would-be bureaucrats creates a demand for them. The growth in administrative complexity is a response to something quite different. It is a response to the enormous growth and proliferation of interest groups. The groups recognize that political decisions are increasingly made in the executive branch rather than in the legislative branch and want not only a share of bureaucratic authority, but also permanent recognition of their claim to bureaucratic authority. They obtain that recognition by seeing to it that agencies are organized in such a way that interest-group demands are institutionally preserved. For example, the effort to create an organizational structure in the Department of Energy based on such analytic concepts as research, production, dissemination, sales, or allocations, was quickly undercut by this process and soon replaced by an administrative structure that reflected commodities: fossil fuels, solar energy, hydroelectric power, whatever. All of the major kinds of commodity had to become the organizational entities of the Department of Energy.

This process is further intensified by the continuing tendency of courts to set policy by creating adversarial proceedings based on an enlarged theory of rights. And in order to deal with that as well as with new laws recognizing the demands of newly organized constituencies, every government agency must be more complex. Agencies must have somebody in charge of each of the issues likely to be demanded by an interest group, insisted upon by Congress, or pressed upon them by the courts—just as all of our universities have become internally more complex as a result of the need felt by the universities to recognize the demands of persons concerned about equal opportunity in hiring, feminism, environmental protection, real estate expansion, and the like.

Conclusion

In comparative perspective, the United States is in some ways the least Orwellean of the major industrial democracies. I say this as a person who has tried to acquire a driver's license in Naples, whose sister-in-law tried to acquire a marriage license in Paris, who tried to mail a parcel home from Milan, who has tried to make a telephone call in the south of France. I can assure you that once you have tried these simple experiments, you are likely to become less worried about the inefficiencies of the American bureaucratic state.

Compared with other Western democracies, our bureaucratic agencies that deal with the average citizen are markedly less bureaucratic: we make it much easier to get a driver's license or passport or apply for Social Security benefits. We place much tighter controls on the discretionary authority of the police and the schools.

Our bureaucratic agencies that deal with firms and other formal organizations are less bureaucratic in the sense of wielding discretionary authority, but much more bureaucratic in the sense of internal complexity and the multiplication of rules and regulations. Every scholar who has written about environmental regulation here and abroad concludes that in the United States, such regulations are written and implemented in a highly formalistic, rule-driven manner. By contrast, in much of Western Europe and in Japan these regulations are devised and enforced in a more flexible, consultative, and nonadversarial fashion. The chief reason for the difference seems to be that in our fragmented constitutional system and under the influence of our rights-oriented political culture, the exercise of bureaucratic discretion over important matters is not tolerated. As a consequence, a business firm finds it relatively easy to comply with social regulations in England or Sweden but much harder to comply in the United States, even though the net effect of the regulations (in terms of, say, improving air quality) is about the same in both places.

This suggests a paradox: a citizen (or in this case, a firm) can experience contact with a government agency as more "bureaucratic" when the agency has *little* discretion (but much internal complexity) and less "bureaucratic" when it has *much* discretion (but few formal rules). What determines whether a rule-bound agency or a discretionary agency is experienced as more "bureaucratic" seems to be the degree to which there is a mutuality of interest between agency and client. When we share the goals of an agency, agency discretion is welcome (like-minded people can get together and "do the right thing"); when we are at cross-purposes with these goals, formal rules are demanded (opposed parties want to "know where they stand").

The heavy emphasis on rules in many U.S. agencies is of fairly recent origin. At one time, we gave a great deal of discretion to the Federal Communications Commission, the Civil Aeronautics Board, the local police, and the public schools. But a wider range of interests are now politically mobilized, with the result that more groups are party to any agency decision. To balance the pressures on them, legislatures and courts enact more rules by which agency behavior must be governed. To minimize conflict and maintain support, members of those agencies adopt rules of their own and further forfeit their discretion. As a consequence, the U.S. government is becoming more bureaucratic in the sense of internal complexity and the multiplication of rules at the very time that it is becoming less bureaucratic in the sense of vesting discretionary authority in government agencies.

I do not think that any of the three theories—public choice, social control, or interest-group liberalism—adequately captures this complex process.

Notes

1. A.V. Dicey, *Introduction to the Study of the Law of the Constitution* [1885] (London: Macmillan, 1965), ch. 4; Theodore J. Lowi, *The End of Liberalism: The Second Republic of the United States*, 2d ed. (New York: W.W. Norton, 1979), ch. 11.

2. Ibid., ch. 3.

3. Michael Lipsky, *Street-Level Bureaucracy: Dilemmas of the Individual in Public Services* (New York: Russell Sage, 1980).

4. Hugh Heclo, "Issue Networks and the Executive Establishment," in *The New American Political System,* ed. Anthony King (Washington, DC: American Enterprise Institute for Public Policy Research, 1978), p. 114.

10

Catastrophic Errors and the Changing Shape of Bureaucracy

Martin Landau

Having had an opportunity to review a spate of economic forecasts, and to compare anticipation with outcome, I find it obvious that the practitioners of our "most developed social science" do not exhibit any distinctive predictive power.[1] Their performance record emboldens me to prophecy fearlessly about the future of American bureaucracy. I must confess, however, that my valor is somewhat constrained when I consider the sobering thoughts of that remarkable twentieth-century sage, Samuel Goldwyn: "Never make forecasts, especially about the future." But I do not wish to shirk my tasks, so I plunge ahead now with only slightly diminished audacity.

General Predictions and Theoretical Assumptions

In some definite though for now undeterminable future, bureaucracies will be less hierarchical, more pragmatic, less rule-bound, more redundant, more competitive internally, more experimental, and more appreciative of the therapeutic significance of error. Measures of effectiveness will replace those of efficiency; experimental decisions will precede terminal decisions; and premature programming, the cause of so many errors, will diminish as our public organizations become less synoptic in mode and more inventive in their operations. Where control is now a responsibility of sheer incumbency, it will come to be seen as a causal factor that can only be employed effectively on the foundations of knowledge. This means that our notions of accountability will change. As fact continues to displace value in the making of decisions, and at an accelerating pace, decision makers will be held responsible for their empirical claims, not simply for their good will or political disposition. Even now we are beginning to see the emergence of the concept of "empirical accountability," a concept that will only grow stronger. That is because *all policies* contain high empirical content and their success depends on the corpus of knowledge upon which they are based.

My argument is as follows.

It takes but a moment's reflection to conclude that the only actions we can control are future actions. That is why we make policy. To make policy is to engage the future. The object involved is to create a stated condition or direct a course of events yet to come and to reduce the incidence of random behavior attending those events. We can do nothing about the past; and when we decide to do something about today, our actions occur in the tomorrow.

Policies, accordingly, are *hypotheses*. That is what they are, and that is the way they must be treated. Hypotheses are assertions of fact; they are empirical claims of the "if–then" form, and the real problem is to determine their validity. Indeed, the one sure thing we do know about hypotheses is that their validity has not been established. Hypotheses belong, thus, to the class of unverified propositions and they cannot be accepted *a priori*, or by the principle of *senatus consultum*.

Catastrophic Errors and Bureaucratic Knowledge

Once validated, a policy becomes a solution set, a specific, a formula that can be applied by rote to the class of problems it covers. A policy then becomes a terminal decision. Unvalidated, it remains problematic, and the actions directed by the policy are clearly experimental. But the experimental character of policies is frequently lost. I need not dwell on the reasons for this: partisan advantage, self-serving interest, symbolic politics, ideological blindness, bias, ignorance, power plays, status and position—these and more are involved.

Whatever the reasons, the plain fact is that every program courts error. Some errors are nuisances easily tolerated, some are quite costly but tolerable, and some are disasters. This society has now reached a point where there are bureaucratic errors that can no longer be tolerated. Some errors may be disastrous by orders of magnitude beyond anything we have yet experienced. Generally speaking, bureaucracies learn by experimentation, which necessarily involves error. But nobody wants to experiment with dropping 500 atomic bombs to find out whether this will, indeed, produce a nuclear winter. Nobody wants to experiment with what will happen if, in fact, there is a core meltdown in a major nuclear reactor. We reach the point where in so many areas the errors that occur are not simply amplified as they go up the chain, but they are errors of the sort that create problems that are beyond our comprehension. This will occur even in the "soft" areas, not just the high-technology areas. I have in mind the sorts of soft areas that gave rise to such phrases as the "culture of poverty." It may very well be, for example, that the welfare system we established in this country during the 1960s as a compassionate reform was an error of an order of magnitude that we are only now beginning to appreciate when we talk of such things as the culture of poverty or point to the fact that large numbers of families have now been on welfare for as long as four generations.

One of our major difficulties today is the extraordinary ability of bureaucracies to hide error, to refuse to acknowledge error, and to search for scapegoats when error is exposed. And because we do not really grasp the knowledge-producing power of error detection and correction methodologies, the practice of "covering your ass" is not only ubiquitous, but has been elevated to a principle of bureaucratic behavior. When nature, which is our primary "whistle blower," then presents us with the inescapable consequences of our folly—that is, when it holds us accountable for our actions, the cost is there for all to see.

Increasingly, that cost looms larger than life. It may be that the scale and the complexity of our programmatic actions ordain that our errors will be transformed into calamity. Perhaps. Whatever the reason, we know of *Challenger*, of the Savings and Loan crisis, of nuclear weapons plants that are nightmares, of horrendous budget deficits, of widespread functional illiteracy, and of that "bright and shining lie." We know these, and more.

When we investigate, more often than not the search is for a villain. There are villains, and finding them may be good for the soul. But such discovery does not erase the fact that calamitous and catastrophic errors derive from an absence of knowledge, the misuse of knowledge, and a general failure to hold ourselves empirically accountable. That is why, in the Comptroller General's language, "we spend billions attempting to design and install government computer systems . . . yet wind up with systems that do not work."[2] Or with Sergeant York, the Army's spectacularly unsuccessful—and costly—antiaircraft gun. We make terminal decisions when we do not know, and we then hide the inevitable errors that occur and rationalize upon their exposure. The result is a loss of legitimacy, widespread cynicism, and a pervasive fear that curbs the intelligent risk taking through which mankind progresses. It is not likely that this state of affairs can be maintained indefinitely.

We do well to recall, as Robert Merton once put it, that bureaucracy is a system of control on the basis of knowledge. That is the meaning of a merit system. Organizations recruit those who possess the necessary skills and technical competencies. Such actors provide solution sets. Solution sets take the form of rules that are to be applied to specified classes of problems as medicine is applied to a class of disease. Rules are ordered; they are formed into a logic that constitutes the structure of the organization. And that structure invariably takes the shape of a formal theory. The structure is asymmetric and transitive, exactly equivalent to a formalized body of knowledge. That is why we say *formal* organization: it is ordered, predictive, and causal; and the structure of the organization constitutes its body of knowledge. Its operations, its actions, its functioning provide information. In this usage, the concept of information is entirely different from that presented by Theodore Lowi in chapter 8. My usage bears clarification.

Knowledge, that is, formal knowledge, is inversely related to information. The development of a corpus of knowledge in a given area is tantamount to a progressive reduction of information in that area. Or, said alternatively, the higher the information level of a field, the less the knowledge in that field.

On first reading, this appears strange. It becomes clear, and intuitively acceptable, when it is understood that in the formal discipline that studies it, information is defined in terms of surprise, anomaly, and news. It is measured by its news value. If one tells a person something already known to that person, no information is transmitted. The something may be a fact, but to the person who knows it, no information is gained. Information is transmitted only when one hears something new, when one is surprised, when unexpected events occur. Where a field of knowledge, say mechanics, can be ordered into a closed set of variables, and where the rules describing the interactions of these variables are known, or where the system is "fully analyzable," little or no information is generated. For example, Cal Tech's Jet Propulsion Laboratory reported, on January 24, 1986, that *Voyager* had reached a point 50,000 miles from the blue-green clouds of Uranus at exactly 12:59 P.M. eastern standard time. This was only one minute off the prediction made by JPL five years and a billion miles before. *Voyager* weighed 1,800 pounds and raced to Uranus at 45,000 mph.[3] Such was the power of the theoretical knowledge that warranted the launch.

What would have happened, however, if *Voyager* had not behaved as expected? The violation of expectation would immediately have *informed* us that the knowledge base was faulty—that errors had been made. And the search would have been directed toward the elimination of anomaly, toward the reduction of information, toward control and predictability. All of us know what happened when "cold fusion" was announced. This was so unexpected a finding, against the prevailing theories, so momentous a piece of news that physicists the world over ran to their labs to evaluate and test. It was information indeed—of such magnitude as to defy the fundamental expectations of atomic theory. If the information had been correct, it would have informed us that the theory was wrong.

Catastrophic Errors and the Quest for Bureaucratic Reliability

Now our textbooks in public administration tell us that bureaucracies organize behavior, banish randomness, produce predictability, and thereby render outcomes controllable and expectable. Presumably, they lower the information level of the fields over which they have jurisdiction. If the knowledge carried in the structure of an organization were powerful enough to immunize against anomaly—that is, against faulty predictions or error—this would mean that the organization operated on the basis of perfect knowledge, and its rule-governed decisions would always be correct. Prediction and outcome would be the same. We know, of course, that organizations are not fault free. We know that they operate with imperfect knowledge. We know this despite the fact that they are prematurely programmed. We know that, while their structures present the appearance of a powerful theoretical corpus, they are heavily and seriously flawed. It is the flaws that create tension between structure (the body of knowledge) and function (the set of operations). And because the knowledge base is much less than appearance would suggest, operations continually produce news, surprise, and anomalies—all of which take form as predictive errors.

Such errors are information and they *inform* us that the knowledge base is inadequate. If our managements were scientific, as they surely are not, error potential would be recognized as a fact of life, and the study of error would be seen as the path to knowledge—as in the case of the National Transportation Safety Board. What we have now are dogmatic assertions of certainty that, imbedded in the structure of hierarchy, block the path to corrective action. Subjective certainty triumphs over an objective certainty that can only be had when we frame our policies and programs so that they are empirically accountable—a condition that can only obtain when we frame them so as to make error detectable. Instead, our bureaucracies suffer from practices that invariably produce "institutional self-deception." The crime involved does not derive from the error itself, but from the silence that surrounds it.

But we have now reached a time when the cost of error tears at the fabric of our system. Some costs are of an order of magnitude that is literally staggering. Errors occur as part and parcel of contemporary experience, and they introduce gross discontinuities in our polity, threaten our marketplace, afflict our environment, weaken our defenses, randomize our street scenes, and transform a citizenry into an audience. Horror pictures are what our citizen audience watches.

The increasing potential for catastrophe will force our public administration to change. Management fads will not help us; they have not helped in the past. But knowledge will. Knowledge will help even with thorny moral problems, for it takes knowledge of the consequence of our actions to be moral persons.

It is unfortunate that our organizational leaders are seen as executives, administrators, and managers. It is even more unfortunate that they take their behavioral cues from these terms. The result is a failure to appreciate that, in their first estate, they direct searches for knowledge. Our bureaucracies are important producers of knowledge; if only they were organized to capture and to apply it.

Conclusion

We have before us a dramatic and vivid illustration of the collapse of a system that institutionalized self-deception. The Soviet Union was founded on subjective certainty—an ideology. Catastrophe followed on calamity as Soviet agencies legislated fictions, ignored and suppressed information, and remained deaf to nature's whistles.

For us, the lesson is clear. Knowledge does not inhere in doctrine or in high office. It inheres in experiment. Our bureaucracies will have to learn to experiment; there is no other way to reduce the informational level in a task domain. When bureaucracies behave experimentally, hierarchy will diminish because talent, intelligence, creativity, and imagination are variably and unevenly distributed in every organization. Standards of reliability and effectiveness will replace those of efficiency as organizations become more sensitive to error potential. Silly slogans addressed to duplication and overlap will lose their currency as organizations introduce appropriate redundancies. As they do, error will cease to be regarded as sin.

We now hide error for as long as we can because we judge the cost of exposure to be high. The reasons are clear enough: the exposure of error reveals misfeasance and incompetence, it threatens coalition stability, it opens vital information to antagonistic forces, it weakens credibility before authorizing agencies, it results in loss of status and power, and it begets punishment. We think we lose when error is exposed, but the simple fact is that the cost of concealment is infinitely higher. A Congress or an investigating committee can be stone-walled, but nature cannot, and nature often exacts a high price for our follies. Our record of disasters, many of which were so clearly avoidable, dictates that our bureaucratic pattern must change. The pattern will change as a matter of necessity. As the pattern changes, policy will become corrigible and programs will become experimental. We will design systems that are "error tolerant," and we will move away from "success-oriented strategies" to "failure-avoidance strategies."[4]

I believe that none of these predictions is utopian. Nonetheless, the political "realists" among us are likely to assert that partisan advantage will serve to insure the maintenance of the present state of affairs indefinitely. If they are correct, we shall go the way of the Soviet Union. That is because every determinate system must change as time passes so that its structure is characterized by the lessons of its experiences, by the information it generates—not by its initial state.[5] If change does not occur, if our bureaucratic system clings to its initial state, it will assume an immunity from error that is guaranteed to produce catastrophe.

Notes

1. Martin Landau, "Epistemological Status of Forecasting." Plenary paper presented to the Sixth International Symposium on Forecasting, Paris, June 1986.

2. See Comptroller General's *Annual Report, 1989*; and see *Reports and Testimony* (Washington, DC: U.S. General Accounting Office, 1990), p. 35.

3. *New York Times*, January 25, 1986.

4. A full discussion of this concept can be found in Martin Landau and Donald Chisholm, "Fault Analysis, Professional Football, and the Arrogance of Optimism: An Essay on the Practical Methodology of Administration" (unpublished manuscript, January 1991).

5. See W.R. Ashby, "The Effect of Experience on a Determinate Dynamic System," *Behavioral Science* 1 (1956): 35–42.

11

American Exceptionalism: Government without Bureaucracy

Francis E. Rourke

I want to discuss what can be described as the American quest for a government without bureaucracy—a quest that is only one aspect of a hunger deeply rooted in American political history for a democracy without government. For much of this century, but especially in the period surrounding World War II, predictions about the impending triumph of bureaucracy were common in this country, as they were in other parts of the Western World. Published in 1941, James Burnham's Managerial Revolution was but one example of a spate of books at that time that saw bureaucracy as taking over the reins of power in democratic governments throughout the world.[1] It was a prediction that aroused concern in every free society, but nowhere more deeply than in the United States.

There were differences in the meaning such prophets attached to the rise of bureaucracy. Some saw with dark foreboding the appearance of a new and all-powerful political elite. Amateur statesmen would now be displaced by professional technocrats as the dominant force in national politics. Others were less worried about the effects that bureaucratization might have on the distribution of power within the political system. They were more concerned with its impact on society as a whole: the standardization and routinization that would result, or the dehumanization of interpersonal relationships that a pervasive bureaucratization might bring about.

Thus, one set of doomsday prophets saw bureaucratization as a political catastrophe, shifting control over public policy from elected to nonelected officials and converting democracy into a political system in which a facade of citizen control concealed the fact that it was bureaucrats who were actually pulling the strings of power. Others focused on what they regarded as the calamitous social consequences of bureaucratization. In the workplace people would be expected to take orders in hierarchical settings that would dampen if not stifle individual initiative. At home they would live under tight constraints imposed by government bureaucrats that would gradually leach every vestige of creativity and spontaneity from the body politic.

American Exceptionalism

Over the course of time these doomsday prophecies failed to sink very deep roots into the political culture of most of the world's democracies. The capacity of bureaucracy and democracy to adapt to one another had been grossly underestimated. Citizens in most countries discovered that a bureaucracy could in fact be a very useful instrument for reducing their vulnerability to a variety of personal and social misfortunes, including unemployment, ill health, crime, poverty, crop failures, natural disasters, and a host of other hazards to which humanity is prey. It is hard to think of a human problem anywhere in the world's democratic societies with which some bureaucracy has not been established to cope in the years since World War II. By and large, moreover, bureaucracies were able to serve these various purposes without posing any serious threat to the survival of democracy itself.

In this respect as in many others, however, the United States was different, or what historians might call "exceptional." A deep and abiding antagonism to bureaucracy remained as one of the most distinctive features of the American way of politics. It continues to flourish today even in situations in which Americans express a very positive attitude toward the bureaucratic organization with which they have the most direct contact, or on which they most strongly depend for assistance.[2] It is hard to think of any subject on which a broader political consensus presently exists in the United States than the common view that government bureaucracy is at best a nuisance and at worst a threat to historic American freedoms.

The fact that antibureaucratic sentiment has been strong among American conservatives is hardly surprising. In this country as elsewhere conservatives have always argued that bureaucrats only aggravate the difficulties of the people they are trying to help when they seek to solve humanity's problems. From the conservative perspective all bureaucratic organizations have the iatrogenic characteristic sometimes alleged to be characteristic of hospitals—doing harm when they try to do good. Bureaucracy has come under relentless attack from neoconservatives in the United States on just this score in recent decades. These critics have shown particular hostility toward public agencies that are trying to improve the lot of the poor or to assist disadvantaged minorities within American society.

Much more surprising, however, has been the recent strength of antibureaucratic sentiment in the somewhat smaller sector of American politics inhabited by liberals. Until recently, advocates of liberal causes in this country had always looked upon bureaucratic organizations as instruments for the achievement of some of their most cherished objectives. The conservationists in the Progressive period saw the Forest Service under Gifford Pinchot in this light, and their liberal descendants in the New Deal period were no less devout in their belief that organizations such as the Tennessee Valley Authority, the National Labor Relations Board, and the Farm Security Administration stood on very high moral ground in their unselfish service to the public.

Far otherwise is the situation today. Bureaucracy is now more commonly seen by liberal political activists as the enemy rather than the friend of reform. Contemporary liberals tend to believe that bureaucracies serve their own interests or the interests of some predatory group in American society rather than the needs of the people whose welfare they were established to protect or promote. Ralph Nader and other public interest advocates working in behalf of liberal causes have led the way in an attack on government regulatory agencies, which they regard as having been captured by the very industries they were created to regulate.

Building a Bureaucracy-free Society

Today Americans live in a society in which reformers on both the right and the left are assiduously trying to find solutions for pressing social problems through nonbureaucratic means—to build, if they can, a bureaucracy-free society. For American conservatives, market decision making is now, as in the past, much to be preferred to an economy shaped in accord with bureaucratic rules and regulations. The strength of the conservatives' conviction in this regard has been greatly reinforced by the dismal failure of regulated economies in Eastern Europe, especially in the Soviet Union. Their preferred alternative to bureaucratization is deregulation—the removal of government controls over economic activity whenever possible. There is also widespread support among conservatives for privatization—turning public functions over to private entrepreneurs.

Liberals have sometimes joined forces with conservatives in their attempts to scale down the role of bureaucracy in American society. Liberals have, for example, played a leading role in some areas of economic deregulation, not in order to free business from government control, but because they see such deregulation as being of benefit to ordinary consumers. They have also joined conservatives in supporting the establishment of voucher systems under which citizens would be given the wherewithal to purchase such services as education or housing that they might otherwise have to depend upon some public agency to provide.

In other areas, however, the efforts of liberals to reform bureaucracy have been aimed at bringing its power under public control rather than dissolving it altogether. In some sectors of domestic policy making, liberals have strongly supported arrangements under which ordinary citizens can participate in bureaucratic decision making. This strategy was expected to keep the policies followed by governmental agencies in closer harmony with the views of their constituents. In the arena of foreign policy, liberals have sought with only partial success to rein in the power of national security agencies, especially those engaged in intelligence activities. Their chief strategy for doing so has been to advocate procedures that would expose the activities of these agencies to greater public scrutiny.

The Decline of American Bureaucracy

The prominent place that bureaucracy began to assume in the structure of American government during the New Deal period in the 1930s rested essentially on two pillars of power. The first was the growing dependence of elected officials and of the public that put them in office on the information and advice that bureaucrats alone seemed able to provide in shaping the development of national policy in an increasingly complex and rapidly changing world. The second pillar of bureaucratic power was the capacity that bureaucratic organizations developed to convert the dreams of policy makers into the reality of successful programs. In the kind of language that bureaucrats have themselves generated, theirs was the power of implementation.

As a result of the efforts of both conservative and liberal reformers, the role and influence of bureaucracy in each of these areas—the formulation of policy and its implementation—has progressively diminished. Increasingly in recent years, bureaucratic organizations in every area of governmental operation have lost the position of primacy they once enjoyed in providing information and advice to policy makers both in the Oval Office and in Congress. Their place has been taken by a variety of advisory institutions and sources in both government and the outside world to which elected officials can now turn when they are looking for help in appraising old policies or designing new programs.

Within government, both the president and the Congress have built up formidable advisory systems of their own. Presidents have created an advisory apparatus within the corridors of the White House itself in the form of a staff that can provide daily advice to the chief executive across nearly the whole spectrum of national policy. Each congressional office now has a variety of aides to help legislators meet their responsibilities, and Congress itself has established four specialized advisory institutions to assist all its members in grappling with the issues they confront.

National policy makers have also fallen into the habit of creating advisory commissions or other temporary organizations within government to consider and give advice on major policy issues or problems.[3] These officials also turn to sources outside of government for this kind of assistance. A striking aspect of recent American political history has been the leading role played by such outsiders at crucial turning points in the recent development of national policy. Task forces dominated by outsiders were instrumental in charting the direction of President Lyndon Johnson's Great Society programs in the 1960s. And such private organizations as the Heritage Foundation played a leading role in providing both ideas and personnel for Ronald Reagan's conservative counterrevolution in the 1980s. Each of these periods saw a radical restructuring of national policy in the United States. Hence, when elected officials need advice and information at critical junctures in contemporary policy development, they ignore bureaucracy and turn to new institutions that they regard as better-suited to provide such assistance.

The other traditional source of bureaucratic influence over policy development—the ability of bureaucrats to carry out or implement the goals of policy makers—has also been greatly weakened by recent developments. A feature of the national policy process in the United States that is becoming more and more important is an arrangement under which government provides the financial support needed to achieve desirable social purposes but turns over the task of implementing these objectives to nonprofit organizations in the private sector—"third-party government," as it has been called.

Moreover, presidents are now able to use their appointing power to infiltrate their own appointees deep within the ranks of bureaucracy in each executive agency throughout the government. Such presidential surrogates become heavily involved in the internal affairs of these organizations and can eventually control day-to-day decisions throughout the bureaucracy. Marissa Golden provides an arresting description of the way in which Assistant Attorney General William Bradford Reynolds, President Reagan's choice to run the Civil Rights Division of the Justice Department, took close control over that agency's operation:

> In terms of the day-to-day running of the agency, Reynolds ruled the Civil Rights Division with an iron hand, centralizing control of the agency in the Assistant Attorney General's office, instituting a system under which almost all the work of the career attorneys came to be reviewed by politically appointed special assistants or by Reynolds himself, and generally reducing the autonomy and discretion of the career attorneys. . . . Reynolds also increased the number of political appointees in the agency. . . . The strategy . . . had two chief effects. . . . The first was that the appointees took to handling cases themselves, something that had traditionally been done only by the careerists. The second effect of this control strategy was increased review of the careerists' work by the appointees.[4]

It can, of course, be argued that all these changes in the role of bureaucracy in government still leave reformers far short of achieving their dream of extinguishing bureaucratic power in American democracy. It is an indisputable fact of life that the large tasks of government today require the presence of hefty organizations capable of performing these tasks. Inevitably, they will exercise considerable power while doing so.

At the same time, however, it is equally true that a deep desire to minimize the power of bureaucracy has been the animating force behind some of the most significant changes that have taken place in the recent development of American political institutions. If a dream cannot itself become reality, it may nonetheless have a heavy impact on the shape that reality ultimately takes.

Postbureaucratic Government

What shall we make of the developments traced here, not to mention the events that have recently taken place in Eastern Europe, where, as noted earlier, efforts to dismantle highly bureaucratized political systems have now become the order of the day? It seems no exaggeration to suggest that the United States is living today in what can be called a postbureaucratic era, that some rough beast is slouching toward Bethlehem to be born—whether for good or ill remains to be seen. What we do know with some certainty is that, contrary to many earlier expectations and prophecies, this beast will have much less of a bureaucratic face than we once expected.

But is there a downside to this development? What are we to make of these changes that have had so negative an impact on the reputation and power of bureaucracy in modern government? Will we be better off or worse off in this emerging postbureaucratic world? From the perspective of at least one very clouded crystal ball, the decline of the bureaucratic role in the framing of public policy poses some real hazards for the health of the American political system.

One thing that a strong bureaucracy does provide is a certain measure of stability and continuity in policy development. Admirers of this country's use of in-and-out political appointees to play leading roles in its policy-making system have always claimed that this practice leads to more innovative policies. What they tend to neglect is that it leads just as inevitably to the placing of the task of policy making in inexperienced hands.

In some cases the task may even end up under the control of people who are very poorly informed in the areas of decision making for which they have suddenly been given responsibility. In international trade negotiations, for example, the United States mainly relies on political appointees in the office of the United States Trade Representative to protect its interests, while the other countries with which it is in economic competition, especially Germany and Japan, depend instead on the well-honed abilities of highly experienced career officials in such trade talks.

The experience and expertise that bureaucrats bring to the deliberative process are not their only contributions to effective policy making. As their role in policy making is reduced, we will also make the belated discovery of another advantage we derive from the participation of bureaucrats in policy discussions—the fact that they provide one of the principal checks we have in the governmental process on the flights of fancy on policy matters to which political officeholders are prone.

Some of this adventurism on the part of political appointees comes from the fact that they are often beholden to political movements outside of government with "far-out" ideas on social or economic policy. There is, for example, the possibility that this country's position on population policy abroad might draw its primary inspiration in the postbureaucratic era from "right to life" movements in the United States, at a time when overpopulation and hunger are major problems in Third World countries. It is far less likely that this country would have adopted such an unrealistic stance in the period when career officials with extensive knowledge and experience with the famine and population problems of Africa and Asia were still playing a significant role in forging policy options.

President Bush once described the economic proposals of Ronald Reagan, his more conservative predecessor in the White House, as "voodoo economics." Describing some of the population policy proposals entertained by administration appointees in recent years as "voodoo demography" would be no less accurate.

Finally, when assessing the performance of American bureaucracy in recent years, one ought to bear in mind that while bureaucrats have shouldered much of the blame for conspicuous failures in American policy in Vietnam, the War on Poverty, and elsewhere, the real blame for such policy failures can very often be assigned to the elected officials who originally conceived these ill-fated ventures rather than to the bureaucrats who were unable to carry them out. It is what bureaucrats are given to do, rather than what they choose to do, that often gets them into the most trouble and brings them into the greatest public disrepute.

Notes

1. James Burnham, *The Managerial Revolution: What Is Happening in the World* (New York: John Day, 1941).
2. The evidence to this effect is summarized in Charles T. Goodsell, *The Case for Bureaucracy: A Public Administration Polemic* (Chatham, NJ: Chatham House, 1983), pp. 16–37.
3. See Francis E. Rourke and Paul R. Schulman, "Adhocracy in Policy Development," *The Social Science Journal* 26 (1989): 131–42.
4. Marissa Martino Golden, "Exit, Voice and Loyalty: Bureaucratic Responses to Presidential Control during the Reagan Administration." Paper presented at the 1990 meeting of the American Political Science Association, San Francisco, 1990, pp. 6–7.

Index